Festivals and the Cultural Public Sphere

Festivals and the Cultural Public Sphere provides the first major social-scientific study of contemporary arts festivals in the wake of their explosion in popularity over the past decade. It explores the cultural significance of these festivals from their location within the cultural public sphere, examining them as sites for contestation and democratic debate and as examples of a particular aesthetic cosmopolitanism.

The book approaches contemporary festivals as relatively autonomous social texts that need interpretation and contextualization. This perspective, combined with a diversified set of theoretical approaches and research methods, and guided by a common thematic rationale, places the volume squarely within some of the most debated topics in current social sciences. Furthermore, the multifaceted nature of festivals allows for unusual but useful connections to be made across several fields of social inquiry.

This timely edited collection brings together contributions from key figures across the social sciences, and is valuable reading for undergraduate students, postgraduates and professionals working within the areas of contemporary social theory, cultural theory and visual culture.

Liana Giorgi is the coordinator of the EURO-FESTIVAL project on European arts festivals. She is co-author and co-editor of *Democracy in the European Union: Towards the Emergence of a European Public Sphere* (Routledge, 2006).

Monica Sassatelli is Lecturer in the Sociology Department at Goldsmiths College. She has published in the sociology of culture and of Europe, as well as classical and contemporary social theory. She is the author of *Becoming Europeans: Cultural Identity and Cultural Policies* (Palgrave, 2009).

Gerard Delanty is Professor of Sociology and of Social and Political Thought at the University of Sussex. He is the author of twelve books and editor of seven, including *The Handbook of Contemporary European Social Theory* (Routledge, 2006). His most recent publication is *The Cosmopolitan Imagination: The Renewal of Critical Social Theory* (Cambridge University Press, 2009).

Routledge Advances in Sociology

Festivals and the Cultural Public Sphere

Edited by
**Liana Giorgi, Monica Sassatelli
and Gerard Delanty**

Routledge
Taylor & Francis Group

LONDON AND NEW YORK

First published 2011
by Routledge
2 Park Square, Milton Park, Abingdon, Oxon, OX14 4RN

Simultaneously published in the USA and Canada
by Routledge
711 Third Avenue, New York, NY 10017

Routledge is an imprint of the Taylor & Francis Group, an informa business

British Library Cataloguing in Publication Data
A catalogue record for this book is available from the British Library

Library of Congress Cataloging in Publication Data
    Festivals and the cultural public sphere/edited by Liana Giorgi,
    Monica Sassatelli and Gerard Delanty.
        p. cm.
    1. Festivals–Social aspects. I. Giorgi, Liana. II. Sassatelli, Monica.
    III. Delanty, Gerard.
    GT3930.F483 2011
    394.26–dc22   2010048558

ISBN: 978-0-415-71496-9 (pbk)
ISBN: 978-0-415-58730-3 (hbk)
ISBN: 978-0-203-81878-7 (ebk)
Typeset in Bembo by Sunrise Setting Ltd, Torquay, UK

First issued in paperback 2013

Contents

Contributors

Andy Bennett is Professor of Cultural Sociology and Director of the Centre for Public Culture and Ideas at Griffith University, Australia. He has authored and edited numerous books including *Popular Music and Youth Culture, Cultures of Popular Music, Remembering Woodstock, After Subculture* and *Music Scenes.*

Christine Blumauer is a political scientist currently enrolled in the master's programme for peace and security studies at the University of Hamburg. She specializes in conflict resolution in the South Caucasus. Her master's thesis deals with the issue of Turko-Armenian relations.

Jasper Chalcraft is currently a Research Fellow working in the University of Sussex's Sociology department, and he also works for the Istituto Carlo Cattaneo in Bologna. Beyond music festivals, his research interests and publications cover cultural cosmopolitanism, ethnoarchaeology and heritage and memory institutions.

Joanne Cummings completed her PhD in Sociology at the University of Western Sydney, Australia in 2007. Her thesis involved an ethnographic study of Australian indie music festivals. Her main areas of interest are environmental sociology, youth culture, popular music festivals and the sociology of everyday life.

Gerard Delanty is Professor of Sociology and of Social and Political Thought at the University of Sussex. His most recent publications include *The Cosmopolitan Imagination: The Renewal of Critical Social Theory* (Cambridge University Press, 2009) and, edited with Stephen Turner, *The Handbook of Contemporary Social and Political Theory* (Routledge, 2011).

James F. English is Professor of English and of Comparative Literature and Literary Theory at the University of Pennsylvania. His recent publications include *A Concise Companion to Contemporary British Fiction* (Blackwell, 2005) and *The Economy of Prestige: Prizes, Awards, and the Circulation of Cultural Value* (Harvard, 2005).

Jean-Louis Fabiani is Senior professor of Sociology and Social Anthropology at Central European University in Budapest and *directeur d'études à l'Ecole des* *hautes études en sciences sociales* in Paris. Recent publications include *Après la culture legitime. Objets, publics, autorités* (L'Harmattan, 2007) and *l'Education populaire et le théâtre. Le festival d'Avignon en action* (Presses Universitaires de Grenoble, 2008).

Liana Giorgi is the coordinator of the EURO-FESTIVAL project, in the framework of which the present volume was conceptualized. She has published extensively on European public policy.

Paolo Magaudda is a postdoctoral Research Fellow in Sociology at the University of Padova, where he works on the consumption of media and technology in everyday life. In the musical field he has published articles and chapters on the themes of musical technologies, consumption practices, independent music and musical subcultures.

Meredith Martin is an Associate Researcher in the school of Culture and Communication at the University of Melbourne. Her doctoral research explored the persistence of cultural reform as a solution to urban blight and social exclusion from late-nineteenth-century London to contemporary northern England.

Jim McGuigan is Professor of Cultural Analysis in the Department of Social Sciences at Loughborough University, UK. His latest books are *Cool Capitalism* (Pluto, 2009) and *Cultural Analysis* (Sage, 2010).

Nikos Papastergiadis is Professor at the School of Culture and Communication at the University of Melbourne. Recent publications include *Spatial Aesthetics: Art, Place and the Everyday* (Rivers Oram Press, 2006) and *Empire, Ruins and Networks* (co-edited with Scott McQuire, Melbourne University Press, 2005).

Motti Regev is Associate Professor of Sociology at the Open University of Israel. He is a sociologist of culture and art, whose major research interest is in popular music studies. In this field he has published among other things *Popular Music and National Culture in Israel* (University of California Press, 2004, co-authored with Edwin Seroussi).

Maurice Roche is Chair in Sociology at the University of Sheffield. His main interests are in the sociologies of Europe, social policy, popular culture and citizenship. His books include *Mega-Events and Modernity: Olympics and Expos in the Growth of Global Culture* (Routledge, 2000) and, most recently, *Exploring the Sociology of Europe* (Sage, 2010).

Monica Sassatelli is Lecturer in the Sociology Department at Goldsmiths College. She has published in the sociology of culture and of Europe, as well as classical and contemporary social theory. She is the author of *Becoming Europeans: Cultural Identity and Cultural Policies* (Palgrave, 2009).

Jérôme Segal is Assistant Professor at the University of Paris-Sorbonne and senior researcher at the Interdisciplinary Centre for Comparative Research in the Social Sciences in Vienna. His publications are available online (http://jerome-segal.de).

Ian Woodward is Senior Lecturer in Sociology in the School of Humanities at Griffith University, Australia. He has written on cosmopolitanism, consumption practices, subject–object relations and material culture. He is the author of *Understanding Material Culture* (Sage, 2007) and co-author of *The Sociology of Cosmopolitanism* (Palgrave, 2009).

Introduction

Liana Giorgi and Monica Sassatelli

In the early days of sociological inquiry, beginning with Durkheim ([1912] 1995), festivals began to be recognized as instances of 'collective effervescence', and therefore as channels for expressing and consolidating a sense of community. This was as true of the arts festivals in ancient Athens (Ober 2008) as of the revolutionary festivals at the time of the French Revolution (Shiner 2001). Traditional festivals organized in various rural communities across the centuries to mark the change of seasons fulfilled a similar purpose. In contrast, contemporary festivals receive little attention from the social sciences other than as ritual performances in the context of anthropological studies or as impact factors in the framework of socio-economic assessments of the so-called cultural industry.

Yet, following Raymond Williams ([1961] 2001), one of the central figures in the sociology of culture, understanding societies is concomitant to exploring the ways in which people form communities. The study of communities is at the same time the study of communication in its various forms – whether in the political or legal–constitutional arena as proposed by Habermas (1992); in the context of social institutions such as religion, the school, the workplace or the social movement, as in traditional sociological inquiry (Giddens 1993); in the context of the old and new media or, indeed, in the framework of cultural exchanges and encounters. Moreover, culture is not to be understood only with reference to 'national identity' or even multiculturalism, but more broadly as including aesthetic forms of cultural expression, and hence also the arts. This is perhaps even more important today in view of globalization and the associated more general trans-national flows of capital, people and resources.

Against the above background, the present volume represents the first comprehensive social-scientific study of contemporary arts festivals. Besides looking at how arts festivals negotiate and communicate collective identities – how they have done so in history and how they do so today – we advance a new perspective by locating arts festivals as instances of the cultural public sphere. The latter concept is here used to refer to the articulation of politics and societal issues as contested domains through aesthetic modes of communication. In other words, we study arts festivals as instances of communication and community-building and we are also particularly interested in the ways in which they foster political opinion formation and political identities.

This is a very timely publication. During the past few decades there has been an explosion of festivals throughout the world and especially in Europe. This is the consequence of several factors: migration, cultural globalization and the erosion of the distinction between high and low cultures through the wider democratization of cultural taste, as well as related changes in the nature of the public and the audience. Some festivals are explicitly defined as sites for contestation and democratic debate; almost all carry political messages one way or another. In addition, post-traditional festivals are channels for experiencing and reflecting on internationalism and cosmopolitanism.

The authors consider examples of contemporary international arts festivals as relatively autonomous social texts or scenes that need interpretation and contextualization. Combined with a diversified set of theoretical approaches and research methods, and guided by a common thematic rationale, this places the volume squarely within some of the most debated topics in current social sciences. In this introductory chapter we elaborate on the main themes that underlie the book, and also present its plan and a summary of the individual chapters.

Public culture

'Popular culture' is a redundant expression: all culture is 'popular' in some sense; it would simply fade away if it were meaningful to nobody (Griswold 1997). This is even more the case for '*public* culture', since we can certainly say that all culture is public: meanings are, by definition, shared understandings that we learn, produce and reproduce in and for interaction; even subcultures are public in this sense, although their reach may be more limited and self-enclosed. At the same time the concept of public culture is useful because the cultural sphere, unlike the political one, is associated with the private domain, especially in terms of the disengaged consumption of culture industry entertainment (Hartley and Green 2006; Gray 2006). Crucial in the idea of public culture is the constitutive dimension of reception or interpretation within the production of culture itself. Moreover, the notion emphasizes those dimensions of the multifaceted and contested concept of culture that precede and question the idea of *ex post* depictions or representations of social life, instrumental to the orderly divisions of the latter into separate groups (identified by culture as discrete units of 'way of life'). By insisting on the public dimension of culture, we are also forcing ourselves to recognize that culture – in its aesthetic forms as well – can be appropriated and influenced from different standpoints, and by different actors, agendas and taste preferences.

In this sense the notion of public culture is both more specific and more inclusive than the related, and recently much theorized and studied, one of 'public sphere'. It is more specific because it concentrates on the cultural dimension, whilst the public sphere encompasses others, and has a strong focus on the political dimension in particular. It is more inclusive because it is less predicated on the national configuration as a term of reference – as studies on the public sphere have been – seeing it as a distinctive feature of modern, national (and mostly Western) societies. Not surprisingly, therefore, it has proven difficult to rework the notion of the public sphere to apply to a world no longer exclusively organized according to national cultures and canons. This is probably most evident in the European context: whilst several models of a European public sphere have been put forward – ranging from a supra-national, overarching and EU-based public sphere through the idea of Europeanized, but still nationally based, public spheres to that of inter- or cross-connecting public spheres emerging mainly from sharing debates and the cross-fertilization of discourses (Delanty and Rumford 2005; Eder 2006; Giorgi *et al.* 2006) – none seems to have settled the matter. The very notion of a sphere, with its implicit suggestion of wholeness and exhaustiveness, hardly fits with the ever-changing, unfinished process of Europeanization that, as an increasing amount of research demonstrates, contains processes both of convergence and of increased pluralization and can mean different things in different contexts and for different agencies – as some of the chapters on European cases in this book also show.

Indeed, within the public sphere, some aspects have been more studied than others. Particular attention has been given to those related to strong institutions, such as religious or political ones, that have always been conceived of as primary sources of identity formation and therefore terrains of key debate. However, there are other milieux that can be thematized as sites of public culture. Among the most neglected, until recently, were those related to artistic or cultural expressions in the restricted sense of aesthetic artefacts and activities, since these were considered as mere epiphenomena. It is somewhat ironic that this should be the case, given that the very notion of the public sphere as formulated by Habermas in the 1960s took inspiration from literary criticism (Habermas [1962] 1989). He elaborated the concept of the public sphere – the mediating instance between the private and public authority, through the vehicle of public opinion as the product of the free debate taking place in the discursive space the public sphere creates – referring to the literary critical discussion that found a home in London's coffee houses, France's *salons* and Germany's *Tischgesellschaften*. It is from this initial 'literary public sphere' that a public sphere proper developed, where the civil society of the rising bourgeoisie allowed the 'public use of reason'. This literary origin of the public sphere, however, has not been the subject of as much critical attention as other aspects have been (mainly its dimension of exclusion and inequality: see Fraser 1990). The same is true of Habermas's account of the decline of that sphere under the pressure of cultural industry and media development and the related shift from a 'reasoning' to a 'consuming' public, clearly under the influence of Horkheimer's and Adorno's original critique of the culture industry. The diagnosis of the decline of a culture-debating in favour of a culture-consuming public sphere has opened the way for the dismissal of the cultural dimension as merely an illustrative example and not the real thing. Today this dismissal is less tenable, not least because the standard notion of the public sphere that is premised on the sharing of a common culture (so that a domain of common concern can be identified and inclusivity made available, at least in principle) has become much more problematic in the current conditions of cultural fragmentation. Public sphere theory can be significantly revived by a renewed interest in its link with cultural forms (Jones 2007). A cultural public sphere, as argued by Jim McGuigan – and as he explores further with specific reference to festivals in his contribution to this volume – 'refers to the articulation of politics, public and personal, as a contested terrain through affective (aesthetic and emotional) modes of communication' (McGuigan 2004: 435). This volume contributes to investigating this link, both theoretically and by offering a range of empirical cases of post-traditional festivals.

Post-traditional festivals

Now, what do we mean by post-traditional festivals, and why is it important to concentrate on them as sites of the cultural public sphere: that is, on their cultural significance? As with all 'posts', the term suggests a critical relationship with forerunners and, in particular, with the role they were given in (allegedly 'traditional') societies and are still given in the study of them. Indeed, one could equally, and more simply, say 'contemporary festivals'; however, by implying in a way that all contemporary festivals are by definition non-traditional, this apparently less controversial expression betrays a more evaluative notion of tradition (or lack of it).

> Traditional feasts and festivals constitute, symbolically, a renewal of the past in the present, a way of recalling the origins – whether mythical or historical – of a community of men [sic]; they are occasions when cultural and national identity can be re-asserted and feelings of self-awareness and participation in common experiences reaffirmed … Feasts played an important role in the past and nowadays there is a new interest in their sociocultural function as the quest for self-identity and self-assertion unfolds within modern societies.
>
> (Metraux 1976: 7)

Taken from the introduction to an early double issue of the UNESCO journal *Cultures* that was dedicated to festivals, and although still formulated in a prepostmodernist language (little aware of gender issues or challenges to the nation as the taken for granted site of identification), this quotation is illustrative on a number of levels. Most importantly it shows how deep-seated is the idea that festivals are important to social and cultural (re)production. Secondly, it advances the idea that this does not only apply to traditional festivals and traditional societies.

Unfortunately, the subsequent observation by the author, that unlike festivals in 'traditional communities' their heirs' significance for contemporary society has not really been investigated by social scientists, remains true over thirty years on. The point, of course, is not only to study the 'survival' of traditional festivals within contemporary society, as this author still recommends, but to study the significance of contemporary, post-traditional festivals as well, treasuring the lessons from that socio-anthropological approach so successfully applied to traditional ones. Traditional festivals have been considered relevant and revealing of the societies they emanate from; this can and should be taken up for contemporary festivals as well – these, too, can be seen as revealing of the modern societies they emanate from. The tendency within some academic circles to assume the decline of culture (and of festivals) because of the growing influence of the market and the cultural industry has led to their dismissal as irrelevant in terms of community building, cultural debate, and also politics. Even if this were the case, it ought to be shown through empirical inquiry rather than hastily assumed in the course of a normative debate.

Festival narratives and conflicting realities

As James English puts it in his contribution to the present volume, there are two apparently conflicting views of arts festivals – as there are more generally of the public sphere or of the notion of 'publicity', understood broadly to refer to all means of communication, mediatized or not. The first is through the lens of an optimistic reading of Habermas, in terms of communicative action, i.e. as opportunities for realizing a discourse about public good(s). The second is through the more competitive lenses of Bourdieu (1995), which emphasize structure and the means of drawing and reproducing distinctions within societies. According to Giorgi *et al.* (2006) writing on the emerging European public sphere, these different views of the public sphere are not necessarily to be treated as inherently contradictory. Rather, as suggested by Appiah (2005), following Kant, they can be judged as differences in perspective (cf. Giorgi 2009). The communicative action approach is a theory of action – as its name suggests – and therefore places the emphasis on agency. By contrast, the field approach is a descriptive–analytical theory, which is more interested in understanding patterns and structures and the power relations between them. Both approaches are valid, and both have something to contribute to the understanding of the dynamics of the public sphere, as well as of the cultural public sphere and hence also of festivals. The first approach demonstrates how ideas, beliefs and norms inform festival organization and shows that only on this basis is it possible to create content, which, in turn, brings forth 'effervescent' experiences. The second approach shows the way in which these contents (often idealistic) are embedded in the real world of industrial power-relations, networks and scarce resources. The latter act as constraining factors, limiting the scope and outreach of content and determining what can and cannot be realized. But, ultimately, it is the underlying beliefs, norms and values – however watered down they might sometimes become through their insertion in the real world of power relations – that enable persons as citizens to abstract themselves from their specific and individual viewpoints and participate in activities that contribute to the building of (political) communities – national or trans-national.

All contributors to this volume struggle with this duality – and, unsurprisingly, given their different value orientations as persons, citizens or professional social scientists – they all display different preferences when concentrating on their subject of study, i.e. one or another arts festival, or when assuming a comparative perspective. But the main added value of the present volume is the way in which it starkly demonstrates how both of these approaches are valid and important for understanding the dynamics within the emerging global public culture and how it plays out in different nations, cities, genres, audiences and other group collectives. It is not possible at this stage to entirely specify the contours and boundaries of this public culture or the political identities these might eventually bring about. But what can be said is that contemporary societies, and especially the educated middle classes, which have grown in numbers as a result of social democratic policies over the last half century, are 'culture hungry' – to borrow a term from Bennett (1999) writing about the foundation of the Cheltenham literature festival back in 1949. What is more, the 'culture' that is craved cannot be easily classified into the traditional canonical configurations of high- or low-brow, or by nationality, genre or orientation. There is a certain conspicuousness in the idea of festivals and their audiences – which some sociologists of culture like to refer to as 'omnivorousness' (see also Regev in this volume) in order to emphasize its never-gratifying character – but what this also denotes is an excess of curiosity. How deep or sustainable this curiosity is and what it ends up implying in terms of our future societies and polities can perhaps not yet be established; but what it does suggest is that – unlike what cultural pessimists or those who herald the end of both history and democracy might fear – it is not a negative notion and is certainly a necessary, even if not sufficient, condition for radical political thought.

Plan of the book

The present volume is based on empirical research carried out by different authors in different contexts. The first couple of chapters, by the authors of this introduction, present the overall theoretical framework. Based on this, the subsequent contributors examine different festivals and advance their own theoretical reflections. Different perspectives are offered by different authors: thus Papastergiadis and Martin consider also the changing role and function of the festival curator; McGuigan looks at the role of corporate sponsorship; English considers the social geography of festivals and, in particular, of the film industry; Fabiani and Regev explore the expectations of festival audiences, whilst Roche as well as Cummings *et al.* concentrate their attention on the cosmopolitan values mediated by festivals. Finally, Segal and Blumauer as well as Chalcraft and Magaudda reflect on the impact of festivals on specific artistic genres – film and music respectively. In his concluding chapter, Gerard Delanty recaps the book's main arguments and draws conclusions for the future of aesthetic cosmopolitanism and public culture.

In summary, the book's chapters advance the following arguments.

Echoing what was said in the previous section, in the first chapter of this volume *Monica Sassatelli* questions the frequent normative assumption in socio-logical studies of festivals that post-traditional festivals are 'less' than traditional festivals in the sense of displaying a 'loss' in terms of 'authenticity'. Using Simmel's concept of sociability, developed in his short analysis of world exhi-bitions at the end of the nineteenth century, she reminds us that sociology had always had problems with its attitude to 'entertainment', especially when the latter began to get entangled with the modern relations of economic produc-tion and consumption. Simmel, on the other hand, chose to view world exhi-bitions as 'social phenomena that continue to exist after the original function for which they emerged fades' and as phenomena that tell us something about the specific 'modern' form of sociability within urban spaces. These are not only spaces of alienation, as they have often been depicted in literature (think, for instance, of Dickens); they are also spaces of diversity and over-stimulation, with all the positive and negative connotations this might entail. Festivals, sug-gests Sassatelli, ought to be studied in a similar manner, i.e. not as 'time out of time' experiences (Falassi 1987) but rather as social phenomena to be contex-tualized in the particular settings and contradictions of modern societies. It is also for this reason that it is counterproductive to always think of festivals, or public culture more generally, in terms of dichotomous either/or categories, i.e. either as economic urban regeneration projects or as instances of aesthetic and reflexive cosmopolitanism.

Taking up this perspective, *Liana Giorgi* takes a look at literature festivals, focusing especially on the Hay-on-Wye Festival, the International Literature Festival Berlin and the Borderlands Festival. Literature festivals are comparative latecomers in the festival scene, and yet they display several similarities, in terms of rituals and objectives, to the literary salons of the eighteenth and nine-teenth centuries that paved the way for the emergence of representative democ-racy and the democratic public sphere of the twentieth century. Obviously, Giorgi argues, the contemporary literature festival is a different 'social fact', in Durkheim's sense, from the literary salon – not least because the social and eco-nomic conditions of the late twentieth and early twenty-first centuries are very different from those of earlier times. In both times, however, the function ful-filled by literary events is that of creating a space for discussions and debates that transcend the purely political, social or personal and rather seek their dialectic intersection. It is also for this reason that it would be wrong to see literature festivals – and festivals more generally – as mere expressions of the profit-making logic of capitalist societies as it spills over into the cultural realm.

A similar viewpoint is adopted by *Nikos Papastergiadis* and *Meredith Martin*, who explore the explosion of the art biennale across first- and second-tier cities around Europe and Asia by considering the multiple ways in which this phe-nomenon is situated in contemporary urban and cultural landscapes. Today, the authors argue, culture is used for promoting both urban regeneration and social integration – in the ways indicated by McGuigan and Fabiani (see below) – but it would be wrong to view it merely as a mirror of processes of capital flow and cultural exchange. Rather, culture critically takes on these processes, and it is for this reason that global public culture has no fixed identity – neither territorially nor administratively, and also not with respect to value commitments. This is also well reflected in the genealogy of the Venice Biennale, which grew out of the 'salon era' of international pavilions into a multidisciplinary survey of contemporary trends in visual arts. This change is partly driven by – but is also driving – the role of the curator. His or her function is no longer that of interpreting, classifying or even canonizing art forms, but rather that of creating a platform for a dialogue as to what art is or might become.

Taking a more critical view, *James English* considers that festivals can be viewed in one of two ways: seen through the early Habermas lens, they represent vehicles of communicative action, providing an international arena for the exchange of new cultural forms and the broadening of tastes; viewed through the lenses of Bourdieu, they are instead instruments for the reproduction of relations of economic domination and for the exploitative deployment of symbolic capital. By exploring the emergence and growth of African film festivals during the last few decades – largely through the economic and symbolic support of French cinema – he shows how both of these approaches are correct and legitimate in a way, with one or the other dominating at different points in time. At present, however, and insofar as African film is concerned, there is definitely an asymmetry in favour of Western (French) national cultural politics. The fact that many African countries are not supportive environments for individual artists aggravates this trend. It is for this reason that in this specific case colonization continues to be a useful and applicable narrative for understanding the operation of the festival circuit. This is what English calls the 'unhappy features of cinema's [current] symbolic geography', which does not mean that it does not also nurture small, minor and third cinema.

In a similar vein, *Jim McGuigan* undertakes a critique of the regenerative festival idea, which informs much contemporary economic investment in cultural mega-events in old and new urban spaces. Culture, including popular culture, sometimes articulates issues that are marginalized in mainstream and traditional political discourse, and thus entails an awareness raising or even a potential radicalization, at least in the long term. However, cultural policy is today much more concerned with economic efficiency based on commercial and promotional assumptions than it is with cultural enlightenment. It is for this reason that the 'regenerative festival' intervention logic cannot be taken at face value but must always be questioned and scrutinized anew. McGuigan does this with reference to the 2000 Millennium Dome project in London and Liverpool's 2008 European Capital of Culture festival. His research shows that the Millennium Dome project in London was dominated by corporate sponsorships dressed up as public–private partnerships, of which only very few were 'associative' in character, i.e. not directly seeking to influence content and representation. In Liverpool the situation was slightly better, but still, overall, the event was used primarily to advance regeneration according to the neoliberal economic logic.

Jean-Louis Fabiani, relying on research carried out on French festivals, in particular the Cannes Film Festival and the Avignon Festival, views cultural events as spaces driven by dialogic reason, created to expand national citizenship in the democratic sense while still maintaining the nation-state as their main cultural reference. Their targeted audiences are the educated middle classes, and, considering the expansion of the latter over the years, it would seem that the democratization logic driving festivals is working as intended. At the same time, the asymmetry between the artist (as the producer of knowledge or aesthetics) and the audience (as the passive recipient of this artistic codified experience) is maintained and reproduced. The expanding cultural diversification of festivals is, however, leading to the shift of the national–international boundary frame originally used to legitimize (French) festivals' identities as 'national' objects engaged in cultural (international) diplomacy. In turn, this creates a new or different framework for the understanding of citizenship.

Motti Regev is also interested in the festival audience. His research, which focused on four Israeli festivals, namely the Israel Festival Jerusalem, the Red Sea Jazz Festival, the Haifa International Film Festival and the Jerusalem International Film Festival, reveals the ways in which international cosmopolitan festivals serve the cultural tastes of the educated middle classes, which are best described as 'omnivorous' in their conspicuousness, i.e. their abundance and extravagance. Festivals, according to Regev, are conspicuous in terms of their rites of display and consumption – just consider the concentration of so many 'shows' from so many countries in so few days – and in their dramatization of events as 'special' either with respect to representing prominence or for featuring the less well known. It is also not surprising, argues Regev, that small countries, as also second-tier cities, are especially interested in launching arts festivals. Internationalism is the opposite, perhaps, but also an important reference point for national culture (Cinar 2010); therefore, without the enlightened eclecticism and humanist openness that characterizes the omnivorous cosmopolitan middle classes (and their festivals) it is also no longer possible to sustain the distinction, as such, of nationality – an oxymoron perhaps, but one that underlines the contradictory nature of modern civilizations.

Maurice Roche, writing about the historic development of mega-events such as world Expos and the Olympics, thinks that their cultural significance lies in their minimalist cosmopolitanism, namely in representing instances of peaceful coexistence or the proof, perhaps, that the latter is possible. In addition, their proclamation and advancement of human rights, multiculturalism and anti-racism are not mere marketing strategies but authentic symbolic representations. In this respect, the significance of such events is not diminished but is rather amplified through mediatization. Through modern means of communication the 'public' or audience of such events is increased many times over, thus also increasing the scope and extent of this 'mediated cosmopolitanism'.

Joanne Cummings, Ian Woodward and *Andy Bennett* look at the ways in which festivals – and music festivals especially – are contributing to raising young people's awareness about environmental sustainability and a low-carbon society. Their conclusions are based on research carried out on five Australian festivals, the Peat's Ridge Festival, the Big Day Out, the Falls Festival, the Homebake Festival and Splendour in the Green Festival. All of the festivals employ or advertise various environmental sustainability approaches such as organic waste composting, recycling or the use of biodegradable cutlery. The authors consider this 'greenism' of festivals an expression of cosmopolitanism understood as placing local interests in the context of global concerns. Music festivals have been pioneering in this respect.

Jérôme Segal and *Christine Blumauer* trace the development of the Cannes Film Festival since its inception following the end of the Second World War, and show how this grew out of a project of French cultural diplomacy into an arena serving both political and economic (film-industrial) interests. At the same time the festival is a ground – and a leading one at that – for presenting and discovering new talent and new film genres or approaches. It has achieved this by placing a strong emphasis on the *'cinema d'auteur'* and by allowing the parallel running of different sections or programmes. Besides the official section, which is used to attract and present prominent film and stars, the several parallel sections such as the 'Directors' Fortnight' or 'Cinéfondation' provide the opportunity to new directors from around the world to present their work and find distribution channels.

Finally, *Jasper Chalcraft* and *Paolo Magaudda* report on their research on two world-acclaimed music festivals – the WOMAD festival of world music, which has several localities, and the Sónar Festival of electronic music, which takes place in Barcelona. They show how music festivals, however different they might be, are not only locally embedded – both in defining their localities as public spaces and also in that they are dependent on the local scenes of cultural institutions and networks for their existence – but, at the same time, really global in helping ferment music scenes that transcend national borders. This might be especially important within the contemporary music field, given that revenues from labels are on the decline, thus raising once again the value of live performance.

The present volume hopes to engage and reinvigorate a social-scientific and theoretical interest in arts festivals and their meanings and implications for cultural citizenship in the twenty-first century.

References

Appiah, K. A. (2005) *The Ethics of Identity*. New York: Princeton University Press.
Bennett, N. (1999) *Speaking Volumes: A History of the Cheltenham Festival of Literature*. Cheltenham: Sutton Publishing.

Bourdieu, P. (1995) *The Rules of Art: Genesis and Structure of the Literary Field*. Stanford: Stanford University Press.

Cinar, A. (2010) Founding Ideology and the Erasing of the Local in Turkey. *Theory, Culture and Society* 27(4): 90–118.

Delanty, G. and Rumford, C. (2005) *Rethinking Europe: Social Theory and the Implications of Europeanization*. London: Routledge.

Durkheim, E. ([1912] 1995) *The Elementary Forms of Religious Life*. Glencoe: Free Press.

Eder, K. (2006) Europe's Borders: The Narrative Construction of the Boundaries of Europe. *European Journal of Social Theory* 9: 255–271.

Falassi, A. (1987) Festival: Definition and Morphology. In Falassi, A. (ed.) *Time out of Time: Essays on the Festival*. Albuquerque: University of New Mexico Press.

Fraser, N. (1990) Rethinking the Public Sphere: A Contribution to the Critique of Actually Existing Democracy. *Social Text* 25/26: 56–80.

Giddens, A. (1993) *Sociology*. Cambridge: Polity Press.

Giorgi, L., von Homeyer, I. and Parsons, W. (eds.) (2006) *Democracy in the European Union: Towards the Emergence of a Public Sphere*. London: Routledge.

Giorgi, L. (2009) Tariq Ramadan vs. Daniel Cohn-Bendit or Why a European Model of Society based on Weak Citizenship is not Such a Good Idea. *European Journal of Social Theory* 12(4): 465–81.

Gray, J. (2006) *Watching with the Simpsons: Television, Parody, and Intertextuality*. New York: Routledge.

Griswold, W. (1997) *Cultures and Societies in a Changing World*. London: Sage.

Habermas, J. ([1962] 1989) *Strukturwandel der Öffentlichkeit; Untersuchungen zu einer Kategorie der bürgerlichen Gesellschaft*. Frankfurt am Main: Suhrkamp.

Habermas, J. (1992) *Between Facts and Norms: Contributions to a Discourse Theory of Law and Democracy*. Cambridge MA: MIT Press.

Hartley, J. and Green, J. (2006) The Public Sphere on the Beach. *European Journal of Cultural Studies* 9(3): 341–62.

Jones, P. (2007) Cosmopolitanism and Europe: Describing Elites or Challenging Inequalities? In Rumford, C. (ed.) *Cosmopolitanism and Europe*. Liverpool: Liverpool University Press.

McGuigan, J. (2004) *Rethinking Cultural Policy*. Milton Keynes: Open University Press.

Metraux, G. S. (1976) Editorial: of Feasts and Carnivals …. *Cultures* 3(1): 7–10.

Ober, J. (2008) *Democracy and Knowledge: Innovation and Learning in Classical Athens*. New York: Princeton University Press.

Shiner, L. (2001) *The Invention of Art; A Cultural History*. Chicago: Chicago University Press.

Williams, R. ([1961] 2001) *The Long Revolution*. London: The Broadview Press.

1 Urban festivals and the cultural public sphere

Cosmopolitanism between ethics and aesthetics

Monica Sassatelli

The relatively scarce social science material on contemporary festivals is on the whole dominated by a fundamental narrative of falling from grace with respect to pre-modern (temporally or conceptually) festivals. Implicitly or explicitly, it draws on master narratives of modernization as secularization and disenchantment, or, even more critically, commodification and one-dimensionality. When not exclusively focused on 'impact evaluation' and management issues, this literature has mainly posited a directly proportional relationship between the growing professionalization, commercialization and basically popular success of festivals and their becoming both less critical and less significant in terms of their role within wider social life. The exponential growth of festivals in recent decades and their enduring relationship with their location and, in particular, with urban settings lies behind a still timid, but growing, academic interest. However, this is still hardly attuned, if not in open contrast, to the substantial literature on traditional, often rural, festivals, developed especially by anthropology and folklore studies, which instead conceives of festivals as organic expressions of so-called traditional societies and platforms for the representation and reproduction of their cultural repertoires and, thus, identities.

This chapter aims at questioning this common normative stance, which sees contemporary festivals in terms of what they lack in comparison with their forebears or – taking the lead from the theory of the public sphere – as an example of the shift from a 'culture debating' to a 'culture consuming' public sphere. The conceptual tool that allows for such a critique is that of the more focused and articulated *cultural public sphere* that this volume concentrates on (Jones 2007; McGuigan 2005). The notion will be substantiated here by showing the limits of dominant approaches in research on festivals and the promise of alternative ones. Such a critical programme is important because, whilst master narratives of modernization have been discredited in their cruder versions, they lie quite comfortably at the basis of the literature on festivals because unacknowledged.

In order to unveil this, both the classical vision of the traditional festival and the mainstream vision of contemporary festivals will be considered. The analysis proceeds from a consideration of how the cultural significance of festivals, in their more far-reaching aspects as sites for the re-enactment and reproduction of 'community', has been thematized, from the classic studies by Durkheim on. As a corrective to the dismissive attitude to contemporary festivals somehow implicit in this approach, the critical and engaged position of Simmel, who is often overlooked, will be presented. Simmel's snapshots of world exhibitions and his concept of sociability in particular are relevant for the cultural public sphere and provide a possible counterweight to the critical and dismissive position of the Frankfurt school towards mass culture. The latter still informs rigid dichotomies at the basis of festival research, as well as of a similar stance in public sphere theory, especially in its original formulation by Habermas. We then consider how the study of contemporary urban festivals, too, is dominated by such dichotomies, showing especially how even those who do take festivals seriously, i.e. cultural policy researchers, have explained the increasing recent success of urban festivals in Europe as levers for economic regeneration and, by the same token, as possible agents of standardization. Most of the time this leads to bypassing urban festivals' cultural significance, which, as we shall see, is rather better understood in terms of 'festive sociability' as the type of experience informing the cultural public sphere. Finally, the chapter goes beyond its critical objective, applying the notion of this emerging cultural public sphere to interpreting the significance of post-traditional urban festivals as expressions of contemporary society, with particular reference to the notion of cosmopolitanism, often theorized as an aspect of urban experience itself, and in its aesthetic declination a key ingredient of urban festivals. Here, too, the notion of the cultural public sphere allows the evaluative distinction between ethical and aesthetic cosmopolitanism, which is often just the premise for dismissing the latter, to be overcome. Although this chapter mainly advances a critical theoretical argument, examples will be drawn from major urban festivals, and in particular from the European Capital of Culture programme, a long-lasting research interest of mine (Sassatelli 2002, 2009), as well as insights on mixed arts urban festivals in Europe from ongoing research forming the basis for the publication of this volume (Sassatelli 2008; Giorgi and Segal 2009).

Festivals and modern experience

That contemporary sociology has dismissed the study of festivals is somewhat ironic, since virtually no study of them ever fails to cite Emile Durkheim's pioneering work on festivals as intensification of the collective being. Indeed, even today Durkheim's work remains the point of departure. In festivals Durkheim saw a form of 'collective effervescence', in which the solidarity of collective consciousness found both expression and consolidation. Developed in his study on *The Elementary Forms of the Religious Life* (Durkheim 1912 [1995]), this referred to equally 'primitive' societies held together by mechanical solidarity.[1] This is because festivals can be seen as a space and time separated from the profane dimension of daily life and actualizing the sacred. Durkheim's approach was then taken up and accorded long-lasting impact through the work of Marcel Mauss and others (see also Caillois 1958). 'For Durkheim, as for Caillois, the festive process ... generates a collective excitement that frees society from its everyday ups and downs, engaging the social substance in its sacred substrate' (Piette 1992: 40). To describe this social effervescence, Durkheim stressed the moments of exaltation, passion and loss of control (however planned) that, transcending daily life and its rules, established contact with the transcendent in general and with creative moments of rule-making. In this French school of sociology, festival theories derive from within the sociology of religion. Within the latter, and in Durkheimian fashion, the festival becomes an exclusively serious space–time, and little room is left for ambiguity and alternative voices apart from those of the order reinforced through sanctioned transgression. Based on such rigid dichotomies as that between sacred and profane, this type of approach is likely to interpret divergent forms as non-equally serious and therefore irrelevant. Even approaches based on the more recent, but already 'classic', study of rituals by Turner (1982), whilst they stress festivals as polyvocal performances rather than as unified signifiers of a consensual collective conscience, characterized by plural and contrasting rituals,[2] still seem to have serious, 'traditional' festivals in mind as being on the right side of the distinction.

It is perhaps because contemporary, post-traditional festivals have lost their close association with religion that they have escaped the sociologist's attention and have been dismissed as not equally revelatory of society's self-representation when compared with their traditional forebears. More interestingly, given that contemporary society is itself allegedly secularized, festivals are dismissed as remnants of earlier, more *Gemeinshaft* types of social relations and not really representative of modernity, now that they are emptied of that deep, organic meaning. The conceptualization of festivals – or lack of it – can thus be read in the light of this master narrative of modernization. However, an often overlooked approach that can be useful in teasing out this equally often overlooked connection is to be seen in the work of another founder of sociology, Georg Simmel. This is the case in particular in his short essay on the Berlin Exhibition of 1896, one of the many articles Simmel wrote intervening in the 'public sphere' of his time.[3] It is admittedly little more than a cursory glance at festivals, although one that shows their relevance for some of Simmel's key themes such as sociability, the blasé attitude and the shifting relationship between objective and subjective culture in modernity. Simmel explicitly classifies world exhibitions as one of the clearest examples of social phenomena that continue to exist after the original, specific function for which they emerged fades as a result of changing social conditions. What is left is not empty of meaning; rather it is taken over by 'sociability', a more generic, but still sociologically fundamental, form of sociation, and still a crucial indicator of a society's character according to the specific forms it assumes.

> Alongside the very process of sociation, there is also, as a by-product, the sociable meaning of society. The latter is always a meeting point for the most diverse formation of interest groups, and thus remains as the sole

integrating force even when the original reasons for consociation have lost their effectiveness. The history of world exhibitions, which originated from annual fairs, is one of the clearest examples of this most fundamental type of human sociation.

(Simmel 1896 [1991]: 119)

Such sweeping comments may have become rare in contemporary research on festivals (or in general); often, however, the result is only to make the broad generalizations at their basis implicit. So although clear-cut dichotomies and unilinear master narratives of modernity have been amply criticized in social theory (for a review, see Delanty 2006), in research on festivals, as in other cases of cultural production and consumption, they tend to remain as unchallenged and unspoken. Contemporary society is seen as not needing, wanting or being able to reproduce the conditions for 'organic' festivals as codified social phenomena expressing and reinforcing a (well-defined) collective identity, as described by Durkheim. Simmel's account is refreshingly explicit, whilst at the same time allowing acknowledgement of the historical fact of the transformation of festivals, not necessarily in terms of inexorable loss of authenticity, but in terms of the sociability function they continue to perform, a particular sociability that could be, as we shall see, the key to festivals' specific public sphere, or better to their *cultural public sphere*. Indeed, even if 'amusement' is the key to understanding these kaleidoscopic events, according to Simmel, this is not a way to dismiss them, but rather an insight into the specific, modern experience of sociability through its forms of (cultural) production and consumption. In what we would today call mega-events, the common denominator one can grasp amidst the excess of stimuli, the overall message, is that 'one is here to amuse oneself' (Simmel 1896 [1991]: 119). The fact that amusement should take this spectacularized and heterogeneous form is not frowned upon as a sign of the corruption of previously more serious, 'finer' cultural entertainments – an attitude implicitly or explicitly at the basis of much contemporary research on festivals – it is instead linked to the very foundation of modern society, to the predominant 'blasé' psychological condition and to the emergence of what already at the turn of the twentieth century were called 'world cities'. In keeping with his subtle analysis of the modern experience epitomized in the metropolis, Simmel describes how 'overstimulated nerves' need this richness and variety of impressions, thus creating a sort of inverted proportion between 'modern man's one-sided and monotonous role in the division of labour [and] consumption and enjoyment through the growing pressure of heterogeneous impressions' (Simmel 1896 [1991]: 120). In a way taking up the Durkheimian topic of modernity as characterized by division of labour, specialization and differentiation, Simmel here observes a corollary in cultural life (a theme that he developed in a number of key essays; see especially Simmel 1903 [2000], 1918 [1997]), where consumption instead becomes characterized by ever-growing diversity as well as quantity of stimuli. At the same time, fragmentation is avoided through the superficial, but still meaningful, unity of being part of the same event, reaching an aesthetic and sociable, if certainly not cognitive or rational, coherence. This outward unity emerging from contrasts and variety also has a specific modern character in that the ambition of such big celebrations is to be representative of a whole city, and of the whole world within that; in these events 'a city can represent itself as a copy and a sample of the manufacturing forces of world culture' (Simmel 1896 [1991]: 121).

Although not really developed, and found in an occasional paper focused on world exhibitions, these remarks are useful because, instead of pointing out easy distinctions between ethics and aesthetics, authentic and inauthentic, they take the new meanings that festivals may acquire seriously by trying to tease out the relationship with wider societal trends. One may challenge Simmel's conclusion, but the task remains for any serious research on festivals. It is a task that is often made more difficult by a tendency to consider festivals as worlds in themselves. Indeed, a risk that both Durkheimian and Turnerian approaches run is that by conceiving festivals as containing whole worlds that have their own kind of parallel reality – the much quoted 'time out of time' of Falassi's definition (Falassi 1987) – they end up actually forgetting festivals' equally relevant contextualization into the world 'outside'. As a result,

> many studies of festivals, in both theoretical and empirical terms, are marked by tightly defined boundaries of their immediate social context, with an emphasis upon closed spaces, fixed times, indigenous social actors, internal regimes and symbolic contexts, and bounded rituals. Fewer studies have sought to position festivals in a context that is fluid, open to different scopes of (transnational) society and cultural vectors, and that resonates with the realities of ongoing change.
>
> (Picard and Robinson 2006: 4–5)

Other useful analytical tools to avoid these shortcomings come from another field of studies that can be brought to bear on that of festivals and may have much to say about cultural production, display and consumption in general. This concerns studies of cultural displays, which have been developed mainly with regard to museums and visual arts exhibitions, but which can be, and have been, also applied to festival settings. This is well exemplified by a trail-blazing volume edited for the Smithsonian institute on *Exhibiting Cultures* (Karp and Levine 1991). The book considers cultural displays in general as contested arenas for competing meanings, 'settings in which different parties dispute both the control of exhibitions and assertions of identity made in and experienced through visual displays' (Karp 1991: 279). Turning to festivals, here they are defined as inclusive, celebratory events (with little attention to their commercial side), with a view to 'examining how festivals present yet another public forum in which cultural displays tend to produce disputes over meaning' (Ibid.). Indeed, especially when contrasted with museums, festivals are characterized by their 'living' dimension. Unlike museums, festivals are seen as sites of more unrestrained sensory experience, whilst museums rely on distance (they convey an idea of preciousness, rarity and high cultural and financial value, all of which is related to authenticity). Festivals, too, are about authenticity, but in a different way; '[f]estivals communicate messages about authenticity while they also invoke pleasurable, sensual experiences that more totally involve the person' (Ibid.: 282) – a totalizing participation that engages all senses and behaviours, and that some describe as 'blowout': 'The stance that is stressed in festivals is active rather than passive, encouraging involvement rather than contemplation.' (Ibid.)

At the same time, cultural display has a high potential for empowerment, and an underlying question remains as to who exactly is empowered in given cases (an observed positive effect of festivals is raising the status of despised groups of performers, often reaching beyond the event to the context the performers come from). Festivals have a more democratic and non-judgemental participatory and sensory aesthetics than do museums; as such the distinction between museums and festivals is seen as basically reproducing that between elite and popular culture. This observation is obviously more relevant with folk festivals in mind; however, its corollary might be worth considering also in the case of our contemporary, international festivals:

> Elite culture tells a story of cultivation that has universal implications. [...] Festivals tell stories that deny or ignore the universalizing themes of elite culture, in that they often entail just those cultural experiences and groups that resist the universal. Universal stories lead to tidy events; particularizing stories do not allow their tellers to wrap them up into neat packages.
>
> (Ibid.: 283–4)

By taking traditional festivals very seriously, classic sociology and anthropology may have contributed to the dismissal of contemporary arts festivals, creating the grounds for the dichotomous visions that still dominate the field: in particular that of authentic versus commercial festivals, and the related one of critical or engaged versus 'mere spectacularisation',[4] a theme particularly taken up in the critique of the cultural industry more generally. In a way, the fact that a good proportion of the scarce literature on contemporary festivals has been driven by economic research focusing exclusively on economic returns, and thus on an instrumental vision of festivals, has also contributed to reinforcing the idea that contemporary festivals are – from a cultural point of view – of little relevance, as they are dominated by commercial, 'inauthentic' logics. However, as we have seen in Simmel and in studies of cultural displays, nothing prevents us from taking contemporary festivals seriously either, and not only in economic terms, but precisely by virtue of their sociability and experiential form. In doing so, we can trace the complex, polyvocal, discursive and relational field that festivals generate, and thus see in them a litmus test of contemporary public culture, providing an interpretative key to some important issues within it.

Contemporary festivals and urbanity

One good example that shows how binary logics may be too reductive and may struggle to interpret festivals satisfactorily is the peculiar relation of festivals to place, and to cities in particular. Festivals are place specific, as they are performance based (even those that concern non-performative arts), and have a concentrated space–time frame: they create the sense of unique, one-off experiences, for which it is important to say 'I was there', and which therefore bear their own authenticity. It is an authenticity, though, that is less connected to notions of 'purity' than to hybridity – at least, this seems to be the case with contemporary festivals, where experience is the result of an array of different, hybrid stimuli. (For hybridity as the rule of cultural production now, see Regev in this volume.) As festivals have something to do with place, and as 'place' includes a cultural dimension,[5]

> successful festivals create a powerful but curious sense of place, which is local, as the festival takes place in a locality or region, but which often makes an appeal to a global culture in order to attract both participants and audiences.
>
> (Waterman 1998: 58)

This seems to be the case in particular with urban festivals and other major urban events such as World Expos and, more recently, the 'European Capital of Culture', all of which take the name of the city hosting them and develop a complex, circular relation to it.

According to Boissevain (1992), the recent explosion of festivals in European cities is connected and stimulated by secularization, migrations, democratization or, in general, by increased mobility and change. Historical accounts have already stressed the role of festivals as a connecting thread for the social fabric, so their parallel transformation should not come as a surprise. In particular Muir (1997) has analyzed in a European context and historically the importance of public festivities across Europe from the twelfth to the eighteenth centuries, i.e. the period during which 'civic consciousness, or the identification of individuals with their home town, came to be one of the distinguishing characteristics of European civilisation' (Quinn 2005: 928). One of Muir's key examples is Venice's ability to reassert its political dominance over the surrounding cities and regions by imposing its rituals and symbols so as to consolidate civic identity. Indeed, to this day Venice's lion of St Mark is ubiquitous in the public spaces of what used to be Venice's controlled provinces – as well as having become the logo of the contemporary city festival, the Venice Biennale. This is relevant here since it would seem to establish a clear discontinuity with contemporary festivals, which are instead seen as mainly linked to economic and 'regeneration' objectives, especially since the 1980s, when a festival rush was identified, driven by local authorities looking for 'place promotion'. However, Venice's example is interesting precisely because the Venice Biennale itself, although established in non-suspect times as one of the oldest European festivals (its art component dates back to 1895), was clearly, and quite blatantly, an operation to rescue a dying star in the European cultural firmament, especially when the Cinema section was established in the 1930s to prolong and salvage the seaside holiday season of Venice Lido (Papastergiadis and Martin also comment on that in this volume). Regeneration was there long before the 'city marketing' of the 1980s; however, political or cultural diplomacy objectives were also there, co-existing rather than as alternatives. Venice is not an exceptional or isolated case; even when we look at a much more recent, but still established, festival (preceding by far the festival rush of the end of the twentieth century), such as Brighton's in the UK – launched in the late 1960s and now the biggest in England – this one, too, had the unmistakeable aim of relaunching the seaside resort and extending its 'season', according to its own founders. At the same time, this original motor or lever cannot account alone for the festival's significance, or for its success (Giorgi and Segal 2009).

However, the interpretation of urban festivals according to phases of local cultural policy[6] has attained an impressive dominance in the literature. In 'Arts Festivals and the City', Bernadette Quinn (2005) focuses on this relationship of festivals with their urban settings and the multiple instrumentalities of culture; she concludes that we need more, and more multidimensional, research on festivals to assess whether they meet 'their undoubted potential in animating communities, celebrating diversity and improving quality of life' (Quinn 2005: 927). Observing the remarkable rise in the number of arts festivals in cities throughout Europe in recent decades and since the late 1970s and 1980s in particular (PAYE 2008; Allen and Shaw 2000), this is connected with the industrial to post-industrial shift of many major European cities and their quest for ways to 'regenerate' themselves. However, the actual capacity of festivals to meet regeneration objectives remains a moot issue, with quite a number of researchers arguing that using festivals for city marketing and place distinctiveness may be counterproductive, since they run the risk of becoming formulaic and standardized, a form of 'serial reproduction' (Richards and Wilson 2004; Evans 2001). Hard evidence of the regeneration effects is in short supply and narrowly concentrates on the economic impact. Moreover, 'the long-term social impact of culture-led urban regeneration remains something of a mystery' (Quinn 2005: 931), and this is even more so for cultural impact in terms of '[w]hat roles ... the arts festival [has] played in advancing urban policy, contributing to urban life and facilitating the expression of cultural identities' (Ibid.).

Lacking research to provide evidence, studies often rely on commentaries around a set of common macro-sociological distinctions. In particular, it is common to contrast commodification and globalization with the production of spaces for creativity and difference; tourist orientation with authenticity; and reproduction of consolidated social distinctions with countercultural expression within the festivals. An example of such commentaries is Kirstie Jamieson's (2004) article on Edinburgh as a 'festival city'. Jamieson builds around what can be considered the common stance taken by critical social scientists vis-à-vis the often too enthusiastic and uncritical ideas of festivals as sources of regeneration and 'freedom of expression'. The target of the critique is that contemporary arts festivals do not lead to an actual challenge (a carnivalesque subversion) of the everyday and established differentials of access to cultural production and consumption, because they only provide a tourist, commodified 'encounter with the unexpected', a pseudo-transgression that celebrates difference, but actually aestheticizes it and glosses over – thus in fact excluding – actual social differences within the city. This critique also commonly highlights a romantic 'nostalgia for a more sociable and public mode of urban living' (Ibid.: 73), found among audiences and organizers alike. However, the critique itself seems equally gripped by nostalgia for 'traditional' or 'authentic' festivals, rather than questioning the dichotomy, and by a romantic view of community versus society.

Finkel (2004) also well represents this common critique. Drawing on survey research on festivals in the UK as well as a qualitative component (a postal survey with festival organizers across the UK and interviews with policy makers and selected festival organizers), she concludes that

> a new 'type' of combined arts festival is emerging that is more standardized and commercialized. This 'type' is partially a result of entrepreneurial local authorities attempting to capitalize on culture and broaden audience inclusion and partly due to combined arts festivals having to conform to consumer demands or funding body regulations to secure capital. These sanitized, more homogenized versions could be detrimental to traditional local festivals as more contenders vie for a decreasing pool of resources, potentially leading to a loss of place-based individuality for combined arts festivals and the uniformity of cultural forms presented.
>
> (Ibid.: 1)

Finkel calls this process 'McFestivalization' and concludes that 'indeed, the reputation of arts festivals to help the reputation of cities may be at the crux of their upsurge' (Ibid.: 3). This is why they seem trapped in a vicious circle of imitation, risking failure in what Finkel sees as 'the role of the arts to resist this very kind of conformity' (Ibid.: 6).

So if festivals seem to owe their recent proliferation to a self-fulfilling prophecy, then, not surprisingly, social scientists have made it their mission to break the spell. However, this has led to a rather dichotomized, or simplified, debate, revolving around whether or not festivals have regenerative effects, whether or not they are sites of more open cultural politics, and whether or not their association with tourism, commodification and globalization necessarily implies a loss of authenticity, specificity and identity. The latter have always remained the domain of 'traditional' festivals. In this black-and-white picture – enhanced by the almost exclusive methodological reliance on mainly quantitative, economic indicators (even when 'cultural impact' is supposedly targeted) – there is usually little space for nuanced analysis. Even if some authors have pointed to the possibilities of re-appropriation that even commodified, invented (traditional) festivals can have for different audiences (de Bres and Davis 2001; Crespi-Valbona and Richards 2007), the opposition between traditional, local and identity-laden events on the one hand, and change, globalization and extra-cultural instrumentality (tourist and regeneration objectives) on the other is never really challenged. As one can see, a mainstream view of globalization (and related phenomena) and identity as 'conflicting trends' in themselves (Castells 1997: 1) is the unchallenged common basis, so rooted at the heart of implicit theoretical positions that no one seems to have ventured to thematize urban, post-traditional festivals as a (cultural) public sphere.

A particularly neat and revealing exemplification of this is the European City of Culture (ECOC) festival, and the way it has usually been thematized in research. Initiated by the EU (then EC) in 1985 and now a clear 'brand' in Europe's cultural calendar, the ECOC is often cited as a paradigmatic instance of the culture-led urban regeneration approach. Ignored in the first years of their existence, ECOCs have attracted growing attention since Glasgow's nomination in 1990 – the first city to adopt an urban regeneration approach within this programme and to commission proper impact studies (Myerscough 1991). Subsequent ECOCs have attracted increasing scholarly attention, which has followed the path opened by the first studies and has looked mainly for evidence of economic impact, neglecting other forms of impact as well as long-term effects. These remain open to debate today. An exception is found in a study of Glasgow 1990 that was carried out over a decade after the events and endeavoured to assess the cultural impact by means of 'soft indicators' such as those emerging from media analysis and interviews with people in the local cultural sector, concluding that the effect on local identities and city image is indeed the strongest and most long-lasting legacy of the event (García 2005). However, this study, too, shares with the rest of the literature on the subject a neglect of the programme's European dimension and of identities beyond a local, static understanding of them. Apart from some passing remarks, the role of the ECOC within the process of Europeanization and as a viewpoint from which to explore trans-national, European identities has been left unexplored (but see also Keohane 1999; Sassatelli 2002, 2009).

In summary, the dominant trend in research on contemporary urban festivals fails to address their peculiar sociability function (to say it à la Simmel), and thus to unravel their specific form of authenticity and the participatory aspects that are the basis of the complex relation to place, and to cities, in particular. The tendency remains to see festivals as a set of abstract *objets d'art* or events rather than focus on how they might reorganize urban places, creating informal spaces for debate and criticism that have their own forms of inclusivity (and therefore exclusions as well, of course; for an exception focusing on fringe festivals' countercultural reputation, see Willems-Brown 1994). In particular, it conceals what, in a study of the Fallas festival in Valencia, Xavier Costa – partly also inspired by Simmel – has called *festive sociability*: 'festive sociability is shown to have its own public sphere in which reflexivity can be expressed through art and play' (Costa 2002: 484). This reflexivity, in other words, is not only that of critical reasoning that characterized Habermas's bourgeois public sphere, but can also take an aesthetic form,[7] where both the type of critical distance created and the type of participation are different:

> Habermas' concentration on argumentation divides people's attitudes into two extremes, with a big gap in the middle: either they focus on a rational thematization to solve a problem (critical argumentation as the way to question) or they routinely take for granted stocks of rules, knowledge, etc., which are deposited in the life world. There is no place for a wider questioning, a 'sociable thematization', which is able to retain its content, but in a subordinate form to sociability. The festive sociability of the Fallas includes this wider, sociable and festive capacity to convey criticism through the medium of jokes, art or play.
>
> (Ibid., 486)

This is not an unprecedented critique, since others have also pointed out the need to recover non-cognitive and, especially, aesthetic and affective dimensions of the public sphere, and indeed that is the main purpose of the concept of the cultural public sphere (for a review and a definition, see, in particular, McGuigan in this volume). It is interesting, however, to see a similar line of thought find its way into the study of festivals, and to observe the way the dichotomy between the culture debating and culture consuming public spheres – as, more generally, the reductive vision of 'reception' established by the mass culture school – fails properly to account for the experience of festivals. Rational argument may certainly not figure high in festivals, which might thus appear as yet another instance of a 'culture consuming', corrupted public sphere, but other forms of cultural criticism and sociability are in place. What contemporary festivals may have lost, to go back to Simmel, is the practical, specific function that spawned them (perhaps religious, or even commercial) but not their sociable one – and the specific forms this sociability takes can indeed be revealing of this reconceptualized cultural public sphere.

Aesthetic versus ethical cosmopolitanism

That critical analysis has accepted at face value the shift from 'cultural' to 'economic' objectives as a general trend in contemporary festivals actually evinces little critical distance from the policies' own objectives and self-evaluation. It also neglects the fact that, regardless of the main, dominant approach within a policy, the cultural, or even symbolic, dimension, as well as the possibility of resistant forms of experiencing them, do not simply fade away. Now mainly commercial (though even the most 'traditional' festivals had commercial aspects, sometimes quite prominent ones), festivals are still public cultural events. Rather than being analytically distinguished, these two dimensions tend to be conflated and confused. Once again, a very clear example is the way the European Capital of Culture's cultural significance is dismissed in passing remarks, such as in the following passage by Ash Amin in an article otherwise dealing with regionalism.

> [W]e can compare two very different versions of cultural connectivity circulating in current debates on multiculturalism. One is a 'consumer' cosmopolitanism, typified by the EU programme on European Cities of Culture, which celebrates cities and regions as cultural gateways, and plays on the virtues of world music, minority ethnic food and festival, regeneration based on multicultures and multiethnic public spaces, and the exoticism of the stranger. A raft of contemporary urban and regional regeneration strategies play on this aspect of belonging in the world in order to re-boot the local economy through new consumption, as well as to demonstrate an openness to multiculturalism and multiethnicity.
>
> (Amin 2004: 42)

This is interesting because, whilst it establishes a connection with cosmopolitanism, currently one of the most debated topics in social theory, it only does so by qualifying it as 'consumer' and distinguishing it from what the writer sees as a more 'ethical' form. The latter refers to a more serious and relevant, we assume,

> cosmopolitan ethos of solidarity and rights that has been growing in different parts of the world as a form of local response to global poverty, ethnic intolerance and Empire. It is based on combating racism, protecting the rights of displaced people and asylum seekers and fostering inter-cultural dialogue and commitment to distant strangers. It frequently involves local groups developing voice and impact through worldwide solidarity networks and social movements in order to shape and influence cultural politics both "at home" and in other regions.
>
> (Ibid.)

That is not an infrequent move. The idea of a non-elite, 'actually existing' cosmopolitanism is accepted, but also dismissed as not being quite the real thing.

This is particularly the case for 'aesthetic cosmopolitanism'. A recent addition to the growing family of 'cosmopolitanisms', aesthetic cosmopolitanism has, on a whole, a negative reputation, precisely because of having been dismissed by some as a form of consumer cosmopolitanism. Two more-or-less simultaneous origins of the expression 'aesthetic cosmopolitanism' in recent times are found in the mid 1990s: on the one hand, within a consideration of cultural globalization (indeed, it has also been equated with 'cultural cosmopolitanism'), as the related capacity and desire to experience or consume the cultural products of 'others'; and on the other hand, within the sociology of tourism, as a similar attitude towards being immersed, through travel, in other cultures. As one can see, the two contexts share much; tourism is a specific form of consumption and cultural practice, and the connection becomes even clearer when we consider that postmodern tourism has been characterized, among other things, as also happening without actual physical displacement (through media experience).

The expression 'aesthetic cosmopolitanism' was probably first used by John Urry in his *Consuming Places* (Urry 1995: 167), and as such it indicated a sort of extension to the wide contemporary tourist class of the aesthetic disposition of openness once reserved for the eighteenth-century aristocracy (in particular the British aristocracy) undertaking the so-called 'Grand Tour': 'a cultural disposition involving an intellectual and aesthetic stance of "openness" towards peoples, places and experiences from different cultures, especially those from different "nations"' (Szerszinski and Urry 2002: 468; see also Hannerz 1990). The idea of cultural diversity being appreciated on aesthetic grounds by cosmopolitans, given their attitude of active engagement with the other, is also relevant here. The cosmopolitan displays an attitude and eagerness to become familiar with other cultures, through experience and reflection. Although Urry is careful to present tourism as a democratization of travel, he is also not totally free from the idea that such democratization involves a measure of corruption, and that an aesthetic cosmopolitanism will never be as profound and engaged as a proper 'ethical' cosmopolitanism.

It is probably in Tomlinson's usage of the expression in *Globalization and Culture* that this aspect is more evident. According to Tomlinson,

> [t]he aesthetic is not, of course, to be confused with the ethical and ... there is no guarantee that the lifting of general cultural horizons, the honing of semiotic skills and the development of hermeneutic sensibilities will be followed by any necessary sense of responsibility for the global totality.
>
> (1999: 202)

Nevertheless, some space for a less binary division between aesthetic and ethical cosmopolitanisms is allowed, in that 'it is perhaps more likely that such a sense will develop *obliquely* from these popular cultural practices, than that it will be directly cultivated in some sort of abstract global-civic ethic' (Ibid.: 202). This 'frequent flyers' cosmopolitanism would also be rather soft, in that the conditions of contemporary travel (hotel chains, airport lounges and all the typical non-places similar everywhere) considerably cushion the impact and the otherness, itself, of the other (Calhoun 2002). So this aesthetic cosmopolitanism belongs to (mass) tourists: passive, kept in a bubble, enjoying commercialized pseudo-events, and screened off from authenticity. Their cosmopolitanism is superficial, not 'ethical'. So are (assumed to be) the audience of festivals, as well as festivals' organizing principles and festivals' culture. 'Commercialized' is also a key word because an even deeper underlying reference is a long-standing distinction between the products of the culture industry, repetitive and passive, and 'real' culture, engaging and challenging. In a sense, the loss of the critical, 'emancipative' function of aesthetic (high) culture is considered the price to be paid so as to dispose of high cultural elitism, and thus a condition for the democratization of culture (Jones 2007: 76).

Concluding remarks

All these distinctions have been criticized individually, but they keep cropping up under new expressions, such as aesthetic and ethical cosmopolitanism. Binary distinctions dominate, too, in research on festivals. Although recent empirical findings on ordinary (or banal, vernacular, etc.) cosmopolitanism all problematize clear-cut distinctions (Kendall *et al.* 2009), combining openness with a sense of place, and ethics with aesthetics, remains one open challenge of a cosmopolitan (cultural) public sphere. Szerszynski and Urry voice a common concern:

> [W]e do not want to appear to suggest that there is an *inevitable* irreconcilability between cosmopolitan openness on the one hand and dwelling in place on the other. Rather, it may simply be the case that we need to explore, both conceptually and practically, alternative kinds of cosmopolitanism in which this tension is avoided or overcome ... Perhaps we need to fashion such a form of 'cosmopolitics' if we are not all to be fated to become mere visitors in our own worlds.
>
> (Szerszynski and Urry 2000: 127–8; see also Latour 2004)

However, being faced with such dilemmas derives from a priori oppositions that remain unquestioned, as we have seen is the case in public sphere theory. Indeed, judged in terms of the 'standard' public sphere, this aesthetic cosmopolitanism of the type found in the ECOC and other festivals is inauthentic and inconsequential, because the only dimension valued is the cognitive (framing the political and ethical) one. If we instead open up to a more inclusive – and yet specific to contemporary cultural manifestations – *cultural* public sphere, it then becomes possible to thematize meaning not in purely cognitive, rational-argumentative terms, but also as the result of multifaceted sociable experience. Moreover, the idea of a unilinear decadence of the public sphere then seems less tenable. In terms of the cultural public sphere, the contemporary festival's enduring sociability, characterized by concentrated stimuli and effervescence, lived experience and now aesthetic cosmopolitanism, is a key starting point instead. Including also (aesthetic) cosmopolitanism in the narrative of decadence means losing from view what the notions of festival sociability and cultural public sphere try to pin down: its alternative critical potential, alternative to participation through rational debate, such as through forms of aesthetic experience. It is not only a matter of there being counter-publics or other forms of public sphere such as the plebeian one that Habermas recently conceded when reviewing his theory of the public sphere. It is rather an issue of a multidimensional approach (considering affective and aesthetic elements as well as cognitive) in the very definition of what a public sphere is, of what, therefore, is worth considering an expression of it, and of what, descriptively or normatively, to expect of it. Aesthetic and ethical components are usefully distinguished not if the distinction is used, as it often has been, normatively to judge one side (the aesthetic) in terms of the other (the ethical), but if it serves the purpose of developing a more articulate notion of cultural public sphere, and concepts more sensitive to its specific forms of participation, reflexivity and sociability – such as those we need to grasp festivals' specific spaces of experience.

Notes

1 It is worth mentioning that Durkheim also commented on the modern celebrations inspired by the French Revolution as renewed collective effervescence, stressing that it is a general feature that we are likely to find again and again, rather than a one-off and then lost forever trait of bygone times; he therefore did not rule out forms of it that would be more in line with modernity's organic solidarity, and briefly considered that possibility (Durkheim 1912 [1995]: 213–216, 430). However, these remarks have not been taken up in Durkheimian studies of modern festivals.

2 For an application to festivals attempting a morphology, see in particular Falassi (1987) and Regev, this volume.

3 The article was first published as a review of the 1896 Berlin Trade Exhibition in *Die Zeit* (7/91, 1896, p. 204) with the title "Berliner Gewerbeausstellung".

4 It is interesting to note, however, that Guy Debord, the father of the theory of the 'society of spectacle' drew a distinction between spectacle and festival: 'The "potlatch", "lazy liberty without content" (Debord 1983: thesis 127) and "festivals" that are "the moment of a community's participation in the luxurious expenditure of life" (Ibid.: thesis 154) were associated by Debord with a prehistorical, pre-political era. Yet they are also evoked throughout situationist literature as (a) images of the kind of society that the situationists wished to create and (b) the inverse of the spectacle, which is portrayed as a society without real festival, without real life and without real liberty.' (Bonnett 2006: 30)

5 According to a 'sociology of place', there are three elements that make a 'place': geographical location, material form and investment with meaning and value (Gieryn 2000).

6 Three phases in local cultural policies have been defined as the *age of reconstruction* (1940s–60s), the *age of participation* (1970s and early 1980s) and finally the *age of city marketing* (from the mid 1980s to the present) (Bianchini 1999). Even though these should not be considered as clear-cut 'phases', but rather as alternative approaches that can coexist and overlap, they tend to separate 'cultural' and 'economic' rationales as characterizing different eras, rather that promoting an analysis of how they interact in concrete cases.

7 Whether or not 'aesthetic reflexivity' can be a relevant component of 'reflexive modernity' is another main object of contention among different theorists (Giddens *et al.* 1994); this, too, goes to show how research on festivals can and should be brought to bear on key open issues in social theory, such as, notably, the need to rethink the notion of public sphere.

References

Allen, K. and Shaw, P. (2000) *Festivals mean Business. The Shape of Arts Festivals in the UK.* London: British Arts Festivals Association.

Amin, A. (2004) Regions Unbound: Towards a New Politics of Space. *Geografiska Annaler* 86 B (1): 33–44.

Bianchini, F. (1999) The Relationship between Cultural Resources and Urban Tourism Policies: Issues from European Debates. In Dodd, D. and van Hemel, A. (eds.) *Planning Cultural Tourism in Europe: A Presentation of Theories and Cases*. Amsterdam: Boekman Foundation.

Boissevain, J. (ed.) (1992) *Revitalizing European Rituals*. London: Routledge.

Bonnett, A. (2006) The Nostalgias of Situationist Subversion. *Theory, Culture and Society* 23(5): 23–48.

Caillois, R. (1958) *Man and the Sacred*. Glencoe: Free Press.

Calhoun, C. (2002) The Class Consciousness of Frequent Travellers: Towards a Critique of Actually Existing Cosmopolitanism. In Vertovec, S. and Cohen, R. (eds.) *Conceiving Cosmopolitanism – Theory, Context, Practice*. Oxford: Oxford University Press.

Castells, M. (1997) *The Information Age: Economy, Society and Culture, Volume II, The Power of Identity*. Oxford: Blackwell.

Costa, X. (2002) Festive traditions in modernity: the public sphere of the festival of the "Fallas" in Valencia. *Sociological Review* 50(4): 482–504.

Crespi-Valbona, M. and Richards, G. (2007) The meaning of cultural festivals. Stakeholder perspectives in Catalunya. *International Journal of Cultural Policy* 13(1): 103–22.

Debord, G. (1983) *Society of the Spectacle*. Detroit: Black and Red.

De Bres, K. and Davis, J. (2001) Celebrating group and place identity: a case study of a new regional festival. *Tourism Geographies* 3(3): 326–37.

Delanty, G. (2006) Modernity and the Escape from Eurocentrism. In *Handbook of Contemporary European Social Theory*. London: Routledge.

Durkheim, E. ([1912] 1995) *The Elementary Forms of Religious Life*. Glencoe: Free Press.

Evans, G. (2001) *Cultural Planning: An Urban Renaissance*. London: Routledge.

Falassi, A. (1987) Festival: definition and morphology. In Falassi, A. (ed.) *Time Out of Time: Essays on the Festival*. Albuquerque: University of New Mexico Press.

Finkel, R. (2004) McFestivalisation? The Role of Combined Arts Festivals in the UK Cultural Economy. *Journeys of Expression Conference*, published in Conference Proceedings, Sheffield Hallam University, UK, CD-ROM.

García, B. (2005) Deconstructing the City of Culture: the Long-Term Cultural Legacies of Glasgow 1990. *Urban Studies* 42(5/6): 841–68.

Giddens, T., Lash, S. and Beck, U. (1994) *Reflexive Modernisation*. Cambridge: Polity Press.

Gieryn, T. (2000) A Space for Place in Sociology. *Annual Review of Sociology* 26: 463–96.

Giorgi, L. and Segal, J. (2009) *European Arts Festivals from a Historical Perspective*. Euro-festival project report.

Hannerz, U. (1990) Cosmopolitans and Locals in World Culture. In Featherstone, M. (ed.) *Global Culture: Nationalism, Globalization and Modernity*. London: Sage.

Hannerz, U. (1996) *Transnational Connections: Culture, People, Places*. London: Routledge.

Jamieson, K. (2004) Edinburgh: the festival gaze and its boundaries. *Space and Culture* 7(1): 64–75.

Jones. P. (2007) Cultural Sociology and an Aesthetic Public Sphere. *Cultural Sociology* 1(1): 73–95.

Karp, I. (1991) Festivals. In Karp and Levine (eds.) (1991).

Karp, I. and Levine, S. D. (eds.) (1991) *Exhibiting Cultures: The Poetics and Politics of Museum Display*. Washington: Smithsonian Institution Press.

Kendall, G., Woodward, I. and Skrbis, Z. (2009) *The Sociology of Cosmopolitanism: Globalization, Identity, Culture and Government*. Basingstoke: Palgrave.

Keohane, K. (1999) Re-Membering the European Citizen: The Social Construction of Collective Memory in Weimar. *Journal of Political Ideologies* 4(1): 39–59.

Latour, B. (2004) Whose Cosmos, Which Cosmopolitics? Comments on the Peace Terms of Ulrich Beck. *Common Knowledge* 10(3): 450–62.

McGuigan, J. (2005) The Cultural Public Sphere. *European Journal of Cultural Studies* 8(4): 427–43.

Muir, E. (1997) *Ritual in Early Modern Europe*. Cambridge: Cambridge University Press.

Myerscough, J. (1991) *Monitoring Glasgow 1990*. Report prepared for Glasgow City Council, Strathclyde Regional Council and Scottish Enterprise.

PAYE (Performing Arts Yearbook for Europe) (2008) Manchester: Impromptu Publishing.

Picard, D. and Robinson, M. (2006) *Festivals, Tourism and Social Change, Remaking Worlds*. Clevedon: Channel view publications.

Piette, A. (1992) Play, reality and fiction. Toward a theoretical and methodological approach to the festival framework. *Qualitative Sociology* 15(1): 37–52.

Quinn, B. (2005) Arts Festivals and the City. *Urban Studies* 42(5/6): 927–43.

Richards, G. (2000) The European Cultural Capital Event: Strategic Weapon in the Cultural Arms Race? *International Journal of Cultural Policy* 6(2):159–81.

Richards, G. and Wilson, J. (2004) The impact of cultural events on city image: Rotterdam, Cultural Capital of Europe 2001. *Urban Studies* 41(10): 1931–51.

Rolfe, H. (1992) *Arts Festivals in the UK*. London: Policy Studies Institute.

Sassatelli, M. (2002) Imagined Europe: The Shaping of a European Cultural Identity through EU Cultural Policy. *European Journal of Social Theory* 5(4): 435–51.

Sassatelli, M. (ed.) (2008) *European Public Culture and Aesthetic Cosmopolitanism*. Euro-festival project report.

Sassatelli, M. (2009) *Becoming Europeans. Cultural Identity and Cultural Policies*. Basingstoke: Palgrave.

Simmel, G. ([1896] 1991) The Berlin Trade Exhibition. *Theory, Culture and Society* 8(3): 119–23.

Simmel, G. ([1903] 2000) The metropolis and mental life. In Farganis, J. (ed.) *Readings in Social Theory: The Classic Tradition to Post-Modernism*, pp. 149–157. New York: McGraw Hill.

Simmel, G. ([1918] 1997) The conflict in modern culture. In Frisby, D. and Featherstone, M. (eds.) *Simmel on Culture*, pp. 75–89. London: Sage.

Stevenson, D. (2003) *Cities and Urban Cultures*. Buckingham: Open University Press.

Szerszynski, B. and Urry, J. (2002) Cultures of Cosmopolitanism. *Sociological Review* 50: 461–81.

Szerszynski, B. and Urry, J. (2006) Visuality, Mobility and the Cosmopolitan: Inhabiting the World from Afar. *British Journal of Sociology*, 57: 113–31.

Tomlinson, J. (1999) *Globalization and Culture*. Cambridge: Polity.

Turner, V. (1982) *Celebration: Studies in Festivity and Ritual*. Washington, DC: Smithsonian Institution Press.

Urry, J. (1995) *Consuming Places*. London: Routledge.

Waterman, S. (1998) Carnivals for elites? The cultural politics of arts festivals. *Progress in Human Geography* 22(1) 55–74.

Willems-Braun, B. (1994) Situating cultural politics: fringe festivals and the production of spaces of intersubjectivity. *Environment and Planning D: Society and Space* 12(1) 75–104.

2 Between tradition, vision and imagination

The public sphere of literature festivals

Liana Giorgi

A neglected aspect of the theory and research on the public sphere is the aesthetic public sphere, or aesthetic public culture. Unlike other social and cultural institutions such as 'the church' (religion), 'the school' (education) or 'the community centre' (the local) that have been widely explored as sites of identity formation and discursive practice, the arts have received little attention from this angle. This is probably because culture and the arts – whether with 'high-brow' or 'low-brow' connotations – are still considered primarily as depictions of social reality. The recognition that they are autonomous social fields is long established in cultural sociology but not as yet in democratic studies. If, however, following Chaney (2002: 163), we acknowledge that 'cultural objects of performance are shifting from functioning as representations or depictions of social life to constituting the contexts or terms of everyday life', their exploration as public spaces and constituent elements of the democratic public sphere becomes imperative.

The contemporary relative neglect of the study of the role of arts in society has in part to do with the supremacy, within sociology, of the sociology of culture over cultural sociology. The antagonism between the two approaches restates an older cleavage between (historical) materialism and later critical theory, on the one hand, and theories that assign a greater emphasis to ideas and beliefs, or power and status, on the other. For the sociology of culture, what is interesting about the arts is the way in which they are entangled into the processes and patterns of production and consumption characteristic of all markets, and it is perhaps for this reason that the sociology of culture has been mostly interested in the evolution of the popular music industry and the way in which the latter has impacted on cultural taste (Santoro 2008). Cultural sociology takes a more constructivist approach, being more interested in the symbolic domain of cultural practices and their discursive meanings – and hence also more fascinated by performance and visual arts, in addition to film and architecture (Alexander 2005; Alexander *et al.* 2006).

Between the obsession of the sociology of culture with popular forms of music and the fascination of cultural sociology with performance and the visual arts, literature has almost been discarded – today, the sociology of literature is not much more advanced than it was in its early years during the 1960s.

Similarly, within political theory, the early interest in literary events as one of the mediums of enlightenment has given way to law and public policy as testing grounds for democratization.

Against this background, this chapter explores the role of literature within public culture and, by extension, for the public sphere. I start with a review of the early treatment of literature within political and sociological theory before turning to a discussion of contemporary literature festivals. These are discussed from multiple perspectives in order to illustrate the ways in which they relate to phenomena and debates in previous historical periods in addition to anticipating future developments in public culture.

The literary salon in political theory

Beginning in the seventeenth century, literary salons brought together like-minded individuals to discuss arts and politics. Salons were often used for presenting new ideas, read out as papers, which were subsequently published in one of the many literary and political journals appearing around the same time. In *Strukturwandel der Öffentlichkeit*, Habermas ([1960] 1990) saw these literary salons of early modernity as an important facilitator in the emergence of a political public sphere contributing, in its turn, to the process of democratization.

Literary salons displayed a number of features that are worth highlighting. Their 'public' was the educated middle classes, comprising mainly merchants but also craftsmen – i.e. the bourgeoisie. They represented the upcoming urban social class that would question the political and economic forms of organization of aristocratic feudal societies. Their 'setting' was the city, whose dominance, according to Habermas, was consolidated by institutions emerging to take up new functions, such as coffee houses and the print media. Coffee houses grew gradually into an extension of the literary salon encompassing 'the broader strata of the middle class' and thus enabling 'unconstrained access to important circles' (Habermas [1960] 1990: 93, author's translation). Periodicals such as *Tatler*, the *Spectator*, the *Manchester Guardian* and the *Ramble*, which were a mixture of popular journalism, literary criticism and political commentary, became the new media of communication, extending the span of the literary salon even further. Britain, especially, saw the appearance of many periodicals during this time. In an impressive four-volume catalogue, Alvin Sullivan (1983a, 1983b, 1984, 1986) listed and annotated all literary periodicals published between 1698 and 1984 – 90 in the Augustan age (before 1788), 85 in the Romantic Age (until 1836) and over 100 each in the Victorian/ Edwardian (until 1931) and Modern (until 1984) ages respectively. Not many survived for an extensive period of time, most appearing for a few years before vanishing, sometimes to re-emerge under the same or a new title with the same or another publisher.

An especially interesting example was *Cosmopolis; An International Monthly Review*, which was published monthly between 1896 and 1899 in London (by T. Fischer Unwin) and New York (by International News Company).

Cosmopolis was launched with the explicit aim of protecting the intellectual life of Europe from the destructive forces of nationalism. It served as a platform for intellectuals of different political orientations, hosting contributions from Marxists, Fabians, Socialists and Liberals. Each edition comprised an English, French and German issue, presenting features by different authors. In an article entitled 'The True Cosmopolis', written by Frederic Harrison in 1896, the journal's mission was explained as follows.

> An ideal Cosmopolis should from time to time have space for the five chief languages of Western Europe and for contributions from some eight to ten national centres in Europe, and two or three others in North and South America ... The cosmopolitan citizenship of the Medieval University is gone ... The enormous increase of inter-communication due to steam, electricity, railways and the press, does not at all counterbalance the great increase of national pride, jealousy and self-assertion fanned by patriotic dreams of empire, Victory and leadership of the World. This is the ideal Culture of our martial and aggressive age, and it is ex hypothesis a national and not an European culture. [Yet the development of Humanity] needs the joint cooperation of many countries and would languish under any narrow type of national self-sufficiency.
>
> (Harrison 1896: 328–9)

'Cosmopolis' was not the only periodical of the time to follow an explicit political agenda, either in acting explicitly as the mouthpiece of one of the political parties or by pursuing an educative function in the name of enlightenment. Indeed, many of the journals appearing already in the eighteenth century did so in reaction to the rapid diffusion of so-called pamphlet literature, made possible by the new printing technology, but exploited for propaganda purposes (Morrissey 2008). In other words, the literary periodicals of the time had a critical attitude towards the ruling classes, but were equally concerned with the social unrest caused by mobilization on the street. Against this background, the early literary salons had the explicit aim of influencing the public's perception and understanding of specific issues. Over time, this new 'publicity' function of social gatherings such as coffee houses or literary salons forced state institutions to extend their own information policy and, eventually, to take public opinion seriously: 'As a result of the constitutional circumscription of the public sphere and its functions, government bodies began to rethink their organizational procedures towards greater publicity' (Habermas [1960] 1990: 154, author's translation).

With the proliferation of communication technologies in the late nineteenth and early twentieth centuries, literary salons lost their significance as opinion-formation institutions and there was a parallel decline of reading societies, associations and coffee houses as meeting places for exchanging ideas. The Habermas of the 1960s was dismissive of the possibility of the re-emergence of the literary public sphere, thinking, like several of his colleagues from the critical theory school, that modern communication technologies, in conjunction with capitalism-inspired and consumer-oriented leisure behaviour, did not leave much space to safeguard a critical public – hence the shift from a '*kulturräsonierenden zum kulturkonsumierenden Publikum*' or from a culture-reasoning to a culture-consuming public. Habermas did not deny that discussion or debate continued to be valued in advanced democratic societies. On the contrary, he conceded that they might even have increased in number and scope. At the same time, however, they have become institutionalized and compartmentalized.

> Confessional academies, political forums and literary organizations live off discussions and the maintenance of a conversationalist culture that has a need for commentary. Radio stations, publishers and associations run a prosperous secondary trade by organizing podium discussions. The future of discussion thus appears to be secured, and no limits are set to its dissemination. But below the surface much has changed. Discussion is not what it used to be, but has rather assumed the form of a consumer article. Cultural commercialization was, of course, a necessary condition for the emergence of reasoning. But reasoning per se was exempted from bartering ... Roughly speaking, it was always necessary to pay for a lecture, the theatre, a concert or the museum, but not for the conversation about what one had read, heard or seen, or indeed for what one could only appropriate through dialogue. Today we manage and administer dialogue on top of everything else.
>
> (Habermas [1960] 1990: 252–3, author's translation)

It is for this reason that in his follow-up work on democracy from the 1990s, entitled *Between Facts and Norms: Contribution to a Discourse Theory of Law and Democracy*, Habermas was more concerned with the workings and role of constitutional law. This is because the problem faced by democratic societies at the end of the twentieth century is not, as in the eighteenth and nineteenth centuries, that of how to establish a democracy on the basis of representing different interests organized neatly along economic lines; it is, rather, that of how to cope with different social experiences that cut across class or national ideologies. In this social context the public sphere weakens and law assumes a greater role as a medium of societal integration. This does not mean that the public sphere no longer exists, but it is much different from that observed in the eighteenth and nineteenth centuries: 'The currents of public communication are channelled by mass media and flow through different publics that develop informally inside associations; taken together, they form a "wild" complex that resists organization as a whole' (Habermas [1992] 1998: 307–8). This 'wild complex' that makes up the modern public sphere displays advantages and disadvantages. Its main advantage is that it has at its disposal new and 'unrestricted' forms of communication. Its main disadvantage is that 'on account of its anarchic structure ... it is more vulnerable to ... structural violence' (Ibid. 308).

The public sphere has thus been transformed into the civil society comprising non-governmental organizations and associations, which filter and synthesize different views on 'topically specified public opinions' (Ibid. 360), and, in turn, function as a 'warning system' (Ibid. 359). Habermas has nothing to say about the potential role of the literary public sphere in this new pluralistic framework, so we can assume that he either remains pessimistic in view of commercialization or considers its role irrelevant. Nevertheless, his analysis raises one important question: namely the location – if any – for deliberations on issues that are not 'topically specified'. This is, indeed, the main difference between the literary public sphere of the eighteenth century and the civil society of the late twentieth century. The former was characterized by the fusing of the personal, the social and the political; the latter operates at the interface of the three, albeit through the limited lenses of the single-issue or social movement. In that, it is less about the politics of a specific polity and more about policy.

Sociology and the emergence of a pluralist literature scene

For sociology, the history of the arts is one of alternating waves of expansion and specialization as well as of restructuring. One form of this structuring was studied by Bourdieu (1995) in his analysis of the emergence of the French literary field as an autonomous domain during the nineteenth century. Modern literature, Bourdieu argued, was constructed around the self-image of autonomy vis-à-vis cultural policy institutions. This self-understanding of autonomy was not only useful for distinguishing the literary field from other fields, including the field of politics; it was also important for drawing distinctions within each genre.

> [...] [B]etween the beginning of the century, with poetry, and the 1880s with theatre, there develops at the heart of each genre a more autonomous sector – or, if you will, an avant-garde. Each of the genres tends to cleave into a research sector and a commercial sector, two markets between which one must be wary of establishing a clear boundary, since they are merely two poles, defined in and by their antagonistic relationship, of the same space.
>
> (Bourdieu 1995: 114)

This process of differentiation occurred in all artistic fields and explains the potency of the 'duality' construction, which considers that there are only two really relevant fields in the study of the arts, namely 'the pole of pure production, where the products have as clients only other producers (who are also rivals) ... and the pole of large-scale production subordinated to the expectation of a wide audience' (Ibid. 121).

Echoing Habermas's cultural pessimism, Bourdieu considered these two fields as basically antagonistic, and thought that the commercial pole, offering more economic returns, would eventually encroach into the avant-garde pole, where aesthetic quality and prestige reign. This assessment is, of course, not new, but was already central to the discussions taking place in the literary salon of the eighteenth century. According to Löwenthal (1961), Montaigne and Pascal debated the issue in the sixteenth and seventeenth centuries respectively, whilst in the nineteenth century Goethe and Schiller embarked on a classificatory enterprise to characterize all forms of popular or 'inferior' art according to artistic and aesthetic criteria. For the cultural theorist Raymond Williams ([1958] 1983), that these debates are not new is a reminder that the view of culture as a general state of intellectual development linked to a specific way of life is itself a modern construction associated with the interrelated processes of industrialization and democratization. This is confirmed by Larry Shiner's analysis (Shiner 2001) of the history of the arts. Prior to the seventeenth century, Shiner argues, the arts were not distinguished from crafts: both the arts (in the plural) and the crafts were primarily considered valuable in terms of their function – materially or with reference to worshipping the Lord or the king. In the course of the seventeenth century, however, specialization occurred and this was accompanied by the conceptual autonomy of the various genres. In turn, this helped transform the arts into Art (with a capital 'A'), and contributed to the invention of the so-called 'aesthetic experience' that was accessible only to the few.

The emergence of deconstruction within literary studies and philosophy has exacerbated this split by insisting that literary works have to be treated first and foremost as 'texts' of social and linguistic codes. This led Alvin Kernan in 1990 to proclaim the 'Death of Literature', i.e. the demise of 'Literature with a capital "L"', the high romantic literary system that assumed sacred insights of the imagination, the perfection of the work of art, the superiority of symbol and image to rational discourse, the special authority of the poet, the superiority of "art" to practical and useful things'.[1] It is telling that a person like Kernan, who bemoans the death of Literature with a capitalized 'L', is also against linking literature to politics: 'Literature ought to get out of politics. Activism is not its natural business, contemplation and deep consideration of existential and stylistic matters are'.[2]

The 'high-brow' versus 'low-brow' debate on culture continues to inform the social-theoretical interest in literature whereby more recent publications make an explicit attempt to show that this duality is no longer the only driver of contemporary developments – and especially of those linked to internationalization. The first of these recent publications is a book by Pascale Casanova, published originally in French in 2001 and translated into English in 2004, entitled *The World Republic of Letters*. Casanova explores literature as a distinct domain of ideas produced in and through politics, competition and the economy at the interface between the local (national) and the global. Her analysis is based on a socio-ethnographic analysis of metropolitan centres (and mainly Paris of the late nineteenth and early twentieth centuries) as the meeting place of writers and their networks. Casanova's starting argument is that it is not possible to understand the much-celebrated 'world literature' from a historical perspective without acknowledging national rivalries, expressing themselves in rivalries between language and metropolitan centres. Casanova claims that the 'world' literary space is first and foremost structured around language competition and the competition between metropolitan centres, and only at a later stage around the duality of cultural versus economic prestige.

That the opposition between economic prestige and cultural value, which has weighed on the literary field (and its analysis) over centuries, might be gradually becoming outdated, is one of the main arguments of English's (2005) book on *The Economy of Prestige*, dealing with the role of prizes and awards in consecrating and circulating cultural value. English's research is based on the systematic analysis in terms of process and output of several prizes and award systems developed for literature as well as film and music. These include national prizes such as the UK Booker prize for literature or the French Prix Goncourt but also international prizes such as the Nobel. Such prizes, which are often awarded in the context of festivals or special celebratory ceremonies, represent important publicity instruments attached to significant earnings for the book industry. However, it would be wrong, cautions English, to consider prizes as mainly indicative of the ever erosive process of art commodification. The situation is not as clear cut, because even those prizes that begin from a 'pure' commercial position tend over time to 'upgrade', seeking 'symbolic profits' (English 2005: 88). On the other hand, prizes with high cultural prestige seek commercial success and wider publicity. In other words, for the long-term sustainability of prizes both economic and symbolic gains are important. Internationalization strengthens these trends by confirming and at the same time undermining cultural nationalism. It confirms cultural nationalism insofar as it presupposes the existence of national literatures; at the same time, it undermines cultural nationalism by promoting plurality – of language and style but also 'taste' or quality. Literature festivals build on this pluralism and its newly-gained legitimacy.

Bridging the gap by celebration: enter the literature festival

Within the festival domain, literature is a conspicuous latecomer. The first literature festival of the twentieth century was the Cheltenham Literature Festival, which started in 1949. Today's iconic literature festival is the Hay-on-Wye Festival, which was only launched in 1988. The Berlin International Literature Festival (ILB) commenced in 2001. The number of literature festivals has picked up over the last decade – today there are literature festivals in several smaller British towns, in Berlin, Hamburg and Cologne, and in New York as well as in Alhambra, Seville and Mantua – among others. The Borderlands Literature Festival, which focuses on Eastern Europe, takes place in different 'border' cities every year.

Contemporary literature festivals are, of course, not the direct descendants of the earlier literary salon, but they serve similar functions in that they are often established explicitly for promoting the exchange of ideas and to link the arts and politics. Their founders often come from the fields of literature and the arts, and (political) journalists have a key role to play in their promotion. Unlike literary salons, literature festivals are no longer to be found in the private households of their hosts or hostesses. The private salon has been replaced by the local council (Cheltenham), the youth centre[3] (Hay) or the public hall (Berlin), whilst the host has given way to the promoter or director. However, despite the changes in format and organization reflecting changes in social relations, literature festivals also maintain – intentionally or unintentionally – many of the characteristics and rituals associated with literary salons. In addition, they provide the stages for observing the interplay of different forces impacting on contemporary public culture.

The modern literature festival host

The hosts of literary salons in the seventeenth, eighteenth and nineteenth centuries were key figures. These were often women; famous examples include Madame de Staël, Margaret Fuller, Sophie de Condorcet, Elizabeth Montagu and Fanny Mendelssohn (Capper 2008; Holmes 2008; Landes 1988; Lilti 2005). Men are more likely to take centre stage at modern literature festivals, but the host is no less important in terms of both content and organization.

The Hay Festival programme often refers to *Peter Florence*, its director, as the master of ceremonies. Florence is the main driving force behind the Hay Festival in terms of programme and design. He is also an active participant in festival events, often as a presenter and discussant. A theatre actor with a background in modern and medieval literatures, he launched the Hay Literary Festival with his parents in 1988. Since then he has founded literary festivals in Seville, Cartagena and Alhambra, and he is planning further ones in Nairobi and Beirut.

Ulrich Schreiber, the director of the International Literature Festival Berlin, is described by the German media as a foreman and a globetrotter. He was trained as an architect and began his professional career working for his father's construction company before he turned to the study of philosophy and literature. He briefly worked as an arts and politics teacher before turning to cultural management. In 1993 he set up the Peter Weiss Foundation in order to host the ILB.

Ulrich Janetzki, founder of the Borderlands Festival, is the director of the Literary Colloquium Berlin (LCB), an institution established in the tradition of the legendary Group 47, a literary association launched in Berlin after the end of World War II with the aim of advancing democratization through literary exchange. Both the LCB and the Borderlands Festival are devoted to the scholarship of writing and translation with a focus on Eastern Europe.

The role of the media

The success of the literary salons in the seventeenth and eighteenth centuries coincided with the diffusion of the press – newspapers and periodicals representing the new media for the transmission of ideas. The media are equally important for contemporary literature festivals. A widespread format, for instance, is the discussion between a journalist and a writer about the writer's work, but also, more generally, about the socio-economic and political conditions of the creation and reception of a work of literature. The media also contribute directly to the festival organization through sponsorship. The International Literature Festival Berlin lists both *Der Spiegel* and DeutschlandKultur Radio as festival supporters, whilst the Hay Festival initially had *The Times* and currently has the *Guardian* as its eponymous main sponsor.

From the city/country dichotomy to the world

Literary salons were a phenomenon primarily of the cities, which were the home of the 'bourgeoisie' in the eighteenth century. A common assumption is that contemporary book fairs and literature festivals are likewise metropolitan events. This is a distorted view brought about by the fact that the largest book fairs take place in major cities such as Frankfurt, London and Leipzig. Literature festivals of the type considered in the present chapter are rather a mixed lot. Hay-on-Wye is a small city of 2,000 inhabitants situated within the Brecon Beacons National Park, north of the Black Mountains on the border between England and Wales. Cheltenham is a medium-sized city in Gloucestershire, with a population of just over 100,000. Cologne, the home of the lit.Cologne festival, has just under one million. Berlin, the capital of Germany, is a metropolitan city with over three million inhabitants. New York, the location of the PEN World Voices Festival, has a population of eight million. Literature festivals in major cities tend to be international in orientation (Berlin, New York) or commercial (Cologne). Literature festivals in second-tier or smaller cities tell a more mixed story, often representing a 'national' initiative within a more local context.

Contemporary festivals more generally appear to represent a conscious and explicit attempt to overcome the city/country dichotomy brought about by industrialization and the parallel development of the arts as a system bound to fully fledged and integrated institutions such as the museum or the concert hall. Such institutions are brilliant repositories or performance locations for the arts, but their costs are also prohibitive; hence they can often only be maintained financially in major cities, which, by reason of size, also attract the lion's share of public and private investment. Festivals, even if large in scale, are concentrated in time, and this allows cost containment in a way that also makes them attractive as regeneration instruments for second-tier cities; hence also the explosion of urban mixed-arts festivals around the world.

In this context the Hay Literature Festival is a particularly interesting example. It is also interesting for its relationship with Raymond Williams, who wrote extensively about the English novel and also about the country and the city. For Peter Florence, who also decided to settle in the countryside, it has been important to show that cultural and literary life is not concentrated in the capital, London. A similar vision seems to underlie his 'expansion' plans to Alhambra, Bogota, Nairobi or Beirut. The objective is to open new spaces for the exchange of ideas, but in so doing to support writers as well as literary institutions in these countries.

The format of events and the role of entertainment

Literature festivals place an emphasis on entertainment, thus also continuing the tradition of the literary salon, which valued the pursuit of pleasure through intellectual discourse, the performance of the written word through recitation, and the combination of both with food and drink (Lilti 2005). The key difference between the literary salon and the literature festival is the latter's outreach, which, of course, also entails implications in terms of format and contents.

The core idea from which literature festivals derive their imagination and their ability to kindle other people's imagination is simple: namely that of bringing people together to make conversation. Peter Florence often describes how it all started by referring to family get-togethers and 'looking for something enjoyable to do' – and this, for him, includes 'intelligent conversation'.[4] And what could be more fun than getting together with some old and new friends to discuss books, arts and politics? Even if this is a simple idea, its successful implementation is not easy, given that the people brought together to initiate the dialogue, and also those participating, are usually strangers to one another – or know one another only indirectly through the written word. Unlike music, film or the visual arts, literature is therefore also much more difficult to 'stage' as performance for the general public – especially if, unlike theatre, it is supposed to be interactive and informal and yet to do without professional actors. Literature festivals prove this is possible.

Both the Hay Festival and the International Literature Festival Berlin began with a programme biased heavily towards poetry readings. Poetry continues to be the genre in literature that enjoys the highest prestige, but it attracts the lowest audiences. This could not be sustained for a long period of time. The programmes began to diversify after a couple of years, gradually expanding to include commercial fiction and non-fiction, and a children's programme as well as political and scientific debates. Poetry did not disappear, and that in itself is a remarkable phenomenon. In absolute terms, poetry readings have tended to remain stable. However, in an expanded programme they no longer make up 50 per cent of the individual events, but only 10 per cent or less.

In terms of format, festivals continue to focus on the figure of the individual artist-author, and mainly comprise readings by authors or discussions with authors. But over time a shift can be observed in the contents of discussions and presentations, away from the mere presentation of the 'works' to a discussion about the insertion of the 'creative process' into the more general social context.

The link to politics

The objective of literature festivals is not only to present authors and their works, but also to discuss social and political developments with reference to books, scripts or theatre. This also means that literature festivals are equally about presenting and discussing fiction and non-fiction. Political journalism, history, social history, science writing and comedy are as frequently featured as are novels, historical fiction, poetry, short stories or commercial writing (crime or popular psychology). Literature festivals are also often used for discussing contemporary developments in literature or the relationship between literature and politics or even ethics. For instance, since its very beginning the Hay Festival has held a 'Raymond Williams Lecture on Culture and Society'. This is usually given by a poet or literary critic, its objective being to explore the continuing relevance of Raymond Williams's theories about culture and society for modern cultural phenomena.

Ulrich Schreiber, the director of the International Literature Festival Berlin, is, of the festival directors encountered, the one most explicit about linking literature festivals to politics and the arts. The political side of the Berlin Festival is accentuated by its international character. Not only are many of the authors brought together by the festival concerned with the interaction between the personal and the social in their definition and experience of post-national, multicultural or exile identity, but their work is often also used as an opportunity to reflect on Eurocentric perspectives on developing countries or non-white identities. The idealistic vision that guided the foundation of the ILB in 2001 was that of opening the German literary and political public sphere to 'outsider' voices, namely voices from other continents, languages and traditions.

Internationalization, more generally, has contributed to the expansion of literature festival programmes. Since the ILB launch in 2001, two other international literature festivals have made their appearance, both organized by PEN, one in New York and the other in London. The motto of international literature festivals is that of transcending national boundaries towards discovering a 'world' literature.

In this context of the transition from Literature to literatures and considering how this has created a space for debating the politics of representation, diversity, inequality, colonialism or migration policy, what is rather surprising is the subject that is often absent from literature festivals, namely Europe. There are discussions about national politics, international politics and even American politics. But there is little discussion about European politics at literature festivals. Enlargement is perhaps the one exception to the above – by means of the entrance of East European authors to the literary scene, and through them reflections about the implications of enlargement, the transition from Communism and the meaning of European 'belonging' or identity. It is perhaps no surprise that the forerunners in this respect were institutions with a longer tradition in East–West relations, such as the Literary Colloquium Berlin and the Borderlands Festival. This is, however, also the smallest of the literature festivals.

The organization of literature festivals

Assuming Habermas is right, the literature festival does not so much represent the descendant of the literary salon in historical–evolutionary terms, but rather its decadent decline. Obviously, as organizations, literature festivals engage in the logic of exchange that characterizes business relations. However, they are far removed from representing 'prosperous trades', as they are usually run on a not-for-profit basis and extensively rely on voluntary work from the organizers as well as unpaid or underpaid work from writers and artists. The prices charged for admission are also low, ranging from five to ten Euros.

Many literature festivals were launched with very little financial support. In 1949, when the Cheltenham Festival was launched, the Town Improvement and Spa Committee supporting it estimated its total cost at £300, to be 'recompensed by admission charges' (cited in Bennett 1999). John Moore, the first director, worked for the festival for practically no pay during its first three years, while trying, in parallel, to make a living by writing articles, screenplays and short stories. At the time, box office revenues were always celebrated as symbolically noteworthy, but were never really significant in terms of income. The audience was enthusiastic but it was comparatively small, picking up very slowly. In 1949 7,000 seats were sold, and that was a record that was only broken 36 years later, in 1985, when 11,000 seats were sold. The breakthrough only came in the 1990s, when literature festivals began to become popular and were also recognized as useful platforms for a young audience. Since 1992 children and young adults have made up around one-third of the Cheltenham public, with current numbers totalling around 40,000.

The Hay Literature Festival, which was launched in 1986, sells some 65,000 tickets a year[5] – up to 150,000 in 2009[6] – and its programme has expanded over the last years to include a significant component of music and comedy.[7] While ticket sales are also a major income source in this case, the festival would not be sustainable without the sponsorship of the *Guardian* (and previously *The Times*), amounting to around £50,000 per year,[8] and a comparable subsidy from the Wales Arts Council.[9] Several smaller sponsorships in cash or in kind complete the financial basis of the Hay Literature Festival. Meanwhile, the Hay Festival has its own site, made up of several pavilion-tents of different capacities. Peter Florence is also known as a successful 'cultural entrepreneur' and a person to call in for advice when launching a new literature festival. Still, the status of the festival remains one of a non-profit organization, the core team of permanent employees not exceeding 15 people[10] and the rest comprising many volunteers or interns employed for a short period of time.

The 'public' share of financing is more significant in the case of the International Literature Festival of Berlin, and this is also in line with the continental tradition of supporting the arts. In central Europe subsidies are more important for all types of non-governmental activities, including civil society organizations and the arts. This is often justified with reference to 'public interest' and sought by cultural actors on these terms. The argument used by Ulrich

Schreiber to mobilize financial support from the City of Berlin was that, first, literature had to be placed on the cultural map of Berlin (next to music, dance, film and theatre) and, second, openness to world literature was something for which private sponsorship was neither appropriate nor feasible. The ILB, which sells around 30,000 tickets a year and is somewhat smaller than the Hay Festival in terms of scope and length, runs on a budget of around €600,000, of which more than half goes on expenditures incurred for travel and organization. The fees paid to authors are at best symbolic, not exceeding €300. The subsidy from the Cultural Fund of the City of Berlin amounts to €450,000, and the remainder is raised by contributions from federal ministries, embassies and cultural organizations. In Berlin, private sponsorship is limited to mostly in-kind contributions.[11]

The decision as to whether to rely on public or private sources of funding, or, at present, the scope and balance of public–private partnerships, is usually a pragmatic decision linked to the cultural policy of the country in which a literature festival takes place. This does not imply that it is not a difficult one to make for festival organizers. This is best exemplified by the debates within the Cheltenham Literature Festival when, in 1991, it was proposed that the *Daily Telegraph* sponsor the event – in a similar fashion to the sponsorship of the Hay Festival by *The Times*. As Bennett (1999: 82) writes, when the proposal was presented to the festival management committee 'they wanted none of it'. This was not just because the *Daily Telegraph* was a newspaper leaning to the right whereas the festival felt itself to be leaning to the left. 'Some saw the advantage or even necessity for the money and media support that the *Telegraph* could offer, but many were nervous that their festival would be changed beyond recognition.' (Ibid.) Twenty years earlier, in the early 1970s, the suggestion by the local Spa Management Committee to place the festival on a more secure financial basis by commercialization, meaning fewer but more popular events, turned out to be short lived, also because the Arts Council, which was supporting the festival, thought that this was an inappropriate development for a publicly funded arts event. This dilemma recurs time and again within literature festival organizations and compels a constant examination of their identities as institutions and formations of and for literature.

Conclusions: from amateur to professional organizations

All literature festivals began as amateur initiatives and their development into more-or-less professional organizations displays several similarities. To what extent literature festivals develop over time, what challenges and pressures they face and how they deal with external and internal demands tells us something about the development of public culture and how it might evolve in the future.

To reiterate, professionalization has involved a number of other changes.

- All literature festivals began as small-scale projects with little attention paid to issues such as accounting, employment contracts and the like, and tended to resemble 'hobby' activities based on unpaid or voluntary work. That had to change quite rapidly – for taxation reasons in view of revenues from ticket sales; but also, more importantly, to make it possible to benefit from public subsidies. All festivals continue to run on a non-profit or charitable basis, but are registered companies or foundations or parts of bigger organizations (e.g. the literature festival at Cheltenham is part of Cheltenham Arts Festivals, and ILB part of the Berliner Festspiele).

- Expansion has occurred in two ways: with regard to the number of events organized and authors invited, and with regard to the organization of 'sibling' or 'satellite' events in different regions or countries. The expansion is driven by internationalization, but also, in part, by economic pressure. Once festivals grow into organizations with round-the-year employment their costs also sky-rocket, and these can hardly ever be covered by the organization of a single or short event.

- Attracting private sponsors such as newspapers or insurance companies entails the benefit of spreading the financial risk. Over-dependence on public subsidies involves the risk that the festival might gradually or suddenly lose its financial basis. This is, for instance, the constant existential fear of the ILB. The financing of its first event took three years' preparation; its second event was only possible following the mobilization of a significant section of the German and international literary scene, who inundated the Berlin mayor's office with complaint letters. All the same, private sponsorship also has disadvantages. One of these is publicity: private sponsors are more likely to sponsor an activity when publicity is guaranteed or when visitor numbers are high. This, in turn, brings along the pressure for commercialization, which often means 'fewer events, more names'.

The process of professionalization has run a similar course in all literature festivals: from the early phase of idealistic and idyllic gatherings in order to enjoy poetry, to the serial-event structure of literary meetings combining public and commercial interests with the social event culture. The organizational changes did not remain uncontested – either externally or internally. The Hay Festival is often criticized today for being more about event culture than literary culture, whilst the ILB has still to legitimize its existence as a separate event from the many other literature activities taking place in Berlin.

Against this background, the main difference between contemporary literature festivals and the earlier literary salons is that literature festivals are not primarily or explicitly about the edification of the middle classes in the face of populism, on the one hand, and state violence, on the other. Democratization has brought about the expansion of the middle classes and the diversification of cultural taste. In this context, literature festivals serve more as stages for *mediating* different cultural tastes. Through the concentration of events in time and space and the explicit support of plurality and diversity, literature festivals contribute to the partial overcoming of the fragmented public sphere observed by Habermas, in addition to facilitating hybridization, i.e. the mixing of forms, styles and genres, as well as interchange and translation. In turn, this brings about a shift of the rigid distinctions implied in the high- versus low-brow classification, both with respect to the various agents of cultural production and to the audience. This may signal a new phase in the democratization of culture, whereby commercialization remains a fact and yet the new-found permeability of boundaries and the joy in experimentation creates new opportunities for culture-reasoning or even a critical public.

Notes

1　Interview with Michael Shaughnessy at EdNews.org
2　Ibid.
3　The youth centre was the location of the Hay-on-Wye Literature Festival in its early years. Since then, the festival has moved to its new location outside the town. This was necessitated by the dramatic growth in the number of visitors.
4　From an interview with Peter Florence (via email).
5　From an interview with Maggie Robertson, November 2008.
6　Own estimations based on field observation and programme analysis. The 2009 programme lists 358 events, distributed over five sites with capacity of 1000, 800, 400, 200 and 100.
7　Around 55 out of a total of 358 events were music or comedy shows. This is 15 per cent of the total, the largest single category (author's own estimation based on programme analysis).
8　This figure has not been confirmed. It is based on the information about sponsors provided on the Hay Festival's website, supplied in scales.
9　Based on information found on the website of the Arts Council for 2007.
10　Based on information supplied on the website of the Festival and the author's own observation.
11　All the financial information about ILB is based on analysis of the ILB documentation, to which the author was granted access.

References

Alexander, J. (2005) Why Cultural Sociology is not Idealist: A Reply to McLennan. *Theory, Culture and Society* 22(6): 19–29.

Alexander, J., Giesen, B. and Mast, J. C. (2006) *Social Performance, Symbolic Action, Cultural Pragmatics and Ritual.* Cambridge: Cambridge University Press.

Bourdieu, P. (1995) *The Rules of Art: Genesis and Structure of the Literary Field.* Stanford: Stanford University Press.

Bennett, N. (1999) *Speaking Volumes: A History of the Cheltenham Literature Festival.* Cheltenham: Sutton Publishing.

Capper, C. (2008) *Margaret Fuller: An American Romantic Life – The Public Years.* Oxford: Oxford University Press.

Casanova, P. (2004) *The World Republic of Letters.* Cambridge: Harvard University Press (translated from French, *La Republique mondiale des Letters*, Editions du Seuil).

Chaney, D. (2002) Cosmopolitan Art and Cultural Citizenship. *Theory, Culture and Society* 19(1–2): 157–74.

English, J. (2005) *The Economy of Prestige.* Cambridge: Harvard University Press.

Habermas, J. ([1960] 1990) *Strukturwander der Öffentlichkeit: Untersuchungen zu einer Kategorie der bürgerlichen Gesellschaft.* Frankfurt am Main: Suhrkamp.

Habermas, J. ([1992] 1998) *Between Facts and Norms: Contributions to a Discourse Theory of Law and Democracy.* Cambridge MA: MIT Press.

Harrison, F. (1896) The True Cosmopolis. *Cosmopolis: An International Monthly Review* August issue 327–40.

Holmes, R. (2008) The Great de Stael *New York Review of Books.* LVI (9): 13–14.

Landes, J. (1988) *Women and the Public Sphere in the Age of Revolution.* Ithaca: Cornell University Press.

Lilti, A. (2005) *Le Monde des Salons: Sociabilité et mondanité à Paris au XVIII Siècle.* Paris: Fayard.

Löwenthal, L. (1961) *Literature, Popular Culture and Society.* New York: Prentice-Hall.

Morrissey, L. (2008) *The Constitution of Literature: Literary, Democracy and Early English Literary Criticism.* Palo Alto: Stanford University Press.

Santoro, M. (2008) Producing Cultural Sociology: an Interview with Richard A. Peterson. *Cultural Sociology* 2(1): 33–55.

Shiner, L. (2001) *The Invention of Art: A Cultural History.* Chicago: Chicago University Press.

Sullivan, A. (1983a) *British Literary Magazines: The Augustan Age and the Age of Johnson 1698–1788.* Westport Connecticut: Greenwood Press.

Sullivan, A. (1983b) *British Literary Magazines: The Romantic Age 1789–1836.* Westport Connecticut: Greenwood Press.

Sullivan, A. (1984) *British Literary Magazines: The Victorian and Edwardian Age 1837–1931.* Westport Connecticut: Greenwood Press.

Sullivan, A. (1986) *British Literary Magazines: The Modern Age 1914–1984.* Westport Connecticut: Greenwood Press.

Williams, R. ([1958] 1983) *Culture and Society.* New York: Columbia University Press.

3 Art biennales and cities as platforms for global dialogue

Nikos Papastergiadis and Meredith Martin

Capitalizing on culture

In 2003 Liverpool beat five other short-listed cities to be nominated as Britain's contender for the title of the European Union's 'Capital of Culture' for 2008. The director of National Museums Liverpool, Dr David Fleming, welcomed the win – ratified by the European Union in 2004 – as providing Liverpool with the opportunity to create 'the finest city museum service in Europe', and, as a direct corollary, the circumstance that the city could now expect 'more investment, new jobs, new projects of benefit to local people, and a massive boost to the region's tourist industry'.[1] Only a decade earlier Liverpool had still been spectacularized as the 'showcase' of Britain's post-industrial decline.[2] So what happened between the dour forecasts of the 1980s and 90s and Liverpool's urban renaissance as the 'Barcelona of the north' in 2008?

According to George Yúdice, a new epistemic framework of 'culture as resource' has emerged in the intervening years, in which 'ideology and much of what Foucault called disciplinary society are absorbed into an economic ... rationality', and traditional notions of culture are emptied out (Yúdice 2003: 12). In this new era of cultural expediency, culture no longer simply serves as a realm of legitimation, but, rather, must itself be legitimated on the basis of its explicit social and economic utility. Ironically enough, it is the state's withdrawal of funding from social programmes that provides the 'condition of continued possibility' for non-profit arts and cultural activities, which are now claimed to 'enhance education, solve racial strife, help reverse urban blight through cultural tourism, create jobs, reduce crime and perhaps even make a profit' (Yúdice 2003: 12). Indeed, the supranational vocabulary of inter-city cultural rivalry for economic infrastructure and development, which underwrites the European Capital of Culture competition, has been described as so pervasive that it may inaugurate a whole new area of what might be termed 'instrumental knowledge' (Boyle and Rogerson 2001: 402).

The Liverpool Biennial has been instrumental in Liverpool's rise as a cultural player on this supranational scale and is deeply entangled in such perceptions of the potential of creative capital to transform urban blight.[3] Liverpool's nomination as the 2008 Capital of Culture was avowedly contingent upon the success of the 2006 Liverpool Biennial: International 06, just as the more recent nomination of Istanbul as the 2009 Capital of Culture arguably rests on the 2005 and 2007 Biennales.[4] Indeed, the role of the biennale in the nexus of culture and economy is expanding exponentially. Until 1984 there were just three biennales and a handful of other large-scale exhibitions that occurred on a periodic basis. By 2008 there was a new biennale opening every fortnight. It is, however, sobering to recall that, just as the Liverpool Biennial in 1998 was marked by the tremendous hope that culture could boost the economy, even the first Venice Biennale in 1895 was partly motivated by the need to arrest the urban decline of this once all-powerful mercantile city and to use the biennale to promote the city as a locus of modernity while also drawing on its museal past.[5]

The aim of this chapter is not so much to adjudicate on culture's capacity to fulfil the twin (and potentially competing) promises of urban regeneration and social integration, but rather to consider the possibility that, in addition to functioning as a symptom of the larger commercialization of culture, the proliferation of biennales might engender multiple sites that critically engage global processes of capital flow and cultural exchange. Whereas the Liverpool Biennial, for instance, may have served to instantiate the city's claims to 'creative city' status on the global stage, under the direction of consultant curators Manray Hsu and Gerardo Mosquera it also addressed the urban myths and bittersweet success of urban regeneration through a historicist and reflexive rumination on the geographic vectors of the imperial enterprise.

We argue that this critical and reflexive disposition is indicative of a new dialogic turn in artistic and curatorial practice that has emerged in parallel with – and is often situated within – the rise of the biennale. This chapter maps the emergence of a discursive biennale model in relation to a wide range of artistic practices that utilize social encounters as the materiality of practice. We consider curatorial practices that have sought to use biennales or other large exhibition formats as a platform for multidisciplinary events that have explicit feedback mechanisms mobilizing multiple forms of public interaction. Whereas Terry Smith argued in 2004 that the post-Documenta 11 biennale was characterized by a reactionary 'retreat from broad-scale engagement', it is suggested here that the biennale is increasingly taking form as one of the most powerful vehicles for articulating the palpable tensions and latent possibilities in contemporary aesthetics and politics.[6]

Biennales as platforms for social exchange

From the outset, biennales have been conceived as providing an alternative to the models of display and knowledge production that were traditionally formed within the museum. The tensions, overlaps and differences in relation to historical narratives, classificatory systems, site specificity and duration are not the focus of this chapter. However, what will be stressed is that, if the biennale is seen as an alternative to the museum, this does not mean that the relationship can be understood as a binary opposition. Neither the museum nor the biennale has a fixed or uniform identity. They are not discrete entities, but are inter-implicated and engaged in a process of interplay that is mutually transformative. As Bruce Ferguson has observed, the methodology informing the biennale does not follow a disciplined or linear process of knowledge formation (Ferguson 2009). It is more accurate to imagine the conceptual terrain within which the biennale operates as a field comprised of a wide variety of approaches and concerns. Indeed, it is arguable that the most salient recurring feature of the biennale is the paradoxical attempt to differentiate each iteration from its own history. While this dynamic generates a context of flux, it is also prone to fits of amnesia and displacing its own boundaries of inclusion and exclusion.

It is the contention here, however, that across this iterative production of differentiation a distinctive modality is taking form, which is characterized by an emphasis on social interaction and a discursive approach to the broad issues surrounding 'art, city and politics in an expanding world'. The reference here is to the title of the proceedings of the 2005 Istanbul Biennial. In the first line of their catalogue, the curators, Charles Esche and Vasif Kortun, declared that it was 'not a survey' (Esche and Kortun 2005). Esche and Kortun, along with the curators Hou Hanru, Charles Esche, Hsu, Okwui Enwezor and Mosquera, who are the focuses of this chapter, have all used the term 'platform' for rethinking the terms of engagement between art, the city in which it is situated, and the emergence of what might constitute a global 'cultural public sphere' (McGuigan 2005). By eschewing the conventional model of selecting and classifying works from across the world that, according to Hsu, produces 'a kind of multiculturalist parallelism that underlines coevality, radical incommensurability of cultures and equal distance and difference', represents a common attempt to utilize the context of the biennale to produce an alternative form of global dialogue that Hsu calls a 'decentralizing cosmopolitanism' (Hsu 2005: 75, 76).

This shift in curatorial strategy has been motivated in part by a recognition that artists are increasingly using the whole of the city as the environment within which their artwork operates, as well as by a desire to distinguish the biennale from generic forms of 'event culture'. Ranjit Hoskote has noted that in our age of hyper-mobility and dematerialized artistic production, the loop between laptop, manufacturing sites and public feedback is not just part of the invisible research and fabrication phase, but also a visible and ongoing feature of the experience of art, so the biennale must be seen both as a joint partner in the collaborative process of community production and what he calls the 'the studio of studios' (Hoskote 2009).

As the city and the biennale are reconfigured as platforms from which viewers can 'launch themselves', we can see how the traditional function of the curator – providing an interpretation and classification of the global trajectories of contemporary art – has been complemented by the task of inviting artists and collectives who activate a critical interface between local citizens and global processes or, to borrow Enwezor's phrase, who use the biennale as a 'space of encounter' (Enwezor 2008). According to Ferguson, these 'biennales that talk about themselves as they present themselves, and take account of the audience in the production of the work' mark the emergence of a new discursive and reflexive trend (Ferguson 2009). Rafal Niemojewski has gone so far as to embrace the shift from discourse on the spectacle to the spectacle of discourse and to assert that a potential model for a future biennale should be an exhibition that is attached to a conference. This is, of course, the reverse of the conventional format of a conference attached to an exhibition (Niemojewski 2009).

Genealogy of the biennale

To appreciate the distinctiveness of this trend, it is worth comparing it with the three models that have dominated debates on the function of biennales. In Lawrence Alloway's account of the origins and development of the Venice Biennale from its inception in 1895 until 1968, the biennale becomes a model or prism through which it is possible to map the 'unsettled problems of art in society' (Alloway 1969: 14). Alloway narrates the Biennale's trajectory in terms of three epochal transitions, which can be categorized in terms of the expansion and contraction of international participation and the waxing and waning of cosmopolitan sensibility. The initial 'salon' era saw an expansion of international pavilions by the end of the 1930s, a growth which was checked during the nationalist hiatus of the wartime Biennales, and then resurged with the new scale of postwar internationalism (Ibid.: 145–6). Writing in the late 1960s, Alloway mapped the Biennale in terms of the rise of a 'new, solid, cosmopolitan art world' (Ibid.: 139) that, in the accumulation of national crossovers and exchanges, promised a 'preliminary global culture' (Ibid.: 146). In short, in the history of the Venice Biennale we can see the articulation of a model that shifts away from the display of national visual cultures in an international frame towards a survey of current trends in art, providing an intimation of global culture.[7]

The second model takes a more explicitly regional, decentralized and anti-Eurocentric perspective (Niemojewski 2009). This approach is credited to the pioneering 1984 Havana Biennial. A central feature of this model is the direct challenge to the metropolitan perspectives and colonial legacies of Western mainstream art institutions. In Havana in 1984, there was a deliberate attempt not only to demonstrate the vitality of the counter-modernities forged in the non-West, but also to create both new cartographies of cultural development and alternative networks of exchange. In the ensuing decade it inspired the development of biennales in Istanbul, Dakar, Brisbane and Johannesburg. This approach gained its distinctive identity through a combination of ideological oppositions – the reversal of stereotypes concerning levels of cultural production in the non-West, the rejection of racial hierarchies that structured the art-historical canon and the desire to break with the dependency on the North by promoting new horizontal networks across the South.

However, as Mosquera, the director of the first two Havana Biennials, acknowledged, it was not sufficient to break with traditional models; a utopian stimulus was also needed to create opportunities for constructing possibilities that had hitherto not yet existed. In his view, the Havana Biennial was more like a multidisciplinary event; it served as a meeting place – an experimental zone for artists from the South. However, with the fall of the Berlin Wall coinciding with the opening of the third Biennial, he noted mournfully that this was also the moment when 'Cuba became a fossil' (Mosquera 2009).

A further shift had occurred by the mid 1990s. The challenge to Eurocentric visions of modernity and notions of cultural development based on the nation-state emerged from a complex mixture of postcolonial critique and a more strident version of globalism.[8] Urban cultural policies were increasingly being designed to gain the attention of global investment flows rather than focus on the civic needs of a local citizenship. During this period there was a rush on the part of second-tier cities to adopt the discourse of creative cities as a mechanism for enhancing their global competitiveness in the field of cultural tourism and, in many cases, to kick-start the process of urban regeneration. With the proliferation of over 200 biennales, most of which are concentrated in Europe and Asia, commentators were quick to adopt a cynical stance and declare that this phenomenon was just another node in neo-liberal networks of leisure and conspicuous consumerism.

The synecdoche between the globalization of the marketplace and the biennalization of the art world relied on the presumed equivalences in the conception of context, subjectivity and modes of communication. Biennales were deemed to be expressive of the cultural logic of globalization because of the putative correspondence between the way in which they offered a context for art that was global in its scope; because they engaged flexible, mobile and multi-skilled artists and curators who were able to work across cultures and mediate between different constituencies; and finally, because the most prominent communicative media privileged interactive and network processes over static objects. The similarities in the processes by which capital reconfigured its work ethic and the practices by which artists and curators operated in the art world encouraged critics to conclude that these aesthetic practices were at best extending the frontiers of capital – either by going into places of unrest, where the social services and private sector had failed, or by creating a new 'atmosphere' amid the post-industrial ruins – and at worst legitimizing the precarious conditions of contemporary society, by providing global capital with a necessary 'facelift' (Arrhenius 2007: 101).

However, there is also a counter-position, one that upholds the more balanced view that the opportunity for criticality is not entirely absorbed by the expansive phase of late capitalism, but actually enhanced by the increase in resources and the venues in which it now circulates. Although the marketing departments of biennale offices go to extreme lengths to demonstrate their events' financial and symbolic benefits, curators tend to reject the claim that the motivation and interest in biennales is sustained by economic return alone.[9] Hoskote, for instance, views the biennale as a hybrid creature, one that was born in the era of industrial capitalism and driven by the same imperial appetite for novelty evident in the formation of museums, expositions and fairs. Yet he also sees more recent manifestations, such as the 2008 Gwanju Biennale he co-curated, as a 'parliament of global contemporary narratives', i.e. not just as a tool by which the margins can reach the centre, but as a space of 'critical transregionality', in which an alternative knowledge of global flows and local engagements is formed (Hoskote 2009). A potent, albeit flawed, example of this trend is the development of Manifesta. Manifesta took on the challenge of redrawing the post-Cold-War European map as an opportunity to engage critically with the new peripheries. Each iteration of Manifesta takes place in a different city and its aim is not only to provoke an alternative aesthetic vision to the local, but also to provide heterotopic sites of emergent cultural production.

'There is nothing' as Henri Lefebvre put it, 'more contradictory than "urban-ness"' (Lefebvre 1991: 386). The extent to which the contradictions of the urban might be critically engaged rather than elided by the biennale model can be neatly encapsulated in the distance travelled between the first and second Moscow Biennales. The 2005 Biennale, the largest international contemporary art fair to be held in post-Soviet Russia, was conceived as a largely commercial endeavour to raise Russia's profile in the contemporary art world. However, the second Moscow Biennale in 2007, curated collectively by a range of guest curators including Joseph Backstein, Nicolas Bourriaud, Hans Ulrich Obrist and Rosa Martinez, with the official theme of 'Footnotes on Geopolitics, Markets and Amnesia', invoked a self-reflexive engagement with the master text of globalization and a critical analysis of the idea of the international biennale itself. In what would at first seem an unlikely venue for the inscription of critical marginalia to macroeconomic battles, the Biennale's flagship event was launched at the Federation Tower, a massive corporate development touted as the tallest building in Europe. If the site suggests a certain irony, it is certainly intentional; as Alexander Osipovich observed rather trenchantly in the *Moscow Times*: 'If you're going to hold an exhibition whose stated aim is to explore the place of art in our globalized, forgetful, capitalist world, what better place than a modern-day Tower of Babel rising out of the petrodollar-fueled bacchanalia of Moskva-City?' (Osipovich 2007).

Indeed, in recounting his response to first learning of the Biennale theme, Bourriaud notes that he 'immediately thought about organizing a section in the shape of a landscape. Global economy's landscape' (Bourriaud 2007). Bourriaud's landscape is palimpsestuous, comprising layers of artists' critical annotations and recodings. Here, the materiality of the urban sphere is not simply an artefact of the flows of global capital; the city is remembered, to quote Lefebvre again, both as a 'setting of struggle' and the 'stakes of that struggle' (1991: 386).

These positive examples of critical practice in the age of neoliberal capital are both laudable and inspiring. They demonstrate that the biennale does not 'completely belong to the system and can give rise to subversive possibilities' (Basualdo 2006: 50). However, as Basualdo notes, due to both the lack of research on the qualitative impact of biennales and the absence of a frame of reference that can be applied across the diverse sites of their proliferation, there is a tendency for critics to draw conclusions that merely follow the value judgements underpinning their general perspective towards cultural practice. So what is left out of these judgements? Basualdo suggests that both of these tendencies – cynically to dismiss or uncritically to embrace – miss something that is palpable and yet almost hidden from view:

> Obviously, it is not difficult to imagine that a case of exhibiting and producing works that is not immediately associated with either galleries or museums – and although it maintains a dialogue with both the market and history, nevertheless does not exactly respond to the expectations of either – may suddenly become at least partially illegible for the system in which it should supposedly operate.
>
> (Ibid.: 44)

It is from the ellipses within the critical framework for registering the authority of the contemporary and against a backdrop of these trends that we now need to situate the biennale as 'symposium' – as a platform generating a critical dialogue about the contradictions of contemporary globalization.

It is within this frame of reference that we would like to position Enwezor's refashioning of the contemporary biennale model in Documenta 11 as a constellation of five 'Platforms'. While Enwezor was attempting to move away from a fetishist economy of display as early as the Johannesburg Biennale of 1997, and Documenta X also signalled a key 'point in art where the field was open to political discourse' (Vesic 2005), Documenta 11 was instrumental in the reconfiguration of the concept of the biennale from a survey of the field to a social network of interlocutors.[10] With the exhibition itself consisting of the outcome of a series of symposia and panel discussions that took place on four continents over the span of 18 months, dialogue becomes more than a trope, and globalization is not simply the conceptual backdrop; both the trope and the abstraction are interrogated as they are reconstituted into the very structure of the biennale through the collaborative and discursive processes that occurred in each locale. Moving away from the 100-day format of past Documenta exhibitions, this extension of the parameters of the exhibition in both spatial and temporal terms constituted a significant attempt to formulate a critical model of a transnational public sphere that joins the heterogeneous cultural and artistic circuits of the global context.[11] This marks a double emphasis on the material dimensions of specific local sites, contexts and practices and the ways in which these dimensions are 'lost and found' in global economic narratives. Critically, the emphasis given to mobility and duration within this model, which subverts the putatively homogenizing tendencies of the biennale, also draws on a series of recent innovations in artistic and curatorial practice.

Yúdice argues that in the contemporary era of 'culture as resource', which is marked by a reciprocal permeation of culture and economy as a 'mode of cognition, social organization, and even attempts at social emancipation', the avant-garde goal of reconciling art and life would seem to 'feed back into the system' it opposes (Yúdice 2003: 27–8). We want to resist this nostalgic and melancholy privileging of the properly political against the 'merely cultural'[12] that this invokes, so as to explore the biennale's potential as a 'space of action' enabling critical intervention in public debate (McGuigan 2005: 436).

Aesthetics and sociability

In 1996 Bourriaud proposed the concept of 'relational aesthetics' in order to identify the common artistic practices that were evident in the exhibition Traffic. He subsequently claimed that the 'interhuman sphere: relationships between people, communities, individuals, groups, social networks, interactivity' that existed in the work of artists such as Pierre Huyghe, Maurizio Cattelan, Gabriel Orozco, Dominique Gonzalez-Forester, Rikrit Tiravanija, Vanessa Beecroft and Liam Gillick was expressive of an emerging and compelling trajectory within the international scene (Bourriaud 2002). The following year, curators Obrist and Hanru launched an open-ended exhibition called 'Cities on the Move'.[13] They proposed a model in which the exhibition would be reinvented in each location. Their aim was to face the dramatic changes in urban development by combining architectural methods for the exhibition design and using collaborations between artists and architects.

In a subsequent partnership with Esche, who had already suggested that a distinctive feature of contemporary art was the redefinition of utopian thinking in the form of what he called a 'modest proposal' (Esche 2005), Hanru described the exhibition space of the 2002 Gwanju Biennale as a platform for initiating new ideas and developing critical social relations. By inviting artists from 25 independent collectives and artist-run spaces to create their own areas within the framework of the biennale, they proposed shifting the focus of an international biennale, from displaying artworks selected on purely aesthetic terms to facilitating the making of 'pertinent works' that address issues arising from the specific cultural realities of everyday life. Hanru and Esche placed faith in the self-organizational and networking skills of the small-scale collectives and were thus willing to devolve power from the central role of the artistic director. By this small step the biennale project opened itself to the challenge of creating a dialogue amongst a diverse range of independent collectives, many of which were meeting for the first time, but also to the opportunity to engender ongoing and unpredictable encounters. Hence, the exhibition space was not conceived as a once-and-for-all event, but more 'like a Pandora's box' that unleashed a wide variety of installations and workshops (Hanru 2002a: 31).

This sense of the biennale as a space of discursive sociability updates and relocates James Clifford's conception of museums as sites of cross-cultural exchange (Clifford 1997). Clifford's more recent work on museums and cultural centres in New Caledonia and Vanuatu, in redeploying Ernesto Laclau's notion of 'articulation', allows for the reality of 'antagonism (us versus them) and alliance (what can we do in common?)' in 'risky, productive, contested sites of socio-cultural activity' (Clifford 2004). In his discussions of fraught cultural sites such as the Tjibaou Cultural Center in Noumea, New Caledonia and the Vanuatu Cultural Center in Port Vila, the museum becomes a space for negotiating the 'opportunities and constraints created by powerful and overlapping cultural, economic, political and historical forces' (Clifford 2004). This refusal to abjure the extent to which these cultural developments are entangled in relations of power – 'exploitation, resistance, accommodation, alliance, subversion' – with national, regional and global forces, and shifting political alignments, means that the work of culture remains 'always political, and relational, marking and mediating insides and outsides, imperfectly negotiating social factions' (Clifford 2004).

We will return to this agonistic sense of the cultural public sphere in our concluding remarks on the Riwaq Biennale. Parenthetically, it is also important to note that this discursive shift in curatorial practice is also aligned to a set of other transformations in the broader context of art production. For well over two decades, art schools, independent artist-run spaces, art magazines and even art fairs have been engaged in critical debates on the interface between art and politics, the role of art in the production of knowledge and the significance of cultural differences in a globalized art world. For the time being, the importance of the recalibration of the biennale will be emphasized in terms of the changing models of artistic engagements with everyday life and the intimations of a global cultural public sphere. Finally, we shall also reflect on how this tendency might function to reclaim the speculative possibility of culture from the expediency of an international spectacular event culture that gives precedence to tourism and economic development.[14]

The aesthetic form and the embedded materiality of social encounters

When Kortun and Esche proposed that the ninth Istanbul Biennial should comprise both avant-garde works, following the tradition of critical engagement with the language of art, and situated, collective and collaborative practices developed by artists who had been invited to reside in Istanbul, they were extending a trajectory in curatorial practice that had been emerging since the mid 1990s. As we have indicated, curators such as Bourriaud and Obrist had been tracking the development of artistic practices that had moved on from what was institutional critique (i.e. an exposure of its structured bias and complicity with capital) towards utilizing these institutions as part of a broader communicational system. The New York collective Group Material, for instance, used exhibition spaces not as sites for display but as locations for public fora. Lucy Orta claims that her work can only bring a certain problem to a point of clarity when there is open debate among different people. In these collaborations, she claims that the museum is adopted to perform new roles:

> I don't see museums as spaces any longer, I see them as part of a larger management team which helps co-ordinate the various collaborations of

the artistic process. ... I have found that an exhibition can form a role to both reflect upon a subject and raise concerns to another level of debate.

(Orta 1999)

A crucial feature of this collaborative practice is the dynamic incorporation of all elements of the museum and gallery structures. This cuts against the hierarchical division that separated the role of the artist and curator from public programming and technical 'support staff'. For Orta, rather than operating according to a Romantic model of creative practice with the artist at the apex of a vertical and sequential chain of command, the preferred mode for developing ideas is by working in an open, horizontal sphere. The realization, fabrication and public dissemination of the work occurs in the process of actualizing the idea, rather than compartmentalizing and distributing it in terms of the exclusive categories of creativity, production and promotion.

These horizontal modes of organization and institutional alliances have been a feature of many collectives forged during the anti-globalization movement and by global anti-racist networks. Most notably, the formation of tactical media centres by transnational groups organized under the banner of No One Is Illegal/Noborder Network were instrumental in defending the human rights of refugees as well as creating fora in which the repressive actions of the State could be exposed and utopian questions could be posed on the freedom of human mobility (Kopp and Schneider 2003). 'Old' museums, 'cool' galleries, or even the networks of 'new' media were no longer the polar extremes of dead and living sites, but nodes that could be utilized for sparking off democratic dialogue. As Hanru has argued, art institutions are not fixed into a permanent state and he rejects the naïve reflex opposition to all institutions 'because society itself is already very institutionalized and there is no way for you to get out of it. Therefore, the only thing you can do is to use the existent institutions and change them from the inside' (Hanru 2002b).

Similarly, Esche has argued that artists are no longer concerned with eschewing the category of art, but with utilizing the various spaces of art to permit new levels of creative exchange. Esche sees these new collaborative models as indicative of a new pragmatic politics that is seeking to convert, co-opt and critique institutions from the inside rather than from a distance. By connecting available material and institutional resources to social aspirations, Esche claims that artists now proceed through a methodology that he terms 'modest proposals':

Modest proposals articulate themselves precisely in terms of 'what might be rather than what is'. They are essentially speculative in that they imagine things other than they are now, yet those speculative gestures are intensely concrete and actual. They avoid the clearly fantastical as well as the hermetic purity of private symbolism in order to deal with real existing conditions and what might be necessary in order to change them.

(Esche 2005: 15)

Esche's reflection on the aesthetic forms and materiality of social encounters in contemporary visual practice highlights the shifts that characterize the new interplay between art and politics. Whilst there is no illusion over the perils and polarizations that have been accentuated by neoliberalism, there has been a fundamental change in the way artists address their adversaries. Artists participating in political activism no longer represent themselves as 'warriors' stepping onto a battlefield in order to eliminate the enemy and capture the ground so as to return it to the oppressed masses. There is now a recognition that the lines of conflict and the affiliations between rival groups in the 'movement of movements' are much fuzzier (Holmes 2007). The role of the public in its relationship with the artist has not only switched from that of witnesses to a spectacle to that of participants in a situation, but has also extended to that of a constitutive partner actively involved in the whole field of meaning. These shifts in the understanding of the roles and responsibilities of producer and consumer redefine both the role of the curator and the utility of the biennale.

The curator as mediator in a global cultural public sphere

In his introductory essay to the 2007 Istanbul Biennial, 'Not Only Possible, But Also Necessary: Optimism in the Age of Global War', Hanru situates the possibilities and problematics of cultural praxis as contingent upon a critical re-examination of 'the promise of modernity', all too often driven by 'liberal capitalism and dominated by Western powers' (Hanru 2007). Turkey, he notes, 'as one of the first non-western modern republics and a key player in the modernization of the developing world has proved to be one of the most radical, spectacular and influential cases in this direction'. Turkey's explosive urban expansion is posed not as a successful outcome of progressive socio-economic 'catch-up' but as the central reference to the conception of the biennale itself. Here the city again becomes a 'battlefield', on which it is possible to 'imagine, test and promote alternative urban and social projects to defend the public sphere and democratic values' from the encroaching privatization of public space. Indeed, this invocation of the politics and potentialities of the urban everyday in the engagement of contemporary art in urban reality is reminiscent of Lefebvre's dialectical understanding of the city of modernity as both an imposed reality and a constant source of subversive action.

We want to suggest that the discursive model of artistic and curatorial practice not only provides a critical inflection on the complex 'ecologies of interdependence', between the global market and the cultural imaginary, but that it has become an aesthetic methodology that is specifically attuned to the emergence of a global cultural public sphere (Lynn 2007: 30). There is no consensus on the potency of this discursive model. Critics such as Blake Stimson and Gregory Sholette, for instance, have expressed affirmative views on the potential of art to produce new political subjectivities. They stress that as contemporary artists adopt collaborative and collective techniques that embrace 'fluctuating identities', hijack the uses of new technologies and establish provisional communal structures, they also produce fleeting social forms that are 'unleashed from geo-political and instrumental norms' (Stimson and Sholette 2007: 4–11). By contrast, the social theorist Susan Buck-Morss struck a more pessimistic note when she expressed the fear that artists were 'hired to assemble publics'; that they merely 'provide atmosphere for the barren planet of finance capital' (Buck-Morss 2003: 133). Indeed, against the more exaggerated claims of many of the anti-globalization protest groups, Raunig has set the cautionary words that the capacity to act in a transnational manner is 'still the ace in the hand of world capital' (Raunig 2002).

There is no denying that the function of the biennale now faces a significant challenge as it confronts the consolidation of commercial interests in the formation of global institutions and discourses. However, it is at the juncture of the apparent expansion of the right to participate in the 'work of the imagination' (Appadurai 2002) and what Lefebvre calls the 'right to the city' (Lefebvre 1996) that the idea of a cosmopolitan cultural sphere is starting to take form. At present, it is impossible to offer a concrete definition of this emergent global cultural public sphere. It has no territorial location, it lacks any administrative entity, and there is not even a coherent community that would claim ownership of the idea. The global public sphere does not exist within conventional geo-political categories. Yet, as Immanuel Wallerstein claims, in biennales, like other recent cultural and political global fora, we can trace the beginnings of a cultural and political imaginary that is moving away from an absolutist and nationalist ideology on cultural identity (Wallerstein 2003). Similarly, while outlining the neo-conservative strategies to control the public imaginary through the imagery of fear, the Retort collective also stressed that it inspired the

> appearance on the world stage of something like a digital 'multitude', a worldwide virtual community, assembled (partly in the short term over the months of warmongering, and partly over the preceding decade, as various new patterns of resistance took advantage of cyberspace) in the interstices of the Net; and that some of the intensity of the moment derived from the experience of seeing – of hearing, feeling, facing up to – an image of refusal become a reality.
>
> (Retort 2006: 4)

We think that the Retort collective is right in stressing that the visuality of the conduct of this war, the witnessing of its mode of representation, was crucial not just in provoking a protest but also as what they call a 'premonition of a politics to come'. This vague definition of the locations, form and constituency of this new politics is echoed further on in their text when they claim that 'something is shifting in the technics and tactics of resistance' (Retort 2006: 12).

We are not so naïve as to rest our case on such faint claims about the potentialities that occur within transitory gatherings. Nor are we so cynical as to assert that art and activism are incapable of making any difference. Between these two extremes there is the more demanding task of teasing out emergent forms and probing the shape of reconfigured structures. The emergence of such 'spheres' is crucial, because without such a common space we would need to ask: in what ways can artists participate in a world that is already saturated by imagery? When both commercial and political spheres have been aestheticized, the formation of a global public sphere takes on greater urgency, as both the destination of art and the focal point for shaping the politics of human life (see Enwezor 2004: 14).

At the forefront of this challenge is the redefinition of the role of curator as a mediator of the contemporary. The function of the curator is no longer confined to being an arbiter of good taste, or the authoritative interpreter of historical trends. As a mediator in a cosmopolitan cultural sphere, the curator is required to set in motion questions that both come from the core of artistic practice and also interact with non–artistic issues. This adds not only a new level of social negotiation to the curatorial agenda, but also a more robust awareness of the interplay between art and politics. It requires not just a capacity to relate to a much wider set of constituents, but also an ability both to read the often contrary ideological and aesthetic value systems and to remain open to the unpredictable feedback resulting from this process. This expanded role and the adoption of an interdisciplinary curatorial framework has been the subject of much criticism. Much of it boils down to accusations of hubris and complaints against the politicization of art. Putting the politics of envy to the side, we think it is more useful to acknowledge idealism as part of the reason, and, as Boris Groys suggests, give due weight to the fact that the art that is primarily made for the biennales is not related to the dictates of the art market, but is for the benefit of an ever-increasing audience of non-buyers. Hence, in a rare outburst of optimism, he concludes that:

> These exhibitions should not be mistaken for mere sites of self-presentation and glorification of the values of the art market. Rather, they try time and again to both create and demonstrate a balance of power between contradictory art trends, aesthetic attitudes, and strategies of representation – to give an idealized, curated image of this balance.
>
> (Groys 2008: 8)[15]

Conclusion

The biennale model that we are cumulatively sketching here exhibits a self-reflexive knowingness with regard to the implication of cultural development in the very processes via which urban transformation produces a range of inequalities – inequalities that are elided in the uncritical celebration of creative capital as a panacea for everything from social anomie to post-industrial decline. Although biennales cannot fix cities, it is equally indulgent to dismiss them as merely the cultural handmaidens of global capital.

We want to conclude with a final example that we think crystallizes Kortun and Esche's conception of the biennale 'not as a tool for selling the city to global capitalism but an agency for presenting it to its citizens and others with eyes awry' (Esche and Kortun 2005: 24), Hanru's emphasis on the 'right to the city' and Enwezor's notion of the discursive platform. The 2007 Riwaq Biennale, which was directed by Khalil Rabah and co-curated by Esche, was structured around a series of ongoing 'Gatherings', consisting of site-specific symposia and workshops aiming at providing visitors and residents alike with an 'alternative set of co-ordinates with which to plot their journeys through the globalized art world' (Rabah 2007).

As in Clifford's model of the cross-cultural exchanges and negotiations of the contact zone, international artists were commissioned to work with the building crafts of Riwaq and gradually install the artistic productions in various Riwaq restoration projects over the longer term. As Rabah argues, given the 'social and territorial fragmentation' of Palestinian territory 'caused by successive Israeli occupations, including the restrictions placed on movement, travel, and international networking within the occupied territories', the whole notion of cultural development and, indeed, of culture as a resource, is somewhat differently inflected (Rabah 2007). Here, the material dimensions of the political cannot be bracketed and displaced to an autonomous and innocent cultural sphere. As Clifford emphasized in his discussion of the fraught colonial context of Noumea, culture's articulations must by necessity be 'always political, and relational, marking and mediating insides and outsides, imperfectly negotiating social factions' (Clifford 2004).

The Riwaq Biennale's 'Gatherings', like Documenta 11's 'Platforms', involve a complex interplay between local and global elements and a willingness to allow this feedback to articulate through an open span of space and time. The biennale thus becomes a process-oriented space of evolving exploration and dialogue, so that, across a two-year exploration period, works begun during the Gatherings could be realized for the multi-sited Third Biennale in 2009. These symposia-in-progress, which range across issues of planning, heritage conservation, architecture and art, initiate a collective, collaborative and situated approach to the very concepts of 'restoration' and 'construction'. Neither the international artist nor the local participant has the authoritative privilege to start or end the conversation. Here, crucially, the issues of how such structures might have creative or artistic functions, and how they relate to the particularities of their immediate surroundings, become entangled in a process of democratic dialogue, thereby instantiating a cultural public sphere.

Notes

1 See the Liverpool European Capital of Culture website, www.liverpool08.com (accessed 30 November 2005).
2 This is epitomized in a quote from the British tabloid the *Daily Mirror* from 1982: 'They should build a fence around [Liverpool] and charge admission. For, sadly, it

has become a "showcase" of everything that has gone wrong in Britain's major cities' (cited in Lane 1987: 11). Twenty years later, Eddie Berg drew our attention to a cartoon depicting a father and son standing together staring down a long row of abandoned factories in the north of England, in which the father turns to his son and says: 'One day son, all this will be a Museum' (Berg 2004).

3 In a press release of 2006, for example, the 2004 Biennial is touted as 'creating an additional £8.3m spend in the city' and lauded for winning the Northwest regional title of Best Tourism Event. See: 'Liverpool Biennial: International 06 Press Release', 9 June 2006, http://www.tate.org.uk/about/pressoffice/pressreleases/2006/tl_biennial_09-06-06.htm (accessed 24 October 2008).

4 Anthony Gardner notes that this 'longing for presence on the global stage partially explains why exhibition events are now a major resource used by many state and corporate stakeholders in order to garner recognition'. He cites the example of Romania, which hosted no fewer than six biennales in the twenty months before its EU accession (Gardner 2009: 953).

5 For the first Liverpool Biennial, see Papastergiadis (2002).

6 Smith frames what is at stake in the future of the biennale around the following question: 'Is the retreat from broad-scale engagement that has characterized all biennales after Documenta 11 a tactical withdrawal to the personal values that harbour the seeds of future community (as at the 2003 Echigo-Tsumari Triennial in Niigata, Japan), or does it indicate that even the biennale, this most inventive exhibition form, is submitting itself to the reactionary, embattled and self-destructive tendencies that currently dominate the "culture at large"?' (Smith 2004: 414)

7 These trends were also influential in the founding of the São Paulo and Sydney Biennales. However, it would also be of great value to investigate how these biennales adapted to fulfil a nationalist agenda that was specific to their own context, as well as articulating the diasporic aspirations of their respective patrons, who, as it turns out, were both from the Veneto region of Italy. Okwui Enwezor has noted that, whilst almost all biennales were founded more from a mixture of economic imperatives and ideological considerations – such as the denazification process in Kassel or the acknowledgement of the democracy movement in Gwanju – the development of biennales also proceeds through an optic of internationalism. For a more detailed, albeit unresolved, account of this contradictory terrain, see Enwezor (2003–04: 102).

8 The emblematic exhibition that embraced this theme was the 2008 Guangzhou Triennial, Farewell to Post-Colonialism, organized by Sarat Maharaj, Gao Shiming and Johnson Chang Tzong-zung.

9 Simon Sheikh, for instance, as curator and critic, sees biennales as places that are capable of maintaining several contradictory representations within a single space; of being both spaces of capital and heterotopic public platforms of hope (Sheikh 2009: 78). Enwezor expresses a similarly positive view of the capacity of the biennale to function as an agent of transformation that leads to the production of a new kind of space and discourse 'of open contestations that spring not merely from resistance but are rather built on an ethics of dissent' (Enwezor 2003–04: 13).

10 Documenta X, curated by Catherine David, was the landmark exhibition that confronted the politics of globalization. A critical component of this exhibition and series of events was the installation of Hybrid Workspace, where The Orangerie was transformed into an open media studio to gather and disseminate information. This 'temporary laboratory' not only recorded and transmitted the viewpoints of

the '100 Days – 100 Guests' programme, but also produced content by its own collaborative team as well as by remote participants who could interact via the Internet. For more information on Hybrid Workspace, a project by Eike Becker and Geert Lovink/Pit Shultz, Micz Flor, Thorsten Schilling, Heike Foll, Moniteurs, Thomas Kaulmann *et al.*, see: http://www.nettime.org/Lists-Archives/nettime-l-9705/msg00008.html. For a discussion of the debates and critical documentation of a number of projects in which art institutions devolved curatorial programming, see Montmann (2006).

11 Platform 1, 'Democracy Unrealized', took place in Vienna from 15 March to 23 April 2001 and continued in Berlin from 9 to 30 October to 2001. Platform 2, 'Experiments with Truth: Transitional Justice and the Processes of Truth and Reconciliation', took place in New Dehli from 7 to 21 May and consisted of five days of public panel discussions, lectures and debates, and a video programme including over 30 documentaries and films. Platform 3, 'Créolité and Creolization', was held on the West Indian Island of St. Lucia in the Caribbean between 12 and 16 January 2002. Platform 4, 'Under Siege: Four African Cities, Freetown, Johannesburg, Kinshasa, Lagos', was held in Lagos from 15 to 21 March 2002, and consisted of public symposia and a workshop entitled 'Urban Processes in Africa'. See http://www.documenta12.de/archiv/d11/data/english/platform1/index.html (accessed 5 February 2009).

12 Here, we refer to Judith Butler's caveat against the tendency in neo-Marxist critiques to equate the 'merely cultural' to the 'never possibly political' (Butler 1998).

13 Cities on the Move opened at Vienna's Secession in 1997 and went on a three-year tour of CAPC Bourdeaux, PS1 New York, Louisiana Museum Denmark, Hayward Gallery London and Kiasma Helsiniki, closing in Bangkok in 1999.

14 See Charles Esche's discussion of the 'caucus' model he developed for the Cork European Capital of Culture project (Vesic 2005).

15 In the now extensive literature on biennales and large-scale exhibitions we have found only one other reference to the discrepancy between art made for biennales and the art market. Carlos Basualdo also notes that the dominant trend of art in biennales is composed of works of an inter-disciplinary and non-objectural nature and he claims that 'the bulk of the financing that concerns the realization of the event and the production of many of the projects is largely independent from collecting (either private or state funded)' (Basualdo 2006: 47).

References

Alloway, L. (1969) *The Venice Biennale 1895–1968: From Salon to Goldfish Bowl*. London: Faber.

Appadurai, A. (2002) The Right to Participate in the Work of the Imagination. In Brouwer, J., Mulder, A. and Martz, L. (eds.) *TransUrbanism*. Rotterdam: V2_Publishing/NAI Publishers.

Arrhenius, S. (2007) Independent Curating Within Institutions Without Walls. In Rand, S. and Kouris, H. (eds.) *Cautionary Tales: Critical Curating*. New York: Apex Art.

Basualdo, C. (2006) The Unstable Institution. In Marincola, P. (ed.) *Questions of Practice: What Makes a Great Exhibition?* Philadelphia: Philadelphia Exhibitions Initiative.

Berg, E. (2004) Venture Culturalism, Or Tales of Culture and Commerce. Paper presented at the conference 'Empires, Ruins + Networks: Art in Real Time Culture', Melbourne, April 2–4.

Bourriaud, N. (2002) *Relational Aesthetics*. Dijon: Les Presses du Reel.

Bourriaud, N. (2007) Stock Zero, Or the Icy Water of Egoistical Calculation. Available at: http://2nd.moscowbiennale.ru/en/main_project/8/ (accessed 05/02/09).

Boyle, M. and Rogerson, R. J. (2001) Power, Discourses and City Trajectories. In Paddison, R. (ed.), *Handbook of Urban Studies*. London: Sage Publications.

Buck-Morss, S. (2003) *Thinking Past Terror*. London: Verso.

Butler, J. (1998) Merely Cultural. *New Left Review* 1(227): 33–44.

Clifford, J. (1997) *Routes: Travel and Translation in the Late Twentieth Century*. Cambridge, Massachusetts: Harvard University Press.

Clifford, J. (2004) Translating Museums, Articulating Heritage: Some Pacific Performances. Paper presented at the conference 'Rebirth of the Museum?' Melbourne, July 8–9.

Enwezor, O. (2003–04) Mega-Exhibitions and the Antinomies of a Transnational Global Forum. *MJ-Manifesta Journal* (Winter–Spring): 6–31.

Enwezor, O. (2004) Documentary/Verite: Bio-Politics, Human Rights and the Figure of "Truth" in Contemporary Art. *Australian and New Zealand Journal of Art* 4/5(1): 12–30.

Enwezor, O. (2008) A Space of Encounter. Interview with Victoria Lynn. *Art & Australia* 46(2).

Esche, C. (2005) *Modest Proposals*. Istanbul: Baglam Publishing.

Esche, C. and Kortun, V. (2005) The World is Yours. In *Art, City Politics in an Expanding World, Writings from the 9th International Istanbul Biennial*. Istanbul: Deniz Unsal.

Ferguson, B. (2009) Biennales as Discursive Models. Paper presented at the conference *To Biennial or Not to Biennial?* Bergen, September 17–20.

Gardner, A. (2009) On the "Evental" Installation: Contemporary Art and the Politics of Presence. In Anderson, J. (ed.) *Crossing Cultures: Conflict, Migration and Convergence*. Melbourne: Miegunyah Press.

Groys, B. (2008) *Art Power*. Cambridge, Massachusetts: MIT Press.

Hanru, H. (2002a) Event City, Pandora's Box. In Esche, C., Hanru, H. and Wan-kyun, S. (eds.) *P A U S E*. Gwanju: Gwanju Biennale Press.

Hanru, H. (2002b) *On The Mid-Ground*. Hong Kong: Timezone 8.

Hanru, H. (2007) Not Only Possible, But Also Necessary: Optimism in the Age of Global War. Available at: http://www.iksv.org/bienal10/english/detail.asp?cid= 3&ac=conceptual (accessed 05/02/09).

Holmes, B. (2007) The Revenge of the Concept: Artistic Exchanges, Networked Resistance. In Bradley, W. and Esche, C. (eds.) *Art and Social Change*. London: Tate Publishing/Afterall.

Hoskote, R. (2009) Biennial Format. Paper presented at the conference *To Biennial or Not to Biennial?* Bergen, September 17–20.

Hsu, M. (2005) Networked Cosmopolitanism – On Cultural Exchange and International Exhibition. In Tsoutas, N. (ed.) *Knowledge + Dialogue + Exchange: Remapping Cultural Globalism from the South*. Sydney: Artspace.

Kopp, H. and Schneider, F. (2003) A Brief History of the Noborder Network. Available at: http://makeworlds.org/node/29 (accessed 22/08/06).

Lane, T. (1987) *Liverpool: Gateway to Empire*. London: Lawrence and Wishart.

Lefebvre, H. (1991) *The Production of Space*. Cambridge, Massachusetts: Blackwell.

Lefebvre, H. (1996) The Right to the City. In Kofman, E. and Lebas, E. (trans. and eds.) *Writings on Cities*. Oxford: Blackwell.

Lynn, V. (2007) We Live in Turbulent Times …. Turbulence Third Auckland Triennial, exhibition catalogue.

McGuigan, J. (2005) The Cultural Public Sphere. *European Journal of Cultural Studies* 8(4): 427–443.

Montmann, N. (ed.) (2006) *Art and its Institutions: Current Conflicts, Critiques and Collaborations*. London: Black Dog Publishing.

Mosquera, G. (2009) The Havana Biennial: A Concrete "Utopia" Paper presented at the conference *To Biennial or Not to Biennial?* Bergen, September 17–20.

Niemojewski, R. (2009) To Biennial and not … Bergen. Paper presented at the conference *To Biennial or Not to Biennial?* Bergen, September 17–20.

Orta, L. (1999) Interview with Hou Hanru. Available at: http://studioorta.free.fr/lucy_orta/TMP-1115468054.htm (accessed 7 October 2005).

Osipovich, A. (2007) Reaching for New Heights. *The Moscow Times*. March 2. Available at: http://www.moscowtimes.ru/arts/2008/06/06/363589.htm (accessed 05/02/09).

Papastergiadis, N. (2002) The Double of Mimesis. In Chuhan, J., Dimitraki, A. and Thomas, E. (eds.) *Re:Trace Dialogues: Essays on Contemporary Art and Culture*. Liverpool: Centre for Art International and Liverpool Biennial.

Rabah, K. (2007) To Set in Motion. Available at: http://riwaqbiennale.org/ (accessed 16/02/09).

Raunig, G. (2002) Transversal Multitudes. Available at: http://eipcp.net/transversal/0303/raunig/en (accessed 13/11/08).

Retort. (2006) *Afflicted Powers. Capital and Spectacle in a New Age of War*. London and New York: Verso.

Sheikh, S. (2009) Marks of Distinction, Vectors of Possibility: Questions for the Biennial. The Biennial as a Global Phenomenon, Special Issue. *Open*, 16.

Smith, T. (2004) Biennales in the Conditions of Contemporaneity. *Art and Australia* 42(3): 406–15.

Stimson, B. and Sholette, G. (2007) Introduction. In Stimson, B. and Sholette, G. (eds.) Collectivism After Modernism. Minneapolis: MIT Press.

Vesic, J. (2005) Interview with Charles Esche. From Prelom Magazine, Belgrade, http://www.iksv.org/bienal/bienal9/english/Page=Curators&sub=Interview&Content=2 (accessed 12/02/09).

Wallerstein, I. (2003) *The Decline of American Power*. New York: New Press.

Yúdice, G. (2003) *The Expediency of Culture: Uses of Culture in the Global Era*. Durham: Duke University Press.

4 Festivals and the geography of culture

African cinema in the 'world space' of its public

James F. English

Festivals have assumed their powerful and seemingly ubiquitous place within the infrastructure of the 'cultural public sphere' (McGuigan 2005) partly by virtue of their consecratory function. Festivals help to constitute publics by organizing the struggles over cultural value and canons of taste by means of which publics come to know themselves. Festivals contribute importantly to the structuring of public reception and debate, producing consensus regarding the 'masters' and 'masterpieces' of a given cultural field, as well as the equally vital forms of dissent – scandal, outrage, controversy – over new, heterodox works or styles.

This consecratory role is obvious for the many festivals that are organized according to a competition format, where juries award prizes to the most outstanding artists or works, these experts' selections often counterposed to the 'people's choices' of the larger festival audience. Such festivals have become the norm in most fields of art and culture, with formerly non-competitive festivals migrating steadily over to the competitive paradigm and established festival awards programmes continually expanding to include more and more prizes in more and more categories. Even festivals that call themselves non-competitive have often found ways to effect a creative compromise with the competition format. Some, for example, have teamed up with a separate, established awards organization or professional association, incorporating some or all of that group's annual prizes into a culminating awards gala on the final night of the festival. Such arrangements can be mutually advantageous, gaining for each institution an increase in consecratory leverage and making its selections more symbolically powerful.

But looking beyond festivals' involvement in the mania for prizes and awards, we can see that all cultural festivals, even those most firmly committed to the ideal of non-competitive cultural celebration – to fostering sentiments of solidarity and mutual belonging through a collective experience of art – depend fundamentally on processes of valuation and judgment. Organizers must apply principles of selection to determine which artists will be feted, which new works will be featured on the programme, which portions of the programme will be scheduled in the most desirable prime-time slots, and even, importantly, which people (on the administrative staff or called in from the outside) will be granted the power to make these various decisions and selections. Every festival thus serves as a means of producing and distributing scarce symbolic resources (recognition, respect, standing, legitimacy) in the form of more-or-less 'bankable' honours: concrete attainments to be listed in one's *palmarès* (if not as 'awards' then as 'festival appearances', 'major exhibitions', 'headline performances', 'international screenings', etc.) and displayed as evidence of one's artistic worth.

For this reason, when we set out to articulate theoretically the relations between festivals, publics, and the struggle for democratized culture, we do well to cross-fertilize our Habermas with some Bourdieu, at least to the point of recognizing that festivals are instruments of *economic* as well as of communicative action. The festival is as much a field for the competitive accumulation and more-or-less exploitative deployment of symbolic capital as it is a forum for the exchange of ideas and the construction of reasoned consensus about art and society.[1]

This symbolic economy, which I have elsewhere called the economy of cultural prestige (English 2005), is no less 'real' than the money economy with which it is interwoven and in which artists and works find their commercial value. The forms of non-monetary capital that circulate within it are as rare and worthy of acquisition as gold coins or Euros, and the economic structure that facilitates their exchange, accumulation, and control is built into the actual world in durable ways that can be measured and mapped. The symbolic economy of culture has, among other things, a specific geography, a relational system of geographic locations comprising centres of accumulated power (large endowments) and more-or-less remote outposts subject in varying degree to symbolic domination by the centres. This geographic dimension of cultural capital and cultural markets has been well described with respect to the literary field by Pascale Casanova in her *Republique Mondiale des Lettres* (Casanova 1999). The object of Casanova's study is not literature as a set of works but literature 'as a *space*: a set of interconnected positions, which must be thought and described in relational terms' (Casanova 2005: 72–3). Festivals – in the other arts as well as in literature – play a critical role in shaping this geography of the symbolic: determining not just a world public but a world space of hierarchically situated publics, not just a global cultural public sphere but a global field of cultural prestige and power. Festivals are after all event-destinations, 'tourist traps', vacation attractions constituting a worldwide system or 'circuit' of more-or-less culturally noteworthy locations into which practically every sizable city or resort town has now inserted itself. Intuitively, we know that the prestige of a festival, the honour it is capable of bestowing on an artist, has much to do with the economics, demographics, and cultural resources of its location. Frankfurt, Hong Kong, London, and New York are teeming metropolitan crossroads rich with every sort of capital, and the festivals in those cities can and do draw upon the cities' broad-based stature or 'world ranking' in establishing their relative importance on the 'circuit'. But, conversely, places of no particular centrality, scale, or cultural prestige can, by virtue of a festival, come to assume tremendous symbolic force and resonance, as has been the case with Hay-on-Wye, Park City, Utah, and so on. The relationship between the location of a festival in ordinary geopolitical or economic terms and its functions and effects within the partly autonomous, symbolic (but real) system of spatial relations constituting the geography of culture is in fact a highly complex one – and has been growing more so in the recent decades of so-called globalization.

As regards the money economy, 'globalization' designates a rapid extension and intensification of transnational networks and itineraries of exchange, with the concomitant emergence of new geographic tensions and clusterings, new forms of centrality and peripherality, and new opportunities to impose or resist economic domination. Some version of these same processes has undoubtedly been reshaping the economy of cultural prestige, as well. But while we have had twenty years of pitched debate about the globalization of commercial and financial capital, there has been relatively little discussion about the forms globalization might be taking with respect to specifically cultural capital. The tendency has been rather to assume that developments in the cultural economy follow a parallel course to those in the sphere of commercial exchange, such that one analytical model (the paradigm of commerce) will provide adequate descriptive and explanatory tools for 'globalization' as a whole. From this perspective, little more has been said than that culture around the world is becoming more Americanized, more blockbuster-obsessed and more homogeneous. An important task for cultural critics today, and especially for those committed (in Bourdieu's terms) to a democratization of the field of cultural power or (in Habermas's) to a relaxation of entry barriers and access restrictions to the cultural public sphere, is to pursue new lines of inquiry that might challenge this reductive economism, which is in fact more of a symptom of neoliberal hegemony than a resource for resisting it. Given the necessarily close involvement of festivals with the business of place-promotion and their recent, rapid expansion onto new terrains worldwide, they offer themselves as prime objects for an inquiry of this kind. The aim of this chapter, therefore, is to offer a small contribution to the major task of 'mapping' the emergent world system of cultural power and cultural power-effects of which festivals are an increasingly prominent and indeed constitutive part.

Location, location, location

Cultural festivals have always been rooted in, and purposively deployed for the benefit of, their locations. The festivals of Ancient Greece, though generally originating in rural ceremony, evolved into prototypical initiatives of urban place promotion. To take one major example, the great Dionysia festival in the city of Athens was consciously aimed at attracting tourists from remote towns and countryside locations into the urban centre, thereby amplifying the city's reputation as a cultural hub throughout the Attic world and, not incidentally, drawing outside money into the local economy. The Athenian Council understood very well the basic principles of place promotion. They made every effort to showcase the biggest names in drama and music from each of the Attic tribes, and offered substantial tax breaks to the private patrons (*choregoi*) who did the organizational legwork and provided the funding for the festivals' huge choral competitions. The events themselves were carefully spaced out – geographically, across various city locations from the Theatre of Dionysios to the Eleusinion, and temporally, from the official 'pomp' and parade of the opening day through to the announcement of winners and awarding of prizes at the closing ceremony a week later – so as to maximize tourists' opportunities to 'enjoy the town' and transfer their money into the coffers of local businesses.

These municipal objectives and strategies are, of course, familiar to us from our own festivals, whose similar rhythm and spacing of events attest to the enduring symbolic and economic interconnectedness of the festival with its immediate location. But modern festivals have tended to promote not just the interests of their host cities, but also, and often more importantly, those of their nation states, which rely on large-scale cultural spectacles to function as collective stagings of national unity and achievement. From the standpoint of the national government, the festival is a doubly useful symbolic event: on the domestic front, it helps to secure nationalist sentiment across lines of internal division, cementing the fragile bonds of 'imagined community'; no less importantly, on the field of international relations, it serves to project a depth and richness of national heritage together with the administrative competence of a properly modern state apparatus. It assists the nation in improving its symbolic position among the many nations of the world.

This can be seen clearly in the early history of film festivals – which are arguably the most important and widespread form of modern cultural festivals, and will serve as the point of focus here. Film festivals were first conceived as touristic attractions very much on the classical model and were heavily promoted by municipal governments and local business associations. Part of the impetus for the Venice Biennale, the international exhibition of art from which the earliest film festival emerged, was to attract tourists into a city that had long been economically dependent on tourism and now saw itself losing ground. The threat came in part from other European cities, which, by founding professional teams and building large new stadiums, were capitalizing on the rapidly growing popularity of interurban and international football, with its ability to attract throngs of free-spending fans on a regular basis. The biannual festival was thus conceived as a kind of cultural World Cup. Cannes, where the second-earliest festival of cinema was founded, was likewise a place already devoted to tourism – a high-end resort town for Europe's leisure class. As Lucy Mazdon has discussed, the fact that the festival was launched there reminds us that the 'link between film festival and tourism', far from being a result of recent commercialization, was 'inextricable ... from the outset' (Mazdon 2007: 17).

But in Venice, Cannes, and other early film-festival cities in Europe, the national cultural ministries also assumed an important role in the organizational framework. Their objectives were not necessarily at odds with the touristic goals of the municipal administrators, but they were distinct. One key aim of the national ministry, for example, was to raise the reputation and enlarge the market for works of the national cinema in the face of rising domination by Hollywood. This was not a particularly urgent concern for the host city, which in most cases was not the primary base of the country's cinema industry and would have preferred a foreign-dominated programme that could fill hotel rooms and theatre seats to a dutifully nationalist one that held little tourist appeal. Nor were the local organizers necessarily committed to the political success of the existing regime or to its particular vision of nationalist belonging and solidarity. Yet, for those regimes themselves, whether the Mussolini government of Fascist Italy or the emerging Cold War democracy of West Germany, the festival was irresistibly attractive as an instrument of national propaganda (Stone 1998: 100–8; Fehrenbach 1995: 235–50). To offer one quick example, the prize for best picture at the 1939 Venice festival – the 'Mussolini Cup', as it was then called – was shared between Riefenstahl's *Olympia* and a film made by Mussolini's own son. The closing ceremony thus served to legitimate Fascist art in Italy and to strengthen the cultural linkages of the Berlin–Rome Axis. In Venice as elsewhere, the festival effected a kind of symbolic shift, whereby the city's desire to become a destination for cinema-tourism was achieved through its domestic repositioning as the symbolic heart of a specifically national, and nationalistic, cinematic field, which could then be further positioned internationally in accordance with the national government's geopolitical agenda. Each destination on the early 'festival circuit' came to be regarded not just as a 'city of cinema' among other such cities, but as its nation's capital in an emergent international geography of symbolic competition and collaboration.

Of course, the simple division of the cinematic field into its distinct national cinemas – a scheme of division that festivals have done much to reinforce and elaborate – was never more than a convenient simplification; the whole history of cinema has absolutely depended on international exchange. But the recent decades of rapidly expanding transnational networks and flows, the revolution of global communications technologies and the worldwide rise of VCR, DVD, and online video, and the increased mobility and interconnectivity of the globe-trotting cosmopolitans alongside the forced unsettlement and exile of the 'vagabond' classes (Bauman 1998: 77–102) have made it harder than ever to understand the system of cinematic production, distribution, consecration, and consumption in terms of national boundaries. The manic proliferation of the festivals themselves, dozens of them crowded into individual countries and many devoted to celebrating the cinemas of other, quite distant, places, has exploded the older model of international rivalry. As various kinds of transnational, regional, ethnic, and exilic film festival have emerged to capture the new touristic flows and to extend the festivals' consecratory power to new subsets or cross-sections of world film production, the resultant map of their relational positions has become much harder to decipher. It has also, I believe, become more autonomous, attaining a wider separation from the maps of commercial and geopolitical relations than is generally recognized. Together with the system of cultural institutions that operate within and through it, the festival circuit has become capable of drawing boundaries and charting itineraries entirely of its own making: not only actively producing new cinemas and new publics (as opposed to merely distributing existing cinemas to existing publics), but producing new kinds of relationship between cinema, cinemagoer, and place – even in a sense, producing new 'places'. This expanding productive power has undoubtedly been harnessed to good intentions, aimed at achieving a more redistributive and potentially emancipatory global economy of cinematic prestige. Yet certain factors, not least of which is their enduring investment in the idea of national cinemas, are continuing to constrain the festivals and to limit the culturally democratizing effects of their expanding world system.

The festival circuit and the situation of Africa

Both the productive dynamism and the limited efficacy of the festival circuit in the current phase of its globalization are manifest in the dramatic multiplication and spreading of African film festivals. Their heady proliferation in recent years raises a number of interconnected questions. What relational position does the term 'African' designate on the festival circuit, and what symbolic advantages or disadvantages does that position entail? Where is the African cinema to be located in the 'world space' of the cinema? (Where is its base? Where are its centres of power? In what 'public sphere', exactly, is its value produced and accumulated?) How does that location differ from Africa's place in the more familiar geography of material production and trade (i.e. in the 'cinema industry')? And finally, what is the role of festivals in determining these matters?

To begin with, very few of the festivals devoted to African cinema are held in Africa. Despite the emergence of a handful of fledgling festivals on that continent in recent years, there are still no more than six or eight reliably annual or biennial events, and even these are by no means all devoted to the promotion of African cinema. Two of the oldest and most firmly established, in Carthage (biennial since 1966) and Cairo (annual since 1976), are strongly oriented towards the Middle East and points beyond rather than towards Africa. Cairo, 'the oldest international festival in the Middle East', serves primarily as a venue for screening independent films from Europe, Asia, and the Americas, its only concessions to a local or regional cinema being occasional sidebar screenings and two awards reserved for Arab films (out of 15 award categories). Carthage does have a much stronger regional emphasis, and screens many more films from African countries. But owing to its Middle Eastern orientation, its African programme leans heavily towards productions from Egypt and the Maghreb rather than the sub-Sahara. Only two films from outside the Arab world have won top honours at Carthage in the last 20 years.

The handful of festivals scattered through the 50 countries of Central and Southern Africa do mostly emphasize local and regional cinemas. But even for an established and well-run regional festival like that of Durban, which dates back to 1979, there has been an increasing tendency to rely on feature films from Europe, North America, India, and East Asia to give the festival screenings broader audience appeal and to project the city's worldliness and cosmopolitan tastes, its connectedness with the metropolitan cultural scene. This is normal, since festivals (and festival cities) must compete with one another for international visibility and esteem on an increasingly congested field. As Jeremy Stringer points out, the various festivals around the world are continually 'measured and compared, high spots differentiated from low spots, glamorous and sexy locations separated out from the not-so-glamorous and not-so-sexy. Inequality is thus built into the very structure of the international film festival circuit' (Stringer 2001: 136).[2]

The State, too, has a clear stake in this unequal struggle to attract and appeal, inasmuch as different countries compete with one another for prominent positions on the map of most practical, affordable, and 'sexy' filming locations (a competition in which South Africa has lately done rather well). Festivals can represent the best opportunity for a national film office to pitch its country's advantages as a location, but only if the festival succeeds in attracting the acknowledgment and participation of big-time global players.

One result of this whole unequal scramble is a tendency for the more peripheral festivals to reinforce hierarchies of value that obtain at the metropolitan core. Of the 21 awards presented at Durban in 2008, only three went to Africans (and only one to a black African). For all their good intentions, such festivals often seem less capable of establishing a place for African cinema than of putting the African cinema *in* its place.

The great exception to this marginalization of African film within African film festivals is FESPACO, the *Festival panafricain du cinema et de la television de Ouagadougou*, founded three years after that of Carthage, in 1969, and today regarded as the premiere showcase for African film in Africa. Held biennially in the capital city of Burkina-Faso, FESPACO screens many dozens of African films (generally about 20 of them feature films) and provides the continent's main gathering place for film professionals as well as its most important venue for the buying and selling of stock footage. Its top prize, the *Etalon d'or de Yennenga* (Golden Stallion of Yennenga), is awarded to the African film that best shows 'African realities', and only one of its various other prize competitions is open to work from beyond Africa: the Paul Robeson Prize for outstanding film by a director of the African diaspora. Yet even at this most concertedly African of festivals, the status of African film and its place in the geography of world cinema are highly ambiguous.

For one thing, the African cinema that is consolidated and consecrated in Ouagadougou, though held to be categorically distinct from the African diasporic cinema (a category with its own separate competition for the Robeson Prize), is almost entirely written, produced, and directed by people living in Europe, particularly in France. It is in effect a subfield of the European independent cinema, based or headquartered in the great capital of world cinema,

Paris. And it is also Paris that – via the French Cultural Ministry, the *Agence de Cooperation Culturelle et Technique* (ACCT), the *Centre National de Cinématographie* (CNC), and other cultural institutions deeply interwoven with the festival circuit – provides much of the funding for FESPACO as well as many of the personnel involved in arranging the programme and selecting winners for the various awards. Going down the list of these winners, one finds the countries of origin, unfailingly African nations, given in parentheses: Algeria, Cameroon, the Democratic Republic of the Congo, Ghana, Ivory Coast, Mali, Mauritania, Morocco, Nigeria, South Africa, and Burkina-Faso itself. But these are practically never the nations that appear in the official production credits; nor are they often the nations of residence for the writer, director, photographer, or producers of the winning film, all of whom are likely to be based in France or elsewhere in Europe.

Even a rare Anglophone film such as Newton Aduaka's *Ezra* (about the trial of a child soldier traumatized by war in Sierra Leone), which won the Golden Stallion in 2007, follows the general pattern. Classified by FESPACO as a Nigerian film, it is listed in the Internet Movie Database (IMDB) as a co-production of five countries, with France and Austria getting top billing. The company credits are given to Arte France of the Franco–German TV network, and to Cinéfacto and CNC of France and Amour Fou Filmproduktion in Vienna. It was Arnaud Louvet, a French producer for Arte, who came up with the original idea for the film and approached Aduaka with a proposal and funding arrangement (Aduaka 2007). The writer, editor, assistant director, and most of the rest of the crew are all French and based in Paris. The cinematographer is a Panamanian trained in Paris. Aduaka himself contributes the sole Anglophone element.[3] He moved to London in 1985 at age 18, attended film school there and then co-founded Granite Film Works to produce his first feature, *Rage*, a film about race, poverty, and hip-hop subculture in Southeast London. (As the first work of the black British cinema funded entirely by a black-owned company, this film has some historic importance in the UK.) But in recent years Aduaka has lived and worked mostly in Paris, where he has enjoyed a position of comfort and prestige – secured not through FESPACO but through his recognition at Cannes – as Filmmaker in Residence at the Cannes Cinéfondation (Bourne 2005: 183–91).

My point here is not that Aduaka and the other filmmakers celebrated at Ouaga and elsewhere on the circuit are 'really', 'merely', or 'simply' Europeans. Aduaka is indeed an 'African filmmaker'. But his status and recognition as such – the very specifications and limits of that term – have less to do with anything going on in Africa than with the work of selection, classification, and promotion done by the festival circuit as a whole. Most instrumental in this regard are the festivals in Europe and North America, which are far more numerous and powerful, and even in fact more invested in the idea of an African cinema (though much less so in the actual emergence of a cinema industry in Africa), than the African ones. The principles of eligibility and the criteria of value that have evolved and been applied in these festivals of the global North, and in their 'sister' or 'partner' festivals elsewhere, are what primarily shape the list of winners at FESPACO. By these principles, a picture's eligibility as 'African' (as also 'Chinese' or indeed 'French' or 'Italian') depends on the director's country of birth and/or parents' citizenship. As Aduaka was born to Africans in Africa, *Ezra* is an African film, as was *Rage* (which appeared on the Planet Africa programme at the Toronto Film Festival and won the award for best first feature at the Pan African Film Festival of Los Angeles before winning the same award at FESPACO).

To be sure, other, alternative, criteria can be found at work in the institutional apparatus of cinematic classification, criteria that allow the occasional uncoupling of films from their directors' national origins in order to consider the sources of funding, the places of residence of the various creative collaborators, the themes and locations and source materials involved – the whole larger system of productive inputs. It is fairly common for festival directors to accept any plausible criterion that justifies 'claiming' a good picture for the expected (if not downright obligatory) programme highlighting domestic films. This explains why *Rage*, screened as an 'African' film in Los Angeles, Amiens, Toronto, Ouagadougou, and elsewhere, was embraced at festivals in London and Edinburgh as a work of the new multicultural British cinema, or why *Ezra* was screened at the Diagonale Festival of Austrian Film in Graz. But these are understood as specially motivated deviations from standard practice, and they do not point to any real flexibility or imagination in the classificatory system. The European festivals long ago lent themselves to the task of constructing world cinema according to a paradigm of individual auteurs belonging to distinct national cinemas, and this scheme is now firmly lodged in the circuit. As Azadeh Farahmand puts it, nationality 'coalesces with authorship in the sense that a filmmaker's authorship is often constituted and found meaningful in relation to its national status; ... star directors "author" their national culture via their films' (Farahmand 2006: 96).

Cinematic production in general is misrepresented by this system, which obscures the medium's profoundly collaborative and transnational nature behind the twin modern ideologemes of the individual genius and the immutable national character. The scheme systematically over-selects for the work of exiles and émigrés – especially those working in Europe (whose films, being Euro-funded, have already secured a modicum of visibility and legitimacy in the world cinema system) – while discounting the kinds of work being produced domestically (which are more obscure, less hooked-in). In this respect, the divisional scheme encourages a deterritorialization of the world cinema.[4] It tends, as well, to over-select (and drive a market for) the kinds of narrative that conflate personal struggle for dignity or redemption with postcolonial struggle towards true nationhood – i.e. meldings of affirmative *Bildungsroman* with national allegory, which have become the generic staple of 'world fictions' both literary and cinematic in the neoliberal era (Slaughter 2003, 2007; Barnard 2008).[5]

Notwithstanding these more general biases of selection, the national-author optic also creates some specific problems in the way it represents the cinematic production of Africa. As a continent whose film industries collectively have fewer resources and produce fewer theatrical feature films than even a relatively small European country, Africa has been counted in this scheme as a single nation – a misfitting of paradigm to reality that the festival industry has often papered over by lazy or even cynical application of the utopian term Pan African.[6] The paradigm also systematically excludes the commodity-movies produced by an industrial system geared for direct-to-DVD distribution. Even where these have not been ruled out by a required 35mm format (which still functions as the main barrier to entry for the 'cinema of quality'), their effectively 'authorless' production weighs heavily against them. Yet this is the one cinematic option that makes economic sense for most nations of sub-Saharan Africa, where even if theatrical distribution were not so completely dominated as it is now by American, Indian, and Hong Kong films, there would still be nowhere near adequate ticket revenues to support domestic or even regional films (Bartlet 2005).

The one thriving movie industry in the sub-Sahara is Nigeria's 'Nollywood', which churns out more than a thousand new DVD titles a year and turns substantial profits on sale prices as low as a dollar per disc. The Nigerian director Lancelot Oduwa Imasuen, for example, though still in his thirties, has made a hundred films, fifty of them in the last five years alone. The sustained domestic success of such directors is inspiring young filmmakers in Sierra Leone, Senegal, Cameroon, and Madagascar to adopt the 'Nigerian model' of production (Bartlet 2010: 220–1). But this decision to embrace the only viable domestic model effectively removes their work from the public sphere of discussion and debate, since that space is constituted by a global festival circuit that systematically withholds recognition from local, popular screen cultures. While it is true that some festivals have lately begun to devote spotlight programmes to video titles from Nollywood, the movies have almost never been accepted into competition – i.e. into the sphere of consecration proper – at FESPACO, Durban, Carthage, or any of the major European and North American festivals. It is the exilic Nigerian Aduaka who is feted on the circuit rather than Nigeria's prodigious local talent, Imasuen.

'African Cinema', then, has been defined according to the auteurist model of the national cinema and put into circulation on those terms within a global circuit of festivals, festivals-within-festivals, and festivals-of-festivals devoted to promoting what amounts to an object of their own construction. This cinema comes for the most part from Europe, but bears the name of an Africa that supports neither its production nor its distribution and reception, and is afforded only the most marginal role in its valuation and consecration, with even FESPACO functioning more as an arm or annex of the French consecratory apparatus than as an autonomous symbolic instrument. The films that constitute this cinema nearly always premiere at festivals of the global North, and, if they are to attain special stature or esteem in the field, will have already embarked on that rise of fortunes (acquiring various prizes, honours, or special mentions) before they ever find their way onto an African screen – if, indeed, they ever do.

This African cinema is a way for 'Africa' to appear in the peculiar cultural geography of the festival circuit (the geography of the production and circulation of cinematic prestige), whose logic demands that Africa appear, and appear to be valued, in the global cinematic public sphere, regardless of the actual circumstances of the cinema and its publics in African nations. This logic of increasing visibility and stature for the other might be seen in terms of a shift of opinion or attention in the global cinematic public sphere, whereby a cosmopolitan politics of multicultural egalitarianism puts pressure on the world cinema's gatekeepers, eventually winning from them a capacity to recognize value outside the West. According to this view, the festival circuit, after some decades of discursive struggle over the world's symbolic as well as material resources, has accepted an obligation to wield its substantial symbolic power in more equitable and anti-imperial ways, distributing its consecratory wealth beyond Europe and North America, and offering the gift of world-cinematic stature to *other* cinemas, after the manner of foreign aid or global philanthropy.

This view is not wholly wrong. But we should also see the circuit's eager pursuit of new, non-Western cinemas – Latin American, Iranian, Hong Kong, Chinese, African – as a response to an autonomous or self-generated demand, driven less by the imposition of a new politics of appreciation in the public sphere than by an internal logic of growth, by the circuit's self-generating need for global expansion as more and more cities, resorts, university towns, and other places seek to establish themselves somewhere on the chain of festal destinations.

Or rather – because we now have multiple and hierarchically differentiated festivals taking place at any given moment, and are thus way past the point of an orderly, sequential calendar of events – not a chain but a *rhizome*: constantly expanding by every available means of replication and subtle differentiation, producing ever more festivals, each one 'new', 'the latest thing', and yet connected, interwoven, and not so different from the others as to break loose from them easily.

Manthia Diawara observed a decade and a half ago that what was happening with respect to Africa was that its cinema industry remained moribund, with 'no production nor distribution structures in place', while 'the cultural industry *around* African cinema [kept] growing larger and larger, generating new festivals in every corner of the world' (Diawara 1994: 386).[7] That lopsided process of expansion has continued and even accelerated, to the point where there are now many more festivals of African cinema than there are theatrical feature films made in Africa (an imbalance that obtains even if we count all the films funded and produced under European and/or American auspices).

There has been, as well, a proliferation of African spotlight programmes or sub-competitions within most of the large international festivals, such as the aforementioned Planet Africa programme at Toronto. Aduaka's *Ezra*, to return to that example, has been screened at more than 50 international festivals, nearly half of them festivals of African cinema, and most of the others scheduling the picture within an African programme.

Yet this is only a small sampling of the full array, which includes dozens more in North America alone: in Atlanta, Berkeley, Boston, Chicago, Denver, Miami, Portland, Vancouver, Washington, and many other cities. The rhizomatic design now covers practically the entire world, the well-established festivals of African film in Amiens (1980), Montreal (1985), Milan (1990), Los Angeles (1990), and New York (1993) replicated not just by the many festivals in other cities of Europe and North America, but also by ones in Rio, Uppsala, Seoul, Buenos Aires, Sydney, and on and on.

As the rhizome has expanded, it has not fostered a more fractured and con-flictual public sphere of cinematic discussion and debate, tossing up rogue fes-tivals, unexpected categories and alternative criteria. On the contrary, it has contained its ever more geographically dispersive public within an ever denser and more seamless tissue of linkages and symbolic norms. The first African film festival in Spain, for example (Tarifa), has entered into partnership with a 'mate-festival' newly established in Mexico City, and it invites other festivals of the Spanish-speaking world to join the network and collaborate on various curatorial and administrative projects. The African Film Festival of New York (AFF) has established 'ongoing partnerships' with festivals in Sudan, Brazil, Trinidad and Tobago, St Kitts and Nevis, and in the Middle East. In recent years, the AFF has curated or co-curated the African Film Festival of Sydney, the African Film Festival of Kingston, Jamaica, and the African CineFest of Barbados. The circuit's expansion appears to be extending and reinforcing the consecratory itineraries of the most powerful festivals, rather than opening new pathways of recognition and symbolic attainment.

Having well exceeded the scale of its object, the 'culture industry around African cinema' nevertheless continues to grow. We might hope to read in this unrelenting expansion a determined international effort to foster, through a relaying of resources from the symbolic to the material economy, some inde-pendent 'production and distribution structures' in Africa. But the circuit's trajectory of growth cannot be accounted for by any collective vision or agenda of autonomy for the cinema cultures on that continent. It points only to the increasing autonomy of the cinematic status system itself, which does not require any change in the industrial relations of material advantage and disadvantage in order to generate its new 'national' cinemas and, correspondingly, its new boutique venues of consecration (the AFFs of Barbados, Berlin, Bilbao, Boston, Buenos Aires, etc.) and its new publics or sub-publics (the now worldwide communities of fans of African cinema). Indeed, as has been suggested, the autonomy of this symbolic world system is such that even the places of esteemed production, the 'nations' highlighted on the map of cinematic value, are in a sense auto-generated by the circuit itself.

But to say that the 'Africa' whose cinematic production has now been so widely recognized by the festivals, its cultural value declared within an expand-ing world-cinematic public sphere and compounded within an expanding sys-tem of global circulation and consecration, is in fact a kind of deterritorialized non-space, a utopian space existing nowhere but in the collective imaginary of the festival public itself, is not to say that the cultural geography of the festival circuit, the geography according to which African cinema commands a place of increasing scale and stature, is simply 'unreal'. We would make an error by thinking that the only reality here is what is happening on the ground, in industrial terms, inside the actual borders of African countries. The reality is a double and contradictory one: an African cinema that has emerged from and is thriving within the festival circuit, with vigorous institutional support, an expanding non- or semi-commercial distribution network, and ever-increasing symbolic credit among the geographically dispersed yet culturally consensual populace of the world-cinema public sphere; but that can find no home, no base, no reliable audience in Africa itself, most of which remains a no-go zone, a kind of gap or hole, in the vast festal rhizome.

Conclusion

In noting these rather unhappy features of the cinema's symbolic geography, we are not merely elaborating an argument against economic globalization. It is not simply a question of festivals effecting a decline from or corruption of the ideal of democratized culture by imposing surreptitiously on the cultural public sphere the values of the mass media, assuring that public recognition and honour tilt towards the very images of Africa that have been pre-approved on the field of commerce. This would be the kind of narrative that was urged upon us by Habermas himself, at least in his original formulation of the problematic.

But even if we were to accept provisionally the opposition of public (good) versus market (evil), we are here speaking of an institution – the festival circuit – that has served, within the larger institution of cinema, as the main bulwark against a fully commoditized film culture and as the main harbour for small, minor, and third cinema. It produces and assures the circulation of non-monetary forms of cinematic value that might otherwise be rapidly eroded and discredited. To the extent that the most elaborate large-scale festivals have tended over time to merge with or replicate the logic of the commercial apparatus, there is also an observable contrary tendency at these very points on the circuit to produce and proliferate new fringe-festivals, counter-festivals and festival slams, a set of alternative or unofficial institutions that seek to guard the democratic vitality of the system and to preserve the very right to 'talk back' that Habermas saw audio–visual media as foreclosing (Habermas 1989: 170–1). While the festivals of African cinema have not yet reached this point of disputatious fracturing, that is likely because, even on their current trajectory of growth and success, they remain at present too modest in economic scale and impact.

In any case, the aim here is not to collapse all distinctions between the festivals and the institutions of Hollywood, or between the scales of symbolic value they represent. It is only to recognize that in performing its consecratory functions, in shaping the economy of world-cinematic prestige and thereby providing the institutional framework of a cultural public sphere with respect to African cinema, the festival circuit shapes a geography of culture that can serve as cover or alibi for zones of the most egregious dispossession. By making African cinema available for consumption and debate by a broad and active public, the festival circuit in effect bypasses the institutions and the publics of Africa itself, cutting them out of the very 'world space' in which they appear to have been winning so much new ground. Indeed, it is fair to say that the circuit's globalization has mainly served the interests of its own sponsors: the local tourist boards and business associations, the national cultural ministries, the established transnational institutions and power-brokers of the European world cinema, the emergent global bureaucracies of inter-festival co-operation and networking. In the course of producing its many winners, the circuit has claimed the most substantial and enduring victory for itself.

Notes

1   For a notably positive assessment of 'the potential of the work of Pierre Bourdieu as a means of extending and deepening Habermas's critique of the public sphere', see Crossley (2004: 88). One should be cautious, however, not to imagine a ready compatibility of the two systems of thought. Though both the theory of communicative action and that of symbolic power are directed toward understanding and enlarging the conditions of possibility of democracy, they are at odds in important respects. One point of fundamental divergence is pithily expressed by Bourdieu in an interview: 'Instead of wondering about the existence of "universal interests", I will ask: who has an interest in the universal? Or rather: what are the social conditions that have to be fulfilled for certain agents to have an interest in the universal?' (Bourdieu 1990: 31). For a clear statement of the intellectual commitment to democratic politics that informs Bourdieu's critique of culture, see Wacquant (2004).

2   This is another reason why festivals cannot disavow their competitive or consecratory function; they are themselves constantly sorted into a hierarchical array, and the films that appear on their programmes are symbolically boosted or advantaged accordingly. I should note here, however, two main points of divergence between Stringer's analysis and my own. First, Stringer sees the frantic competition among festival cities for tourist traffic and for world status as a recent effect of the 'global city' phenomenon influentially described by Sassen (1991), whereas I see it as an originary motive. And second, Stringer believes that the whole spatial dynamic of festivals has ceased to take much account of national boundaries, whereas I argue that the idea of the national cinema remains fundamental to the relational space of the circuit and to its logic of global expansion.

3   So unusual is it for a non-Francophone director to be celebrated at FESPACO that Aduaka began his acceptance speech with an apology for not speaking in French (Calhoun 2007: 4).

4   For an instructive example of this tendency to valorize the exilic producer while constructing a 'national' or 'new national' cinema, see Farahmand (2006) on the rise of the New Iranian Cinema via the festival circuit in the 1980s and 1990s.

5   Since most works of the world cinema, including African cinema, face very bleak prospects for any distribution beyond the festivals, the festival circuit serves in effect as the 'market' for these films, taking the role that, for world literature, is played by publishers and booksellers. According to Slaughter's analysis and Barnard's, both markets dictate that postcolonial societies appear within the cultural public sphere in

the ultra-digestible and essentially liberal form of the *Bildungsroman*-as-national-allegory. In fairness to the festivals, however, I should say that while the most successful and widely consecrated African festival-circuit films, such as *Tsotsi* and *Ezra*, do conform to this generic pattern, they inject far more strain and contradiction into the form than do Hollywood pictures such as *Hotel Rwanda* or *Blood Diamond*.

6 In 1995, Claire Andrade-Watkins estimated that the financial resources available for cinema in all the countries south of the Sahara could not support more than 25 active feature filmmakers (or about one filmmaker for every two countries), and there is little reason to think that number has risen significantly in the intervening years (Andrade-Watkins 1995: 148). France alone funds far more (35mm) 'African' films than the combined nations of Africa do.

7 Along with Nollywood, South Africa's film industry might be regarded as an exception to the rule of industrial stasis. Certainly, the post-apartheid retooling of the country's cinema industry, geared towards producing many fewer films but affording much higher production values, has yielded success on the festival circuit, culminating in the Golden Bear at the 2005 Berlinale for *U-Carmen eKhayelitsha*, as well as major awards off the circuit for Gavin Hood's *Tsotsi* in 2006 and Neill Blomkamp's *District 9* in 2009. But most of the internationally acclaimed films were funded by European or American companies, and most of them were directed by white South Africans, complicating their position in a symbolic space that tends to select for black directors even where this is not an explicit criterion.

References

Aduaka, N. (2007) Park City '07 Interview. *Indiewire* (Jan 11) www.indiewire.com.

Andrade-Watkins, C. (1995) A Mirage in the Desert? African Women Directors at FESPACO. In Martin, M. T. (ed.) *Cinemas of the Black Diaspora: Diversity, Dependence, and Oppositionality*. Detroit: Wayne State University Press.

Barnard, R. (2008) *Tsotsis*: On Law, the Outlaw, and the Postcolonial State. *Contemporary Literature* 49(4): 541–72.

Bartlet, O. (2005) Afrique noire: la fin des salles? *Cahiers du Cinéma* 604(Jan–Mar): 94–103.

Bartlet, O. (2010) The New Paradoxes of Black Africa's Cinemas. In Durovicova, N. and Newman, K. (eds.) *World Cinemas, Transnational Perspectives*. New York: Routledge, 217–25.

Bauman, Z. (1998) *Globalization: The Human Consequences*. New York: Columbia University Press.

Bourdieu, P. (1990) *In Other Words: Essays Towards a Reflexive Sociology*. Stanford: Stanford University Press.

Bourne, S. (2005) Newton I. Aduaka and *Rage*. *Black in the British Frame*. London: Continuum.

Calhoun, D. (2007) Burkina Faso's Film Festival. *Time Out*, online edition, 20 March.

Casanova, P. (2005) Literature as a World. *New Left Review* 31(Jan Feb): 71–90.

Casanova, P. (1999) *La république mondiale des lettres*. Paris: Seuil.

Crossley, N. (2004) On Systematically Distorted Communication: Bourdieu and the Socio-Analysis of Publics. In Habermas, J. Crossley, N. and Roberts, J. M. (eds.) *Habermas: New Perspectives on the Public Sphere*. Oxford: Blackwell.

Diawara, M. (1994) On Tracking World Cinema: African Cinema at Film Festivals. *Public Culture* 6.

English, J. F. (2005) *The Economy of Prestige: Prizes, Awards, and the Circulation of Cultural Value*. Cambridge: Harvard University Press.

Farahmand, A. (2006) At the Crossroads: International Film Festivals and the Constitution of the New Iranian Cinema. Ph.D. dissertation, UCLA.

Fehrenbach, H. (1995) *Cinema in Democratizing Germany: Restructuring National Identity After Hitler*. Chapel Hill: University of North Carolina Press.

Habermas, J. (1989) *Structural Transformation of the Public Sphere*. Cambridge: Polity.

Mazdon, L. (2007) Transnational 'French' Cinema: The Cannes Film Festival. *Modern and Contemporary France* 15: 9–20.

McGuigan, J. (2005) The Cultural Public Sphere. *European Journal of Cultural Studies* 8.4: 427–43.

Sassen, S. (1991) *The Global City: New York, London, Tokyo*. Princeton, NJ: Princeton University Press.

Slaughter, J. (2003) *Clef à Roman*: Some Uses of Human Rights and the *Bildungsroman*. *Politics and Culture* 3.

Slaughter, J. (2007) *Human Rights, Inc.*. New York: Fordham University Press.

Stone, M. S. (1998) *The Patron State: Culture and Politics in Fascist Italy*. Princeton, NJ: Princeton University Press.

Stringer, J. (2001) Global Cities and the International Film Festival Economy. In Shiel, M. and Fitzmorris, T. (eds.) *Cinema and the City: Film and Urban Studies in a Global Context*. Oxford: Blackwell.

Wacquant, L. (2004) Pointers on Pierre Bourdieu and Democratic Politics. *Constellations* 11.1.

5   The cultural public sphere –
a critical measure of public
culture?

Jim McGuigan

The public sphere is readily dismissed as an unrealistic notion with no credible purchase on reality. Apart from the cynicism and, indeed, nihilism of such a dismissal, the public sphere is at the very least defensible as an ideal type: that is, a typification of certain essential features of a phenomenon existing to some extent at some time, in some place and somewhere. Moreover, without any idea of a preferable condition, something better than that which currently prevails, there are no grounds to question or possibly change present conditions. Such an idea, then, provides a principle of judgment. In this case, it is no less than an official principle implicit in claims to democracy, the practical implementation of which may be called to account with impeccable legitimacy. This is not some unrealistically radical notion at all. The public sphere is supposed to be the arena of critical dispute, free and open debate of a reasonable kind about issues of interest shared by citizens. It is meant to be a space in which opinions are formed and articulated concerning public interests that should, therefore, be consequential for the political process in a democracy. To paraphrase Lippmann ([1922] 1997), the public sphere is a dogma of modern liberal democracy.

If the foregoing assumptions are correct, public-sphere theory is clearly relevant to policy-oriented research, combining a focus of analysis and an evaluative criterion, for instance in cultural policy studies. Such research is usually constrained by administrative considerations associated with the source of funding. Although we might like to think that properly critical research of a scientifically valid kind should not be thus restricted, this is an especially difficult orientation for research today, and possibly always, when there is an overwhelming pressure to produce recipe knowledge of immediately practical utility, which may simply legitimize conventional wisdom. The most obviously conventional wisdom in the present field is a belief in the economic efficacy of cultural investment for urban regeneration, supportive of which are a cluster of interests wedded to neoliberal ideology, which displaces consideration of the specifically cultural value of such investment from the public agenda.

In this chapter I wish to apply public-sphere theory to the phenomenon of the regenerative festival via my own formulation of the cultural public sphere.

The aim is to propose a critical measure of such a phenomenon, illustrated by cases with which I have more or less detailed familiarity: the New Millennium Experience of the year 2000 and Liverpool 2008, the recent European Capital of Culture. First, however, it is necessary to elaborate how a concept of the cultural public sphere is an addition to public-sphere theory that is especially pertinent to critical research in the field of cultural policy studies.

Political and cultural public spheres

Jurgen Habermas's ([1962] 1989) original thesis on the public sphere, *The Structural Transformation of the Public Sphere*, distinguished between the literary and the political public spheres. While the distinction is not clearly delineated, it is evident that Habermas saw the literary public sphere as a precursor to a fully fledged bourgeois public sphere in the field of politics. He notes how 'private persons putting reason to use' (p. xviii) were represented in early publications during the late seventeenth and early eighteenth centuries, such as the *Spectator* in England, in which cultural criticism had political implications. These publications were not exclusively concerned with events. They featured discussions of ideas that were debated in semi-private settings, most notably the London coffee house and the Parisian salon, where equality of participation was assumed in the process of dialogic argumentation. Publications, of course, reached the intimate sphere of domesticity where women had significant presence. Still, the emerging bourgeois public sphere was largely a masculine affair. However, the principles of rational–critical argument and equality of participation in the debate established protocols that were not ultimately so narrowly contained. In effect, the cat was let out of the bag. The circle of claimants to democratic rights of deliberation would inevitably widen over time to include women, lower classes and colonial subjects.

To some extent, the literary aspect has been lost in the adoption of the idea of the public sphere in modern media studies, where issues of agenda setting and circulation of information have been privileged. A few years ago, Nicholas Garnham (1995) actually suggested, not entirely convincingly, that the public sphere was the key problematic of a critical media studies. Insofar as it is a guiding principle, the main focus is on what might be called cognitive communications directly impinging on politics in the press and broadcasting; and latterly the implications of the internet in this respect. Affective communications are typically marginalized and even treated as a spoiling agent in the public sphere with, say, the reduction or obliteration of serious news to 'infotainment'. Habermas himself is at least partly responsible for this orientation in much of media studies, including both its admitted strengths and its debilitating weaknesses. The second half of *Structural Transformation* completed a rise-and-fall narrative of the public sphere, whereby the media had become excessively commercialized and dominated by the manipulation of public relations over the course of the nineteenth and twentieth centuries. The mass of people were no longer passionately interested in important issues – assuming with some reservation that they had ever been so – and were now distracted by consumer culture and trivializing entertainment, according to the standard mid-twentieth-century account.

Since the publication of an English translation of *Structural Transformation* twenty years ago, Habermas has revised his earlier pessimistic conclusions regarding the fate of the public sphere. There are three especially salient aspects to this revision: first, appreciation of popular culture; second, sensitivity to the exclusion of women; and third, optimism concerning the influence of campaigning social movements on mainstream political agendas. Responding to the 1989 conference on the public sphere held in the USA (Calhoun, ed. 1992), Habermas remarked:

> [O]nly after reading Mikhail Bakhtin's great book *Rabelais and his World* have my eyes been really opened to the inner dynamics of a plebeian culture. This culture of the common people apparently was by no means only a backdrop, that is, a passive echo of the dominant culture; it was also the periodically recurring violent revolt of a counterproject to the hierarchical world of domination, with its official celebrations and everyday disciplines. Only a stereoscopic view of this sort reveals how a mechanism of exclusion that locks out and represses at the same time calls forth countereffects that cannot be neutralized. If we apply the same perspective to the bourgeois public sphere, the exclusion of women from the world dominated by men now looks different to how it appeared to me at the time.
>
> (Habermas 1992: 427)

It is not as though Habermas has actually become a connoisseur of popular culture, whether folk or mass, or himself made a significant contribution to feminist theory, though others have sought to apply discourse ethics to feminism (Gilligan [1982] 1993; Meehan, ed. 1995). Nevertheless, these moments of Habermasian self-criticism have contributed to an enrichment of public-sphere theory.

The third aspect of revision is to do with Habermas's development of what has been described as a 'sluicegate' model of the public sphere (Carleheden and Gabriel 1996). This revised model is detailed in Habermas's 1992 book, *Between Facts and Norms*, where he states:

> The communication structures of the public sphere are linked with the private life spheres in a way that gives the civil-society periphery, in contrast to the political center, the advantage of greater sensitivity in detecting and identifying new problem situations. The great issues of the last decades give evidence for this. Consider, for example, the spiralling nuclear-arms race; consider the risks involved in the peaceful use of atomic energy or in other large-scale technological projects and scientific experimentation, such as genetic engineering; consider the ecological threats involved in an overstrained environment (acid rain, water pollution, species extinction, etc.);

consider the dramatically progressing impoverishment of the Third World and problems of the world economic order; or consider such issues as feminism, increasing immigration, and the associated problems of multi-culturalism. Hardly any of these topics were initially brought up by expo-nents of the state apparatus, large organizations, or functional systems. Instead, they were broached by intellectuals, concerned citizens, radical professionals, self-proclaimed 'advocates', and the like. Moving in from this outermost periphery, such issues force their way into newspapers and interested associations, clubs, professional organizations, academies, and universities. They find forums, citizen initiatives, and other platforms before they catalyze the growth of social movements and new subcultures. The latter can in turn dramatize contributions, presenting them so effectively that the mass media take up the matter. Only through their controversial presentation in the media do such topics reach the larger public and sub-sequently gain a place on the 'public agenda'. Sometimes the support of sensational actions, mass protests, and incessant campaigning is required before an issue can make its way via the surprising election of marginal candidates or radical parties, expanded platforms of 'established' parties, important court decisions, and so on, into the core of the political system and there receive formal consideration.

(Habermas [1992] 1996; 381)

To return now to the distinction between the literary public sphere and the political public sphere: for Habermas, the very practice of criticism was pio-neered in the literary field before it moved into politics proper (Eagleton 1984). In this sense, the literary public sphere was not so much about transient news topics as about complex reflection on the problems of life, meaning and repre-sentation, which is characteristic of art. To this extent, the literary public sphere worked on a different time scale from the emerging political public sphere and its rapid turnover of newsworthy topics. A favourite example of mine to illus-trate what might be meant by the literary public sphere in the eighteenth cen-tury is the function of a text like Voltaire's ([1759] 2006) *Candide*, occasioned, it must be said, by a topical event, the Lisbon tsunami, where in excess of 20,000 people died. That event was news indeed, the object of what we would call today 'disaster management'. Voltaire, however, was interested in deeper issues than those normally treated in a here-today-gone-tomorrow news story, to whit, how to explain the significance of such an event in a priest-ridden culture. In effect, *Candide* was an attack on both religious mystification and uncritical rationalism; and it struck at the heart of modern disquisitions on the meaning of life in an entertainingly novelistic manner.

The novel hardly performs such a function today even for a reading and (literary) festival-going public. Literature is simply not as important a medium in conditions of late modernity as it was during the formation of modernity hundreds of years ago. Since then we have seen the proliferation of media, and changes in literacy that would now have to include media literacy, which typically involves competence in visuality as well as words. That is one reason why an updated theory requires the conception of a cultural public sphere.

Furthermore, critical perspectives on the public sphere have focused much more on cognitive communications than on affective communications and are, therefore, limited in their approach, as some commentators have already noted (Gripsrud 1992; Dahlgren 1995). Accuracy of information and conditions conducive to dialogic reason are normative requirements of genuine democracy. Yet an exclusive attention to cognition would be seriously flawed should we wish to understand popular engagement with lifeworld issues. While active citizenship addressed towards the 'big issues' of politics is desirable, the subject matter of, say, serious news may be apprehended by many people as being irrelevant to their everyday lives. Popular lack of interest in official politics is also understandable when people ordinarily have so little power over what happens at the level of the system. It may seem entirely remote from the lived or imagined relationships and identifications of mundane existence. However, aesthetic and emotional engagement with lifeworld issues might be felt passionately and experienced as especially meaningful. Hence the need for a conception of the public sphere that accounts for affectivity as well as cognition.

The cultural public sphere of late modernity operates through various channels and circuits of mass-popular culture and entertainment, facilitated routinely by mediated aesthetic and emotional reflections on how we live and imagine the good life. The concept of a *cultural public sphere* refers to the articulation of politics, public and personal, as a contested terrain through affective – aesthetic and emotional – modes of communication (McGuigan 2005a: 435, 2007: 255). The cultural public sphere features pleasures and pains that are experienced vicariously through willing suspensions of disbelief. In a mass-popular medium like television, the cultural public sphere is most evident in forms of fiction and entertainment where representation may not be policed so closely as in news and current affairs. In British television, for instance, there are long traditions of political drama and satirical comedy that are notable for articulating issues that are otherwise marginalized in mainstream communications. Of course, not all drama and comedy can be judged positively in this respect. The fact that something engages popular attention does not in itself qualify it as the site of a critical disquisition.

Applying the critical measure to public culture

Peter Golding and Graham Murdock once argued specifically with reference to the political public sphere that

> the idea of the public sphere is worth retaining, providing that we add that it needs to be open enough that all groups in the society can recognise themselves and their aspirations as being fairly represented. This general idea of a communication system as a public cultural space that is open, diverse and accessible, provides the basic yardstick against which critical

political economy measures the performance of existing systems and for-
mulates alternatives.

(Golding and Murdock 1991: 18)

In making this argument about the public sphere as a critical measure, Golding
and Murdock were principally concerned with the politics of information –
if you like, the cognitive mode – not with aesthetic culture, though they
would not deny its importance. This is very much the orientation of critical
media studies and its emphasis not only on what is reported as news and how
it is treated, but also on the political and economic structures and processes
determining cognitive communications in so many ways.

Recently, from within journalistic practice, not academia, Nick Davies
([2008] 2009) has produced a devastating critique along the same lines of what
he calls 'flat earth news'. Falsehood and distortion are prevalent in a journalistic
environment driven overwhelmingly by commercial imperatives that starve
news-gathering of the necessary resources to investigate evidence and check
the veracity of sources thoroughly. To quote Davies:

> [N]ational newspapers and broadcasters across the developed world have
> been taken over by a new generation of corporate owners, who have cut
> their staffing and increased their output, heavily restricting the time avail-
> able for journalists to check the truth of what they write. I found that the
> same owners have caused the disintegration of the old network of local,
> front-line reporters, in domestic and foreign coverage, heavily restricting
> the flow of raw information to ... hard-pressed newsrooms.

(Davies [2008] 2009: 153)

If it is possible to apply the critical measure of the public sphere to affective
communications, then it will tend to be critical of a good deal of what I would
call 'cool-capitalist culture' (McGuigan 2009). However, it is necessary to
appreciate that the public sphere is a liberal concept, not an inherently radical
one, and by no means prescriptive of what should or should not be represented. However, it does offer an argumentative principle, one that is sadly
lacking in present-day cultural discourse, including discourse on the meaning
of festivals. In this respect, the concept of a specifically *cultural* public sphere
might provide some rules for the game to challenge the all-too-pervasive
obstructions to free and open communications. This point may be clarified by
contrasting a cultural measure of public culture with prevailing political, economic and reductively social measures. It would at least permit the question to
be asked: what do festivals mean?

It is quite striking how the prevailing discourse of cultural policy has shifted
from culture to economics, the assumption being that cultural investment must
be justified on economic grounds. This was spurred on hugely in Britain, and
elsewhere throughout Europe, from the 1980s by John Myerscough's (1988)
The Economic Importance of the Arts in Great Britain. More recently, British

governmental rhetoric concerning 'the creative industries', set out in an influential 'mapping document' of the late 1990s (CITF 1998), which was an offshoot of 'information society' and 'knowledge society' ideology, is a leading instance of such economism. Of greater generality than the claimed measurement of cultural investment's contribution to GDP, and open to sometimes ingenious interpretation, is 'impact', a favourite buzzword today for naming diffuse results. The worth of something has to be demonstrated by its impact, which to my mind is an acutely tricky matter in the field of culture. A typical measure is the number of jobs produced in a locality or region, which is at least something that can be counted, though the relation of correlation to causation is always problematic, quite apart from the quality as opposed to the quantity of the jobs allegedly so produced.

While neoliberal economism is dominant in cultural rhetoric and policy now, it is sometimes qualified by reductively social claims. In this respect, an outstanding example is Francois Matarasso's (1997) Comedia report, *Use or Ornament? The Social Impact of Participation in the Arts*. It functioned as a salve to social-democratic conscience. In order to prove impact, Matarasso conducted a survey of 'participatory arts'. His dubious approach was simply to ask participants in such programmes whether or not arts participation had a beneficial impact on them, an exceptionally unreliable method that arguably proves nothing at all (Merli 2002). Methodological inadequacy, however, did not stop governmental spokespeople citing the research as definitive proof of the social impact of cultural investment. This is an illustration of the political use of research, however flawed, to justify an ideological distortion that deflects attention away from the main thrust of public policy. The example of Matarasso's research also illustrates a contemporary tendency to substitute cultural policy for social policy.

It would be naïve to assume that there were no more-or-less hidden agenda in cultural policy that does not have much to do with culture as such. To suggest that something like a festival is political is hardly controversial. However, it is worth asking exactly what political agenda is in play and, also, wise to assume that the latent purpose of a festival may be quite different from its manifest objective.

Festive debate

Several of the general points made so far derive from or were confirmed by my study of the New Millennium Experience, which took place in 2000 with a centrepiece consisting of a year-long exposition in a gigantic fibreglass tent, known colloquially as 'the Millennium Dome', on a peninsula by the Thames. This was a distinctive and, indeed, peculiar event, taking place in a year when Hanover hosted the official world expo, from which the United States absented itself. The United States – or, rather, some of its leading corporations – was not absent from the Millennium Dome: far from it, in spite of claims that the festival presented Britain to the world and celebrated Britishness at the turn of the millennium (McGuigan 2004). Irrespective of its peculiar features, the case of the New Millennium Experience does, nonetheless, exemplify certain widespread tendencies of city-based festivals today, most notably the commercial and promotional assumptions that have crossed over party-political differences in mainstream politics in the recent period, and a curious confusion or failure of cultural purpose.

The 'Meanings of the New Millennium Experience' research project, funded by the Arts and Humanities Research Board (AHRB – now AHRC), employed a multidimensional methodology combining research on the political economy of production, textual analysis of representational ideology and evidence of reception. Research on reception combined market-research data and conversational interviews with visitors. Another aspect of reception was its mass-mediation, which was crucial to making sense of visitor response, since the news media tended to damn the Dome unreservedly, and yet visitors did not. It was routinely reported as a 'disaster', and has gone down in an admittedly short history as an appalling mistake. In fact, the Dome was the biggest news story in Britain throughout the year 2000 (McGuigan 2002). Despite the avalanche of journalistic coverage, neither broadcasting nor the press really plumbed the deeper issues associated with the Dome. In many ways, the public debate engendered by the news media constituted an instance of what Bruce Robbins (1993) has called a 'phantom public sphere'. People talked and argued incessantly about the Dome, but their talk was not well informed; nor did it have any discernible consequence. My research associate and I were persistently told how awful the Dome was by people who had never been there. The evidence from visitor research produced a very different assessment, largely positive, with generous-minded visitors determined to have a good day out regardless of what the news media said about the exposition or what was actually on offer (see McGuigan 2003 for details on the visitor typology and visitor-research findings).

With regard to the political economy of production, it was necessary to investigate the reasons for staging the festival and how it was financed. The Conservative government that originally made the decision cited the Great Exhibition of 1851, at which Britain had showcased its industrial prowess to the world. The incoming Labour government that adopted the Conservative plans referred instead to the 1951 Festival of Britain that was organized by the post-Second World War Labour government. That festival had envisaged the modernist reconstruction of Britain after the devastation of war. The Millennium Experience was also supposed to present a transformation, produced by New Labour following 18 years of Conservative government, whilst simultaneously marking the millennial turning point. The chosen site had previously been that of a coal-fired gas station in a run-down part of East London. Hence, the event had an urban regeneration dimension typical of such projects today. The Conservatives had promised that the festival would not cost the taxpayer any money; it would be funded by revenue from the National Lottery that had been launched in the early 1990s. However, something in the order of £200 million was spent out of core taxation to buy and partially reclaim a deeply toxic site. Lottery funds were to be supplemented by corporate sponsorship, and efforts were made, unsuccessfully, to persuade a private-sector company to run the festival.

As it transpired, corporate sponsorship was not readily forthcoming. It yielded something like £150 million, much of it 'in kind', such as an ice-skating rink donated by Coca Cola. The exact figure is difficult to ascertain, and much of it had not been procured by the time of the opening at the beginning of January. Costs had already escalated from the original projection. Lottery funding eventually amounted to an official figure of £628 million. It is estimated that as much as a further £200 million was spent on the site after the Festival had been closed and before it was given away to a commercial consortium, to become an entertainment venue a few years later. The whole 'amazing thing' eventually cost in excess of a billion pounds, only a tiny fraction of which came from corporate sponsorship.

The New Millennium Experience Company (NMEC) formally had editorial control over the contents of the exposition, most of it in 14 thematic 'zones'. This was manifestly relinquished in at least two cases, Ford's Journey Zone and BT's Talk Zone, on which a great deal more money was spent by the companies involved than was available for any of the other zones from Lottery funds and corporate sponsorship. Several of the transnational companies involved like Coca Cola and Ford had their headquarters in the USA, including the employment agency Manpower, which not only ran the Work Zone but also hired, trained and sought to relocate on closure the 'hosts' working at the exposition. At the time, Manpower was trying to break into the British market. Manpower's strategy proved successful since it subsequently gained nine out the first fifteen contracts for privatised labour exchanges in Britain. It was commonplace for critical journalists to denounce the exposition as a festival of corporate propaganda. That was a reasonable enough criticism, but rather too simplistic to convey the complex ideological processes at work in the New Millennium Experience.

In studying the zones, it was evident that there was a spectrum of corporate construction of meaning, ranging from explicit or obtrusive to implicit or comparatively unobtrusive; and observing rather different criteria regulating the role of sponsorship. The more subtle ideological messages were rather unobtrusive (a particularly interesting example was the Mind Zone – see below). The best instance of old-fashioned associative sponsorship, whereby the sponsor is not supposed to influence content, was Marks and Spencer's Self Portrait Zone, the only zone that did have something to say about Britain and that was not exclusively self aggrandizing.

The Mind Zone was an especially significant instance of deep sponsorship whereby meaning was encoded in a much more subtle manner than in, say, the Work Zone. Sponsorship for the zone was provided by BAe Systems, the second largest arms manufacturer in the world, and its partner company, Marconi. The Mind Zone did not promote its products directly as did Boots's Body Zone. After all, BAe Systems do not sell Hawk jets directly to the public like shampoo. In context, it is important to appreciate that the newly elected Labour government had promised to pursue an 'ethical' foreign policy on coming into office. This rhetoric was soon quietly dropped since armaments manufacture and exports remain such a major part of Britain's 'information' economy. The background to the Mind Zone's funding is interesting enough in itself, but this instance of corporate intrusion into an exposition largely funded by the public is even more interesting once ideological analysis is applied to its meanings. The Mind Zone was designed by the deconstructionist architect, Zaha Hadid. It was the most cerebral of all the zones, manifestly promoting modern engineering in a manner quite unlike that of some of the other zones. It was perhaps most notably devoid of Work's crude propaganda on the new world of work and a 'flexible' labour market. Mind's principal ideological mode was dissimulation (Thompson 1990).

Instead of celebrating warfare technology, the emphasis in Mind was on communication and the networking principle, extolled most influentially in the work of Manuel Castells (1996). Euphemism is commonly used in discourses of war, and Mind was replete with this, with its (post)modern art, internet and ant colony. The Mind Zone was a curiously dehumanized (Lyotard [1988] 1991) space, the coagulation of body and machine, alongside the superior and yet uncreative powers of artificial intelligence. There was, however, a startlingly humanistic exception plonked into the middle of the zone: one of the sculptures that were distributed randomly around the Dome, in this case Ron Mueck's enigmatic *Boy*, with a quizzical and troubled expression on his face. On my several sceptical visits to the exposition, this is where I found something to identify with.

The general approach taken to the Dome research was that of a critical and reflexive cultural policy analysis. It differs from instrumentalism in cultural policy studies by interrogating the assumptions of prevailing policy and administrative practice from a 'disinterested', in the academic sense, point of view. Questioning and unconstrained by pragmatic imperatives, such analysis is not entirely negative, however, since it may seek to engage governmental agencies either directly or indirectly in dialogue over policy options. It is not unusual, of course, for such agencies to resist any criticism at all, however constructive in intent, and so defend themselves, typically though public relations and self-validating research with performance indicators and the like. In itself, this is sufficient reason for asking awkward questions as a matter of critical witness.

Calling a public artefact such as the Millennium Dome into question on grounds somewhat more substantial than all the news media's sniping, albeit after the event, obliges dialogic critique (Calhoun 1995) to explore alternatives both actual and potential so as to establish reasonable debate according to the principle of a critical measure of culture in the public sphere. Quite different ways of marking the millennium from that of the Dome's celebration of corporate power in the neoliberal age were no doubt possible. Moreover, other projects supported by the National Lottery in Britain have been adjudged to have been of greater success than the New Millennium Experience. Cornwall's unbranded and enduring Eden Project is often cited in this regard.

If the exposition in the Dome at Greenwich is still seen as a reasonable undertaking, which is admittedly an extremely debateable proposition, then it remains worth speculating on different contents, even in retrospect. These might have contributed to public debate and social learning in an affective mode rather than supplying officially prescribed amazement at the wonders of technology. An example could have been a critical War Zone instead of the obscurantism of Mind. The Work Zone might have looked at the conditions of sweated labour around the world, making the technological gadgetry that we use so eagerly and fetishize so routinely. The articulation of alternative views in the spirit of rational-critical debate could reasonably have been expected from an exposition largely funded by the public in a democracy. Instead, we got a social-democratic shell for neoliberalism.

Liverpool 2008 is also a regeneration festival, consistent with the turn that the Capital (formerly City) of Culture festival took with Glasgow as long ago as 1990 (Richards 2000; McGuigan 2005b). There is little doubt that Liverpool merited the designation on cultural grounds, not only because of its moneyed heritage of beautiful buildings and art galleries, but, perhaps more so, for its pivotal role in popular culture, which is not reducible to the Beatles. It has a distinguished history of producing comedians as well as pop stars, but also as an entry point for American black music into Europe. The city is, however, sorely in need of something. With the decline of the docks, its population has halved since the Second World War.

Questions should be asked about the class character of Liverpool's regeneration and the role of commercial interests in the festival. The reconstruction of the city centre and inner city is manifestly aimed at attracting members of the professional-managerial class and banishing the working class definitively to the outer suburbs and satellite towns. Moreover, shopping is a major plank of the regeneration strategy with the Duke of Westminster's Paradise Street development taking over much of the city centre and promising to be something of a white elephant in the absence of sufficient shoppers. This shopping centre development has displaced the Quiggins alternative retail centre, to much public protest (Connolly 2008).

Liverpool's year as European Capital of Culture has provided a very limited setting for the cultural public sphere, though a great deal of disgruntlement has been expressed about its purpose. Alternatives to neoliberal regeneration have been few and far between in the city, reduced, in effect, to marginal, albeit honourable, gestures. Malcolm Miles (2008) has reported on three such gestures on the peripheries of the festival. The self-funded and self-styled Institute for the Practice of Dissent at Home put on a free event in their council house in June 2008, which involved a feminist and anti-capitalist adaptation of Strindberg's *Miss Julie*, followed by a party. The house was draped in a red banner and the 'Internationale' was sung before the performance commenced. Miles (2008) comments: 'while most political art and campaigning takes place in public space, they transposed the action to domestic space, making the home a site for radicalism'.

Second, the Royal Standard, an artist-run space in an old Everton factory, put on an exhibition entitled Navigator, which included Oliver Walker's project, *Mr Democracy*. Walker had commissioned the writing of a British constitution at the East China University of Politics and Law. In addition, a thousand plastic dolls fitted with a digital sound device to recite the constitution were manufactured in a Chinese factory and shipped to Liverpool for inclusion in the exhibition. In his paper on these marginal gestures, Miles does not mention the source of funding for the manufacture and transport of the dolls.

Third, Penny Whitehead and Daniel Simkins produced a free newspaper entitled *Future Visions of History*. This included a report on the story and subsequent fate of the 1984 Liverpool Garden Festival, an earlier attempt at urban regeneration for Liverpool, also instigated by the leading Tory politician behind the Dome, Michael Heseltine. Several years later, the site of the Garden Festival remains abandoned, overgrown and derelict, eloquent testimony to the precarious fate of urban regeneration through cultural development. However, there is still some hope of something there. The site has been earmarked for a high-value residential development. *Future Visions* also included an account of a 'Boat University', a waterborne public debate organized in London's Kensington Gardens concerning the building of an Olympic Village for the 2012 Games in East London. Miles (2008) optimistically describes these marginal gestures as 'cases of an emerging, eruptive vernacular culture'. Pessimistically, however, they might be read as a sad coda to dissent in a once-great dissenting city.

References

Calhoun, C. (ed.) (1992) *Habermas and the Public Sphere*. Cambridge, Massachusetts: MIT Press.

Calhoun, C. (1995) *Critical Social Theory*. Cambridge, Massachusetts: Blackwell.

Carleheden, M. and Gabriel, R. (1996) An Interview with Jurgen Habermas. *Theory, Culture & Society* 13.3: 1–17.

Castells, M. (1996) *The Rise of the Network Society*. Malden, Massachusetts: Blackwell.

CITF (Creative Industries Task Force) (1998) *Creative Industries Mapping Document*. London: Department for Culture, Media and Sport.

Connolly, M. (2008) *Capital and Culture – An Investigation into New Labour Cultural Policy and the European Capital of Culture 2008*. PhD thesis, University of Wales, Cardiff.

Dahlgren, P. (1995) *Television and the Public Sphere – Citizenship, Democracy and the Media*. London: Sage.

Davies, N. ([2008] 2009) *Flat Earth News*. London: Vintage.

Eagleton, T. (1984) *The Function of Criticism – From the Spectator to Post-Structuralism*. London: Verso.

Garnham, N. (1995) The Media and Narratives of the Intellectual. *Media, Culture & Society* 17.3: 359–376.

Gilligan, C. ([1982] 1993) *In a Different Voice – Psychological Theory and Women's Development*, second edition. Cambridge Massachusetts: Harvard University Press.

Golding, P. and Murdock, G. (1991) Culture, Communications and Political Economy. In Curran, J. and Gurevitch, M. (eds.) *Mass Media and Society*, pp. 15–32. London: Arnold.

Gripsrud, J. (1992) The Aesthetics and Politics of Melodrama. In Dahlgren, P. and Sparks, C. (eds.) *Journalism and Popular Culture*, pp. 84–95. London: Sage.

Habermas, J. ([1962] 1989) *The Structural Transformation of the Public Sphere – An inquiry into a Category of Bourgeois Society*. Translated by Burger, T. and Lawrence, F. Cambridge: Polity.

Habermas, J. (1992) 'Further Reflections on the Public Sphere', Calhoun, C. (ed.) (1992) *Habermas and the Public Sphere*, pp. 421–461. Cambridge, Massachusetts: MIT Press.

Habermas, J. ([1992] 1996) *Between Facts and Norms – Contributions to Discourse Theory of Law and Democracy*. Translated by Rehg, W. Cambridge: Polity Press.

Lippmann, W. ([1922] 1997) *Public Opinion*. New York: Free Press.

Lyotard, J. F. ([1988] 1991) *The Inhuman-Reflections on Time*, translated by Bennington, G. & R. Bowlby. Cambridge: Polity.

Matarasso, F. (1997) *Use or Ornament? The Social Impact of Participation in the Arts*. London: Comedia.

McGuigan, J. (2002) The Public Sphere. In Hamilton, P. and Thompson, K. (eds.) *The Uses of Sociology*, pp. 81–128. Oxford: Blackwell.

McGuigan, J. (2003) The Social Construction of a Cultural Disaster – New Labour's Millennium Experience. *Cultural Studies* 17.5: 669–690.

McGuigan, J. (2004) A Shell for Neo-Liberalism – New Labour Britain and the Millennium Dome. In Caunce, S, Mazierska, E., Sydney-Smith, S. and Walton, J. (eds.) *Relocating Britishness*, pp. 38–52. Manchester: Manchester University Press.

McGuigan. J. (2005a) The Cultural Public Sphere. *European Journal of Cultural Studies* 8.4: 427–443; and in Benchimol, A. and Maley, W. (eds.) (2007) *Spheres of Influence – Intellectual and Cultural Publics from Shakespeare to Habermas*, pp. 243–263. Bern: Peter Lang.

McGuigan, J. (2005b) Neo-liberalism, Culture and Policy. *International Journal of Cultural Policy* 11.3: 229–242.

McGuigan, J. (2009) *Cool Capitalism*. London: Pluto.

Meehan, J. (ed.) (1995) *Feminists Read Habermas – Gendering the Subject of Discourse*. London: Routledge.

Merli, P. (2002) Evaluating the Social Impact of Participation in Arts Activities. *International Journal of Cultural Policy* 8.1: 107–118.

Miles, M. (2008) Clean City – Urbanism, Aesthetics and Dissent. As yet unpublished paper, unnumbered.

Myerscough, J. (1988) *The Economic Importance of the Arts in Britain*. London: Policy Studies Institute.

Richards, D. (2000) The European Cultural Capital Event – Strategic Weapon in the Cultural Arms Race. *International Journal of Cultural Policy* 6.2: 159–161.

Robbins, B. (ed.) (1993) *The Phantom Public Sphere*. Minneapolis: University of Minnesota Press.

Thompson, J. B. (1990) *Ideology and Modern Culture – Critical Theory in the Era of Mass Communication*. Cambridge: Polity.

Voltaire ([1759] 2006) *Candide and Other Stories*. Translated by Pearson, R. Oxford: Oxford University Press.

6 Festivals, local and global

Critical interventions and the cultural public sphere

Jean-Louis Fabiani

If one considers, with Jim McGuigan, that the current cultural public sphere is divided into 'three broad stances: uncritical populism, radical subversion and critical intervention' (McGuigan 2005), the most important cultural festivals may be identified with the third one: they presuppose a committed and vigilant audience and they allow a fair space for critical discussions, not only about cultural tastes, but also about political issues. Theatre and cinema are a better material than music for such a purpose, of course, but the critical stance is not directly linked to a specific cultural form. It has rather to do with the very format of the festival: unlike the ordinary consumption of cultural goods, festivals allow more time to gather and discuss before and after the show. They produce a fair number of 'regulars' or even 'devotees' who collectively build a critical space of their own.

Although it would be naïve to acknowledge the existence of a full critical stance at every festival, it is worth mentioning that the format of the festival, particularly when it takes place in the summertime and in an open space – in many ways comparable to a classical Greek amphitheatre – triggers genuine experiences, both emotional and discursive. Arts festivals are often first considered as local events: they are supposed to magnify the genius loci, to bring about some effervescence, in the Durkheimian sense, and to transform rather mundane settings into unique places. Although they are now a part of a world circuit of events, major festivals try to preserve the genuine atmosphere of original and somewhat unlikely encounters. The co-presence of spectators with actors, directors and producers, although it may be reduced by security concerns, remains a strong feature of festivals. Festivals imply a specific way of 'consuming culture', i.e. not as mere spectators but as participants.

This chapter is an attempt to illustrate, and to some extent to question, the conceptual model of the cultural public sphere. In late modernity, the public sphere no longer lies in a specific physical space, such as the café, the theatre or the museum, but 'operates through various channels and circuits of mass-popular culture and entertainment, facilitated routinely by mediated aesthetic and emotional reflections on how we live and imagine the good life' (McGuigan 2011). Is the participatory model that the cultural festivals involve a political and aesthetic alternative to the new cultural public sphere, since they retain some features of the classical public sphere and have cultural ambitions? Are the debates important? Do the controversies really matter? As the major festivals now try to reach the status of world events, it is important to analyse the multiple interactions between the more salient features of localities and their global significance.

This chapter is based on both collective and personal research concerning two major festivals in France: the Avignon Theatre Festival and the Cannes Film Festival (Ethis 2000, 2002, 2008; Fabiani 2003, 2005, 2008). Both festivals gained international reputations during the first twenty years of their existence, although they have reached different levels of recognition: Cannes is undoubtedly a world event (with around 5,000 journalists gathered for the press coverage) and attracts all sorts of publics. Avignon is more of a European event and usually reaches an educated audience. In both cases, the local dimension of the festival is central as the material basis of the event, but it is by no means the only one: the most significant part of the festival lies *extra muros*, in the global world. Cannes, of course, is a case in point, because important features of the public display of world cinema have been redesigned to fit television formats. To a lesser extent, Avignon's 'out of site' audience is larger than that consisting of real spectators. Both festivals have already lasted for more than sixty years and do not show any signs of exhaustion, although they are permanently conflictual and have undergone real crises in the past – the most salient being the unrest of May 1968.

Since the beginning of our research, attention has been focused on the study of the public, using both ethnographic methods and quantitative surveys. Beyond the case studies there was a broader scope: improving sociological knowledge about the audience, going further than mere spectator counting and assessing socio-demographical distribution. It is very important to know better how the people in the audience 'live' the festivals, not only as consumers, but also as participating actors. In order to account for the specific public sphere that festivals generate, one first has to analyse the political dimension of cultural festivals. They provide a good example of the politicization of aesthetics, for two main reasons. First, festivals play a significant part in the process of nation building or, more recently, in the attempts to develop a post-national form of cultural citizenship. Second, particularly in France, the festivals have been a way of addressing the issue of equal access to the masterpieces of the world. They are supposed to bring about less elitist modes of relationship between legitimate culture and the lay public. As a cultural public sphere presupposes vivid, and at times controversial, interactions, I will move in the second part of the chapter to the process of dialogic reasoning that is at work in any type of critical intervention: how is a cultural space constructed, and how is it maintained over time? The presentation will be based on an ethnographic analysis of public participation in Avignon. It will thus be possible, in the final section, to integrate the empirical findings into a more conceptual frame.

Festivals as nation builders

Festivals for citizenship

The major festivals in France have a peculiar ideological and political history: since the early days of André Malraux's Ministry of Culture, created by General de Gaulle in 1959, the issue of democratizing access to culture has been central in shaping the national cultural policy, but also in constructing the main socio-logical frame of analysis for cultural objects. As long ago as the early 1960s a Department for Studies and Research was created within the ministry, long before the same services were set up for Education, Transportation or Health. Young and outstanding sociologists were involved in studies that were to become landmarks in French sociological research and help define a national 'style' for the sociology of culture (Bourdieu [1965] 1990; Bourdieu and Darbel [1966] 1991; Moulin 1967; Fabiani 2003). This explains the success of con-cepts such as 'symbolic violence' or 'distinction' used to describe the social and ideological functions of culture in society.

Successive national surveys organized by the ministry on French 'cultural practices' showed great stability in cultural stratification: highbrow culture remained the monopoly of educated classes and this result was not affected by the policy of democratization that Malraux and his followers, among them the flamboyant Socialist Jack Lang in the 1980s, developed in widely advertised campaigns. Disappointment soon grew among the politicians: why were democratizing actions so inefficient? When he entered office, President Sarkozy wrote a 'mission letter' to the newly appointed Minister of Culture, Christine Albanel, asking her to assess the real efficiency of the democratizing actions. Many suspected the President did not favour highbrow culture (he had been seen with undoubtedly lowbrow actors and singers during his campaign for the presidency) and its costs, and he wanted to reorient public spending towards more popular forms of culture. Mrs Albanel had no time to give a proper answer, since she was replaced by Frédéric Mitterrand after less than two years in office. No action was taken.

So politicians and sociologists shared the same concern: the democratization of legitimate culture, to use Bourdieu's Weberian vocabulary. But there was a lot of misunderstanding going on beneath the superficial consensus. Social scientists, mainly trained by Bourdieu, knew that an instant change in cultural behaviour was unthinkable and that a quick transformation of the social basis of cultural audiences was out of reach. In the meantime, Bourdieu's model had become so efficient that it prevented sociologists from taking account of the effective changes occurring in French society (Fabiani 2007). In 1977 I was involved in the first quantitative survey of the attendance of the Pompidou Center in Beaubourg (Paris), and I discovered, together with my colleague Pierre-Michel Menger, that real cultural dynamics existed even in a context of the relative socio-demographical stability of the public. Studying the visitors at Beaubourg, we noticed that the people with two years of tertiary education (after high-school graduation) played an active role, and that the fully educated classes were not as important as in the widely celebrated results shown in *The Love of Art* about European Museums (Bourdieu and Darbel [1966] 1991). Bourdieu was not satisfied by our findings and refused to publish our account in his journal, *Actes de la recherche en sciences sociales*. We published a shorter version in the *Encyclopaedia Universalis* year book (Fabiani and Menger 1978). When we started, almost twenty years later, a quantitative survey on the Theatre Festival in Avignon, we again found a very specific audience, neither as educated nor as wealthy as the public of the *Comédie-Française* in Paris, for instance (Baudouin and Maresca 1997), and provided with a strong local dimension.

The Avignon Festival is neither a 'popular' nor a fully democratic one. Such a statement would imply a perfect homology between global social structure and the composition of the audience. What we call in France 'the popular classes' do not show up under clear Avignon summer skies, and this should not come as a surprise. The audience is mostly composed of professional, upper-middle-class, highly educated people. But what is striking about the festival is the relative scarcity of the urban 'celebrities or notables', who are much more visible in opera houses, at art fairs or even in Parisian theatres. Teachers (primary and high school), university professors, various scientists and high-tech professionals and people holding higher occupations in culture and arts, information and communications together make up 60.6 per cent of the total sample, although that combination accounts for only one-third of the French occupational structure. We must take into account that a large majority of such people are employed in public service, traditionally important in France, as opposed to members of other professions, who engage in private practice (physicians, lawyers and so on); the latter group appears to prefer Paris stage productions. So the Avignon crowd is largely different from the public of the *Comédie-Française*, the oldest and most prestigious French repertory theater. Professionals in private practice, engineers and people holding higher positions in corporations account for 12.2 per cent of the Avignon sample, compared with 19 per cent at the *Comédie-Française*.

These figures, along with the ethnographic research that has been done in Avignon for more than ten years, allow us to be more precise about the peculiarities of the audience there. First, the festival is not a meeting place for the 'celebrities' who embody, in the foyers of famous theaters or opera houses across France, social power and networks. There has never been any dress code at Avignon. The differences in seating categories and in ticket prices, which, strangely enough, were important at the beginning of the festival, have disappeared. Access to the festival, if highly selective, is determined more on a cultural basis that on an economic one. The Avignon audience is the result of a peculiar history, reinforced by the loyalty of a significant part of its membership. What we have here is a committed audience, who come to Avignon to celebrate common values. Hostility to the entertainment business, scorn of the star system, and belief in the democratic and peaceful effects of theatrical experience are still strong features of the public's conception of the festival, as multiple references to festival history and the legendary founding father, Jean Vilar, clearly show.

Most of the time the festival supplies very ascetic rewards. There are few amenities, the plays may last more than nine hours, and late nights can be awfully cold. In these respects Avignon contrasts sharply with other big dates on the European festival circuit. It is far from absurd to link the notion of 'theatre as public service', a term coined by Vilar to justify his work in Avignon and his long directorate at the *Théâtre National Populaire* in Paris, to the fact that French civil servants are so numerous in the audience. The Avignon community shares a belief that public theatre is an essential component of public life. This belief helps explain the acceptance of various hardships in the theatrical experience. Discomfort and boredom are the unwritten rules of the game. Such a tacit knowledge forms a strong basis for audience loyalty. Disappointment and disillusionment almost never cause people to leave; on the contrary, their personal experience of theatre derives from these 'bad' feelings. Avignon is loaded with powerful and effective rituals – Maurice Jarre's trumpets at the beginning of the play, the daily debates with directors and actors in the scarce shade – which undoubtedly have a reassuring effect on festivalgoers and allow them to reconcile the perturbing effects of innovation and aesthetic lapses with fidelity to the festival programme.

Finally, the surveys give fresh information about the contemporary relationship with 'legitimate' culture, as developed by Bourdieu. One should not generalize about the survey results; again, Avignon is a very peculiar cultural gathering. Avignon loyalists show unquestionable cultural good will, but are never zealots. Loyalty to the festival as an institution never leads to quasi-religious involvement in public theatre. We should be very careful when using metaphors about theatrical experience, which is always local and heavily dependent on specific histories and selective activation of collective memories of places and events.

The Nation on display: festivals as political devices

The association of Avignon and Cannes in a single study might be surprising. After all, they are quite different as regards their material and their cultural and aesthetic history. They do not have the same impact on the economic market. Cannes is still the prime venue in the world for the movie business, although the economic film market is seldom mediatized and remains backstage in the Festival Palace. They also differ with respect to the type of relationship that takes place between the spectators and the art forms shown.

We can spot, however, many common features. The first is undoubtedly the strong association between the festivals and the political world. In both cases, what is at stake is to present the world with an image of France: mostly a self-representation in the case of Avignon (a picture of the cultural republic at its best), and the presentation of France to the entire world in the case of Cannes, an image grounded on a cultural diplomacy that has changed in its forms with globalization, but not in its primary goal, to assess France's cultural–political strength. The almost parallel history of both institutions since the aftermath of the Second World War perfectly shows the national and geopolitical groundings of festivals. One can witness how an institution projects itself into space and time through the efficiency of annual rhythm and of reenacted rituals (Ethis 2000; Fabiani 2005). Rites and rhythms produce political efficiency (Fabiani 2005). This symbolic dimension is reinforced by the mediatization of the event and by the archivistic production of memories of the festival: such archives can be installed in the scholarly world, as in Avignon, where the Jean Vilar House is a part of the François Mitterrand National French Library, but they are also market produced, like the stunning photographic portraits of the audience climbing the steps in Cannes done by Traverso, the oldest photographer on the spot, and sold along the Croisette beach every day.

Since the late 1940s Cannes has been viewed as a French stage for the presentation of the whole cinematographic world. Here the festivalgoer, whatever his or her status, is confronted with a vast array of artworks, with heterogeneous cultural references and cinematographic codes, with stars, unknown performers, directors and critics. What we call 'Cannes' is the simultaneous presence of a selected group of films, representative of the whole cinema, of peculiar forms of sociability and of certain celebratory rituals. In fact, many features of this international fête are largely dependent on local conditions, for instance on the codes that dominated casino life in the 1920s and 1930s, as well as on the traditional features of a beach resort. The rites here are stylized forms of social codes that are part and parcel of winter tourism on the French Riviera.

The first attempts to create a movie festival in Cannes appeared just before the Second World War, when the social relationships of a leisured class were rapidly disintegrating. The main events, i.e. the fashionable winter '*fête mondaine*' and an evening at the casino, were losing their significance. Cannes developed after the war when summer bathing tourism was booming on the Mediterranean littoral, the beach becoming a showcase for presenting the (suntanned) self. The elitist conception of winter tourism, with its aristocratic-like manners, soon gave way to a utopian beach democracy. One might describe the Cannes Film Festival as conjoining two main features of the Côte d'Azur resort. On the one hand, the legacy of winter tourism means that the great divide between actors and spectators is maintained according to a precise and ostentatious protocol; on the other hand, the beach democracy has developed its own conventions, which allow, at least formally, an equal access to public space for everyone.

The Avignon Theatre Festival enjoys a unique status in French cultural history. It remains the best example we have of the powerful association between a state policy and an artistic mobilization. The French state has a long tradition of public intervention in cultural life, enabling and certifying cultural products as well as addressing the problem of democratic access to cultural goods, which became a political priority in the course of the twentieth century. Since the

Popular Front of 1936, theatre has been the paradigm of a cultural area, which can and must be transformed by public action. Pascal Ory has neatly shown how the idea that culture should be a decisive element in public service was able to develop and stabilize over time (Ory 1994). Theatre belongs to the spheres of entertainment and public action. Simultaneously fête and discourse, ritual and political performance, it plays a leading role in celebrating ideas. This is particularly true of the idea of the nation, as well as of the notion of people's assembly. Ever since the Enlightenment, and exemplified by such figures as Jules Michelet and Romain Rolland, French theatre has been synonymous with democracy in action. The assembled people are represented on stage and feel the strength of their collective power. An open space under starry skies is very important in this respect, for it is the moment of 'lay communion', far removed both from the preciosity of Court theatre and from the vulgarity of bourgeois theatre. In French political culture, one has come to expect that theatre should be the driving force in changing the relationship between stage plays, authors and audience, for it would appear to equate to or at least hold out the promise of a united community. The hybrid nature of theatre, between play and institution, is sufficient in defining the space of its republican ritualization. One may also add that it fills the void left by the revolutionary fête, emerging as a post-revolutionary ritual designed to reflect the nation back on itself, but doomed in this respect largely to inefficiency. Of course, there is one other element in the progressive ritualization of French theatre. Ever since the first years of the twentieth century, French artists have propagated the ideology of theatre as a public service ('*le théâtre, service public*' as Avignon's founder, Jean Vilar, was fond of saying) because they hoped their creative autonomy would be recognized and guaranteed by the state against the illegitimate taste of bourgeois philistine consumers. This paradox of state-guaranteed autonomy is a central feature of French cultural life and helps to explain the permanent ritual at these festivals of the artistic–political interface.

For long years, theatre and film audiences have been inured to many conventions, such as that of preserving silence during the show and hiding their feelings to some extent. In different ways, the feeling of belonging to a particular type of society and of sharing specific behavioural codes is essential to the felicitous outcome of an event. This does not mean that unanimity is required or that the public must be united. Sharing the festival codes is not the same as approving the selections of the organizers. Factional divisions are part of the game, and to some extent provide the festivals with increased symbolic significance. In Avignon, for instance, the debates surrounding the festival are almost as important as the performances themselves. Avignon's founder, Jean Vilar, worked ceaselessly to create a space for debates that would embody the very essence of public theatre in a modern democracy; the main goal was to change the spectator into a 'participant', an idea that increased the ritual dimension of this summer gathering of theatregoers and made for the closeness between actors and audience by promoting a certain spatial density and intensity of exchanges.

The public reconsidered

Drawing on an ethnographical work devoted to the critical debates taking place at the Avignon Festival (Fabiani 2008), it is worth giving an account of the attitudes that festivalgoers develop toward the peculiarities of programming, the rituals embedded in the daily performances and the interpretative skills they develop, particularly when the supply of theatre is far from being taken for granted. Three issues will be examined in turn: the loyalty of spectators, the debate concerning democratization internal to the festival and the interpretative attempts by the audience.

The importance of being loyal

The spectators' reaction to the programmed supply and to the performances hosted by the festival can be analysed according to two different frames: the first is Michel de Certeau's '*prise de parole*' (speaking up!), developed in the aftermath of May 1968. The second is Albert Hirschman's exit, voice and loyalty. Michel de Certeau analysed the crisis of political representation that triggered the '*prise de parole*': 'In May 1968, the floor was taken exactly as the Bastille was taken in 1789. The imprisoned speech was freed' (Certeau [1968] 1994). According to Certeau, the act of protest is an act of speech. It raises a major question about the difference between speaking and acting in society. Were the people in 1968 ready to take the Bastille or did they just want to talk? Is protest limited to speech? The Avignon Festival was born out of a reference to a utopia: the dream of a national community united, almost certainly for the first time in history, through theatrical interaction and exchange. Jean Vilar, the founding father, asked for the spectators' participation, but he limited it to a silent one. Participation was constrained by the strong discipline applied to the spectators' bodies (the festival was ascetic from the start) and the carefully organized distribution of speech in the public space. The noise made in 1968 and, later, all the forms of protest that developed against the festival or against the cultural state bureaucracy – the most spectacular one being the cancellation of the whole event in 2003 due to a strike by the actors and technicians – were considered by Vilar and his followers as a violation of the original pact. In July 1968, Jean Vilar could no longer recognize his spectators when they seemed to follow the unlikely star of the show, Julian Beck from New York's Living Theatre, who asked them to get naked and to join the actors in order fully to participate in the party. Jean Vilar, truly desperate, died soon afterwards. He left too early to notice that the breach of loyalty had been ephemeral. Julian Beck and Judith Malina quickly disappeared in the hot Provençal summer, stirring up some nostalgia among the young people from Avignon, and a year later the spectators were loyal again. The '*prise de parole*', simultaneously aesthetic and ideological, did not vanish: it was reframed into more disciplined channels, closer to the benevolent participation that Vilar had wanted to create as one of the most striking features of his festival. But the once taken-for-granted adhesion of the audience was now redefined into a more critical space, where the fundamental justifications of the institution were constantly questioned, even by the most faithful among the *'festivaliers'* (festivalgoers)

The development of such a critical space tended to transform the first convention that had bounded the festival and its spectators. Once nicknamed 'the pilgrims', as if their faith was indefatigable, the spectators tended to become critics. Their relationship with the festival changed to a more reflexive attitude towards their own beliefs as well as towards the theatrical supply. Their attitude may be described according to the model developed by Albert Hirschman for firms in the early 1960s (Hirschman 1970). First, one should note that exit can have different forms in a festival: either one does not show up at all in the year following a disappointing festival, or one leaves before the end of the show. The second attitude can be subdivided, too: either the spectator steps out silently, during the intermission or during very dark moments of the performance – with some risk of falling and creating unwanted disorder – or the exit can be a minor form of protest, when the spectator leaves with no real discretion. It is certain that exit is the most common form of disagreement with the organizers in Avignon. It is also, as a rule, a very silent and sometimes invisible disagreement. Voice is not used frequently. It was not unknown during the summer of 2005, when many spectators, stirred up by the daily articles in the national press, showed scorn or even disgust towards the Flemish artist Jan Fabre's bold selection of plays, or even disturbed the performances by yelling at the actors or asking for their money back. Most of the time, however, they were outnumbered by the loyal spectators who supported the people on stage and asked for a more sedate ambiance.

As elsewhere in the legitimate arts, the theatregoing public has been taken out of the creative process. The ideology of creative action in contemporary societies has relegated the audience to the margins of the process. Contemporary artists are not required to allow space for the spectator. This is, of course, a consequence of the long process of autonomization of the artist, frequently described – and sometimes oversimplified – in historical sociology (Bourdieu [1992] 1996; Elias 1993). Loyalty is demanded of the spectator only in the contemporary pact of reception: disappointment is not contractual. That is for the theory. If we look carefully at the festivals, we can see that the apparatus of debates, post-show meetings and late afternoon drinks with the actors, the playwrights and all the people involved on the productive side help ease things; if the misunderstanding or the failure is almost always put on the spectators' shoulders, one can observe a huge ideological effort (Berger 1981) to lower the tensions. This explains why the re-equalization of conditions, albeit most of the time fictitious, is a main condition of felicity for the festivals.

The equalization of conditions

The coexistence of the spectators' loyalty and of the artists' absolute autonomy brings about a strong dissymmetry in their relationship. 'When I am in the process of creation', Jan Fabre said at the very beginning of his discussion with the spectators, 'I never think of the public'. The public admits the fact, as a component of the theatrical convention. In all the debates that I could tape and analyse during different sessions of the festival one would never question the division between autonomous creation and spectators' faithful loyalty. It is a permanent and structuring principle of division. Talking to the artist is a way of making explicit the spectator's weaknesses in deciphering aesthetic intentions as well as criticizing those intentions as such.

In 2005 the choice of presenting, without any real justification, actors in the nude (mostly men) in almost all the plays and dance shows triggered only some surprise among the youngest spectators, who confessed, albeit reluctantly, to a feeling of unease; all the others, who would privately ridicule what they called '*l'année du zizi*' (the year of the penis) never brought the issue into public debates. Anonymous graffiti posted in the Popes' Palace complained that the dimension of the virile members shown did not match the amount of public money put into the festival. During the debates most of the people started by congratulating the artists, even when it was clear that they did not like the show at all. The moment for thanks and gratitude, which opens most of the debates with the artists, is very important for the development of the relationship. Here is a striking example, taken from the discussion with the Belgian artist Wim Wandeckeybus about his multimedia work entitled *Puur* (pure). There is a rather long silence before the first question. A young man, who looks shy, raises his hand, a little embarrassed by the microphone: 'Well, OK. Thank you. I saw *Puur* ... Well (silence), before, well ... I wanted to tell you that, although I did not understand everything and I am still looking for ... Thanks to you, I could dream for two hours, that is it, I was taken by the dance ... and all that stuff; it was wonderful. So, thank you'. The question (if it was one) was followed by a pregnant silence. All the spectators were disconcerted by the play, and the young man seemed exhausted by his short comment. The show was based on biblical references, but everything was blurred, and many spectators did not grasp the allusion to the Massacre of the Innocents as described in Matthew's Gospel. However, the young man's reaction was a nice example of the mix of misunderstanding and aesthetic pleasure that is often displayed by the spectators. One could add that it is an implicit claim for the autonomy of the spectator's pleasure vis-à-vis the artist's intentions, whatever they are. Most of the time the artists reject the rules of the game: they do not want to give an explicit meaning for their works of art. Giving an account of the intentions or of the creative process is never accepted by the artist. The equalization of conditions between the artist and the spectator lies in the following convention: the spectators accept that they cannot fully understand the creative act and that it is beyond their reach. A clear answer from the artist would ruin the specificity of the creative act. In turn, the spectators seek to warrant a right of their own, the right to dream and to misunderstand a meaning that is, by definition, hidden. This type of exchange is extremely frequent in the debates that I could observe and tape.

As we have seen, respect is shown to the artists, and a '*prise de parole*', Bastille-style, would be very unlikely. However, this does not mean that the public has given up all of its democratic ambitions. The right to speak is expressed as the main feature of the festival: the spectators come here not only to watch the actors, but to talk to them. As the autonomy of artistic action is widely shared, almost nobody tries to relocate the shows in the space of ideology, although this was quite common in the 1950s and 1960s. It is admitted that the 'creators' serves only their creations, which are independent of any social commitment. Such a depolitization of aesthetic issues is undoubtedly surprising in the French context, where cultural issues have long been contentious ideological issues. Bertolt Brecht, who was so prominent in the nonprofit theatre in France, seems to be very far away. Distanciation in theatre was designed to reequilibrate the relationships between the spectators and the artists, but it should have brought about a form of political consciousness. In Avignon today, the equalization of the conditions briefly described above certainly implies a re-aestheticization of the theatre.

The space of interpretations

Very often, artists and spectators develop quite parallel comments on the plays and tend to avoid conflicts of interpretation. But sometimes wrong interpretations arise in the debate; they trigger reactions from the artists, but from other spectators, too. Speaking up is sometimes risky. I will give an example taken from the public debate on the Polish director Kristof Warlikowski's *Kroum*. An elderly female spectator who had a long history of discussions in public proposed a full interpretation of the play. She said that the play reminded her, at the age of 72, of her own life story: that she had wanted to free herself from her onerous Jewish family tradition and that she had never got married; she considered that her own attitude was a key to understanding the play. Warlikowski and some spectators gently dismissed her claim. The play was about the relationship between a mother and her son on the universal level, and neither an ethnic nor an individual explanation would fit. Although the moderators of the debates frequently urge the spectators to express their subjective feelings about the works, the artists show a lot of scepticism towards individual emotional explanations. Exhibiting a purely subjective viewpoint, even when it is framed by more general categories (here, the Jewish mother) proves to be very far removed from the language games that artists use when they try to make the theatrical experience explicit.

An example taken from the debate on a very 'intellectualist' presentation of *Hamlet* by a French director, Hubert Colas, may give an idea of the irreducible distance between the spectators and the professionals on stage. This highbrow *Hamlet* had not been well received by the critics, but it raised a lot of interest among the young spectators, mostly students and frequently from Theatre and Arts departments. The production fitted in quite well with the main tradition in Avignon: seriousness and ascetic austerity by a young group against spectacular props and big names. Hubert Colas had decided to introduce the famous monologue 'To be or not to be' in an unostentatious way, so that it was hardly noticed by the listeners. The first question came from a young female student. 'It seems that you don't give any importance to the words "To be or not to be". Am I wrong?' she asked. A man who claimed to have psycho-analytical training added, with more assurance, the following.

> Yes. It is the first time I hear so clearly in a theatre the enigma of the verb 'to be'. That is simply called immanence. Immanence, that simply means 'existing'. The verb 'to be' is problematic. 'To be or not to be' has been pronounced very simply. As spectators, we were all invited to be as well as not to be. We were invited to that death, and, as a matter of fact, we were confronted with the 'contemporaneity' of our bodies, our immanence. I would like to thank Hubert Colas, since it is the first time I have seen a 'To be or not to be' in an immanent frame.

After a moment of deep concentration, Hubert Colas tried to answer, as follows.

> To the various questions about 'To be or not to be' … I think that the energy of the audience is concentrated on this moment, and I wanted to share some irony with the public. About the words that would allow us to get some relief and to enter a neutral space where we can begin to be together to hear the words.

The answer given by the director might not be completely clear, but it triggered a lot of attention from the audience: the spectators' interpretation was fully recognized and the commenters' competencies were confirmed by the artist who had designed the interpretative frame. The language of sharing is highly significant here: the very peculiar way in which the words 'To be or not to be' were pronounced opens up a common space between both sides of the festival, recreating the conditions of the fictional community as the foundation of the collective event.

As Jim McGuigan warned in the context of television shows that open a space for public debate, the critical interventions are 'not necessarily measurable in terms of social impact' (McGuigan 2005: 440). After all, the Avignon Festival is an example of a minority culture, a form of intellectual aristocracy, although it does not think of itself in this way. The debates have not much direct impact on cultural policy and they cannot significantly change the course of contemporary politics. However, as Avignon and Cannes are heavily present in the national media, they maintain what McGuigan calls 'the enduring tradition of independent criticism of dominant power and ideology in the cultural public sphere'. A collective representation of the democratic dispute is defined here; while it is often timid or even awkward, the debate remains a symbol of a political right to culture that is a condition for full citizenship.

When local audiences address the world

The second part of this chapter was deliberately devoted to micro-analysis in order to analyse the different forms of the contemporary pact between the spectator and the artist, when it is framed by the specific form of the festival. Although generalizations are unfeasible, it is possible to broaden the scope, as the main festivals are not limited to their local roots. Is there a new type of political link between the spectators that would replace the Habermasian definition of the bourgeois public sphere (Habermas [1962] 1989) and correspond to a globalized world?

The contemporary status of the spectator

The modern constitution of the spectator involves a contradiction that considerably increased during the twentieth century. The public space opened by cultural institutions has trapped the old model of connoisseurship into new democratic constraints. The aristocratic or even bourgeois model has been removed from the private space where it was happily located (the cabinet or the court) to a new space of interactions. The institution of culture in democracies simultaneously implies that everybody is transformed into a connoisseur – at least a virtual one; i.e. that they all make a free choice of the artforms they like, and that each sees in them the expression of a unique subjectivity. If one saw an 'age of the masses' in the twentieth century and considered the publics of culture as a kind of undifferentiated crowd, one has to keep in mind that all the institutional constructs that were designed to distribute high culture (theatres, museums and, later, festivals) were based on the attempt to create a genuine personality of the spectator as an active member of a social group and as a singular person able to develop real judgments of taste. In the meantime, and perhaps as an unintended consequence of action, such institutions have tended to perform functions of distinction in a socially and culturally highly stratified space. Therefore, they have often played a small part in the construction of a fully democratic and equally aware public.

That is why the Avignon Festival did not really succeed in producing new social types of audience, and should be evaluated mainly with respect to its civic contribution to the national reconstruction of France. If one considers that this goal has been fulfilled, what will happen in a post-national age, when the significance of a national festival has lost ground? In the 1990s many harsh criticics deplored the exclusively French character of Avignon, and the organizers answered them by welcoming many foreign works and artists, mainly from Central Europe and Germany. This has led to a really different type of festival; if it is well accepted by a majority of young spectators who consider the young artists and directors closer to their own artistic interests, quite a few experienced spectators regret that the old gathering of the French theatre now belongs to the past. Avignon is very different from Cannes in this respect: if the national pride that fuelled the first years of the festival still exists (especially when it is compared with its old rival Venice), it has been gradually replaced in Cannes by a very careful attention to changing world sensibilities and emerging forms in culture and politics.

Festivals and politics

How can we define the public of a festival? The collection of spectators assembled in a single space at the same time of the year does not constitute a regressive form of sociation that would lead to an older (or simply mythical) state of the relations among individuals. It is never the expression, even in its more emotional outbursts, of a nostalgia vis-à-vis an undivided moment of the social being (the purest form of 'mechanical solidarity', in Durkheim's terms). Such publics, more than in ordinary theatres, allow the observer to grasp the reflexivity at work in social interactions. The religious metaphor is often tempting when one wants to give an account of the social gatherings triggered by festivals. The crowds look quite like pilgrims, especially when the events take place in open locations during hot summers. Some descriptions earlier in this chapter might lead to the same conclusions: being a spectator often means enduring a genuine physical ordeal, and some may look for a kind of cultural salvation. In fact, this is a misleading comparison. Festivals are an astonishing example of the secularization of culture. This is not surprising; if we use a broad Habermasian frame, we can say that the theatre was one of the most apposite configurations for an emerging public sphere. It has undoubtedly become a minor social activity in the contemporary world, and is now far from the potentialities that Aristotle in his *Poetics* or Bertolt Brecht in his whole work put into it. But the festivalization of theatre has the capacity to revive its explicit political dimension, particularly because it allows a definite space for critical interventions, within the framework of the representation or in the broader configuration of the event. Big festivals are always multi-sited, even if they occur in a single place. They are no longer the place for the affirmation of a cultural unity, either ethnic or national, but are built on the assessment of cultural differences and variations.

The French media and cinema sociologist Pierre Sorlin (Sorlin 1992) gave an accurate definition of the public when he wrote that 'it is a sociation that is never given in advance and that cannot be reduced to the object that constitutes it as a public'. Such a definition is empirically verified and avoids any essentialization of the public. There is no such thing as a universal public that exists independently of objects that assemble people around them. Following one of the most convincing attempts to theorize the concept of public, Michael Warner's *Publics and Counterpublics*, it is possible to say that the publics formed by the spatial and temporal organization of the festivals are examples of embodied fictions (Warner 2002). An audience is the result of the indefinite multiplicity of spectators and the product of contingent histories. A public is always the outcome of a tension between the local (the *hic et nunc* of the performance) and the universal (the *polis* as the political space for the discussion on the ends of action). Such a tension, which allows the emergence of a critical space, does not exist as such in what McGuigan terms 'uncritical populism', although silent appropriations of mass-produced cultural goods may trigger some individual and quasi-clandestine autonomous creativity, as Michel de Certeau beautifully showed. The third stance defined by McGuigan with regard to the politics of the cultural public sphere, 'radical subversion', seems to be more of a momentary effervescence (like the outburst of protest in Avignon and Cannes in 1968) than a real social space defined by a flow of communications directed to a potential audience. Radicalism, if it is taken seriously, stands beyond any critical space, because the answer is given in advance. It is not the case with the model of relationship between the spectator and the cultural good that has been sketched above. Uncertainty dominates the relationship, and the outcome is never sure. Individual spectators may withdraw at any time and keep their freedom as citizens. Such a model can be spotted in Brechtian theatre as well as in Greek tragedy, performed as a democratic ritual in front of all the citizens – excluding slaves, of course. The tragedy implies the representation of society as well as its criticism, expressed by the chorus. It is a form of alienation from the plot that can be compared to some extent with the Brechtian definition of *Verfremdung*; the creation of a critical space between the spectator and the representation is sought through questioning the 'willing suspension of disbelief' that conditions the ordinary situation of the spectator. The specific settings of the festivals tend to reinforce this critical dimension inasmuch as they offer additional space for critical intervention. Very often, the festivals are described in 'communitarian' terms, exaggerating the dimension of symbolic unity and intellectual consensus involved. A community is undoubtedly created in the process, but it is never a flock of true believers: it is a critically divided community. The spectators are never trapped in a univocal link; they may withdraw or leave, sleep or protest. The plot can be unplotted. The availability of the spectator before and after the shows, a feature that differentiates festivals from routine cultural life, allows the development of independent criticism.

In conclusion, it is possible to say that the form of the festival analysed here is on the side of the politicization of aesthetics, as proposed for the reverse of Walter Benjamin's aestheticization of politics. Art becomes an object of public debate and critical interventions. In a globalized world, the discussions have more and more to do with world issues and less and less with local problems. The co-presence of the spectators and the actors that the festival permits does not lead to inwardness: on the contrary, the stage is the world as well as the world being a stage, and global preoccupations become central. Is the festival a metaphor for a new participatory democracy? It would be naïve to display an excessive optimism about a cultural form that is not accessible to all. The world described here is still determined by what the director Antoine Vitez termed 'elitism for all', which means for not that many, at the end of the day. Does it mean that such a critical space is de facto reserved for a conscious minority, and that the big crowds must be content with the cheap aestheticization of politics that pervades contemporary mass culture and mega-events? Up to now, the space for critical intervention as defined by Jim McGuigan looks a little like the suffrage based on property qualification, as in the *monarchie censitaire*, cultural capital here standing for property. This observation is not limited to the case of festivals. But it means that the democratization of the access to critical intervention is still a major issue on the cultural and political agendas.

References

Baudouin, V. and Maresca, B. (1997) *Les Publics de la Comédie française*. Paris: La Documentation française.

Berger, B. M. (1981) *The Survival of a Counterculture: Ideological Work and Everyday Life among Rural Communards*. Berkeley: University of California Press.

Bourdieu, P. ([1965] 1990) *Photography: A Middle-Brow Art*. Stanford: Stanford University Press.

Bourdieu, P. ([1992] 1996) *The Rules of Art: Genesis and Structure of the Literary Field*. Stanford: Stanford University Press.

Bourdieu, P. and Darbel, A. ([1966] 1991) *The Love of Art: European Museums and their Public*. London: Polity Press.

Certeau, M. de ([1968] 1994): *La prise de parole et autres écrits politiques*. Paris: Hachette.

Elias, N. (1993) *Mozart: Portrait of a Genius*. Berkeley: University of California Press.

Ethis, E. (ed.) (2000) *Aux marches du palais: Le Festival de Cannes sous le regard des sciences sociales*. Paris: La Documentation française.

Ethis, E. (ed.) (2002) *Avignon, le Public réinventé: Le Festival sous le regard des sciences sociales*. Paris: La Documentation française.

Ethis, E. (2008) (with Fabiani, J. L. and Malinas, D.) *Le public participant*. Montpellier: L'Entretemps.

Fabiani, J. L. and Menger, P. M. (1978) Le public de Beaubourg *Universalia* 1978, 180–183.

Fabiani, J. L. (2003) Peut-on encore parler de légitimité culturelle? In *Les Publics*, under the direction of Tolila, P. and Donnat, O. Paris: Presses de la FNSP.

Fabiani, J. L. (2005) Should the Sociological Analysis of Art Festivals be Neo-Durkheimian? *Durkheimian Studies* 11: 49–66.

Fabiani, J. L. (2007) *Après la culture légitime: Objets, publics, autorités*. Paris: L'Harmattan.

Fabiani, J. L. (2008) *L'éducation populaire et le théâtre: Le public d'Avignon en action*. Saint-Martin d'Hères: Presses universitaires de Grenoble.

Habermas, J. ([1962] 1989) *The Structural Transformation of the Public Sphere. An Inquiry into a Category of Bourgeois Society*. Cambridge: Polity Press.

Hirschman, A. O. (1970) *Exit, Voice and Loyalty: Responses to Decline in Firms, Organizations and States*. Cambridge, Massachusetts: Harvard University Press.

McGuigan, J. (2005) The cultural public sphere. *European Journal of Cultural Studies* 8: 427–443.

McGuigan, J. (2011) The cultural public sphere – a critical measure of public culture? Chapter in this volume.

Moulin, R. (1967) *Le marché de la peinture en France*. Paris: Editions de Minuithe.

Ory, P. (1994) *La belle illusion: culture et politique sous le signe du Front populaire, 1935–1938*. Paris: Plon.

Sorlin, P. (1992) Le mirage du public. *Revue d'histoire moderne et contemporaine* 39 (January–March).

Warner, M. (2002) *Publics and Counter Publics*. New York: Zone Books.

7 International festivals in a small country

Rites of recognition and cosmopolitanism

Motti Regev

This chapter looks at four annual international festivals that take place in Israel, in order to theorize their cultural meaning in the context of cultural globalization. The core sociological argument is that the festivals serve the quest of certain collective and individual actors – especially the educated upper middle classes, professionals in cultural sectors and related class segments – for status and self-identification as equal participants in what they perceive as the innovative frontiers of world culture. The festivals celebrate the intertwining of national cultural uniqueness and aesthetic cosmopolitanism, and this is also their purpose. If the cultural public sphere, in its national context, is envisaged as an arena in which various social actors interact, compete on and negotiate the meaning of 'national culture', then international festivals of film and the performing arts are one site in which a cosmopolitan standpoint is manifested on national culture in a collective and orchestrated manner.

The premise here is taken from the Durkheimian perspective on festivals, as it has been developed by Victor Turner (1982) and others in anthropology. Inferring from this tradition, Falassi, for example, defines festival as:

> A periodically recurrent, social occasion in which, through a multiplicity of forms and a series of co-ordinated events, participate directly or indirectly and to various degrees, all members of a whole community, united by ethnic, linguistic, religious, historical bonds, and sharing a worldview. Both the social function and the symbolic meaning of the festival are closely related to a series of overt values that the community recognizes as essential to its ideology and worldview, to its social identity, its historical continuity, and to its physical survival, which is ultimately what festival celebrates.
>
> (Falassi 1987: 2)

As they are not congregations of 'all members of a whole community', contemporary international festivals of the performing arts, film and music do not fall squarely within this definition. Nevertheless, I still want to use it, and, based on it, ask: which community is it that gathers at such a festival, and what does this community celebrate?

The answer would be that these communities are members of omnivorous taste cultures, i.e. segments of the population that define their sense of distinction by consuming cultural goods and works of art from a wide range of cultural contexts: popular and 'high-brow'; old and new; local, universal and exotic. These segments are typically composed of members of the upper middle and professional classes (Peterson 1992; Ollivier 2008). At the festivals they celebrate their omnivorous, cosmopolitan taste, thereby claiming and assessing their sense of equal participation and membership of what is generally perceived as the innovative stylistic frontier of world culture. In the following, the emergence of such communities will first be elaborated; they will be called, after Kendall, Woodward and Skribs (2009), 'cosmopolitan omnivores'. Discussion will then move on to the role and structure of international festivals. This will be followed by a presentation and discussion of four international festivals in Israel.

Cosmopolitan omnivores

As it was globally institutionalized in late modernity, the field of cultural production is organized around a perception of art as a constantly changing and evolving realm. Through its specific diffusion channels and production of meaning apparatus, every art form constantly generates new stylistic directions, new works and new artists. Many of these are set within interpretive and evaluative discourses that present them as inventive explorations of the given art form, as expansions of its aesthetic idioms, and as extensions of its expressive possibilities. In the wake of earlier struggles in various artistic fields, the space of creative possibilities and of aesthetic directions has opened up enormously to practitioners of most forms of art in late modernity. Successful struggles have legitimized popular styles as well as aesthetic elements and traditions from almost every region or ethnic group in the world. As a creative practice, hybridity has become the convention, with the result being mixtures of materials and elements taken from 'high-brow' and 'low-brow', old and new, metropolitan and peripheral forms of expression. In addition, past struggles have also legitimized the use of advanced and sophisticated technologies for creative purposes. Taken together, in late modernity the arts present to aspiring and potential audiences a wealth of forms and styles, many of which bear the mark of legitimate cultural value.

The constantly shifting boundaries of stylistic innovations in the arts, as well as the wealth of works and products, are propagated by cultural industries and other channels as the frontiers of expressive culture in modernity. They should therefore be understood, following Fraser, as constituting 'institutional patterns of cultural value' (Fraser 2002). That is, they are patterns that formulate and define hierarchies of worth or importance in the cultural and artistic realms. Basically, the hierarchies they define relegate to a lower status on the scale of modernity those individuals and collective actors whose tastes hardly consist of works from the creative frontiers, actors whose sense of distinction and uniqueness is based on works and styles lagging behind recent stylistic trends, and whose taste is confined to a narrow range of styles and forms. Consequently, individual and collective actors, especially in so-called 'small countries', who aspire to participate as equals in what they perceive as the cultural frontiers of modernity tend to acquire tastes in, and adjust aesthetic sensibilities to, those cultural products hailed by institutional patterns, and to widen their repertoires of acquaintance and knowledge. At the same time, in various artistic fields where such patterns are transformed into dominant criteria of evaluation, artists from such 'small countries' tend to develop their own, locally specific variants of such styles and trends, with an interest in gaining recognition and valorization in the respective global artistic field. These phenomena gain particular intensity in so-called 'small countries' because actors in local fields of cultural production tend to feel remote and peripheral to the scenes and locations presented by institutional patterns as the metropolitan centres of innovation.

Put differently, the growing wealth and variety of cultural products, artistic goods and repertoires of styles in late modernity are not a social coincidence. Sociologically, it should be envisaged along the principle of homology between the supply and demand sides of culture as outlined by Bourdieu (1993). That is, the ascent and expansion of the upper middle classes and cultural professions in many countries propels the worldwide emergence of individual and collective actors who, on the demand side of culture, develop omnivorous tastes for 'the new and innovative', as a way of defining their sense of distinction in terms of contemporariness and modernity. At the same time, as agents who are self-positioned on the supply side of culture in global fields of art, artists and cultural producers develop creative interests in the most recent and latest stylistic trends, as defined and formulated by the production of meaning positions in their respective fields, and as a way to keep up with artistic innovations in the field and thus be able to participate in the struggles for recognition and canonization. The wealth of cultural products and art works and the wide variety of stylistic trends thus emerge from acts of position-taking by artists and cultural producers catering to the status interests of collective actors.

One outcome of this process is the emergence and institutionalization of aesthetic cosmopolitanism as a leading, or even dominant, variant of national cultures. Aesthetic cosmopolitanism is the contemporary cultural condition in which the representation and performance of national uniqueness is largely based on art forms and stylistic elements deliberately drawn from sources exterior to indigenous traditions (for elaboration, see Regev 2007). Aesthetic cosmopolitanism may be divided, however, into inadvertent and advertent cosmopolitanism. Inadvertent aesthetic cosmopolitanism can be referred to, following Billig (1995), as banal aesthetic cosmopolitanism, or as ordinary and mundane (Lamont and Aksartova 2002; Hebdige 1990). This is the widespread form of aesthetic cosmopolitanism, in which the mixing of local or traditional expressive forms and elements with stylistic trends, cultural products and expressive technologies associated with transnational cultural industries is performed through routine cultural consumption and production. Inadvertent cosmopolitans, in other words, do not intentionally engage in nurturing their cosmopolitanism. They become banal cosmopolitans simply by consuming typical products of the cultural industries.

Advertent aesthetic cosmopolitanism, on the other hand – the one in focus here – is reflexive and intentional. This is the type of aesthetic cosmopolitanism in which agents actively and consciously engage in practices of cultural consumption and production that transgress the conventional boundaries of their own ethnic or national cultures. They seek constantly to be updated with the most recent stylistic trends and cultural innovations, especially those praised by the global institutional patterns of cultural value as expansions of existing experiences. They typically want to have similar cultural products in their 'own' national, ethnic or local culture – and they act accordingly, either as producers or consumers. Advertent aesthetic cosmopolitanism thus becomes a set of cultural performances associated with specific groupings or communities.

Indeed, in late modernity many countries have witnessed the emergence of classes and class segments that work to redefine national cultural uniqueness along the lines of aesthetic cosmopolitanism, in the process becoming taste cultures of cosmopolitan omnivores. These groups aim to produce and consume art works and cultural goods that shift national cultures into a condition of aesthetic cosmopolitanism. This aim goes hand in hand with the development of omnivorous tastes within and across cultural forms. Recent research has empirically assessed the major presence of cosmopolitan omnivores on the cultural market. Thus, following work on omnivorous cultural consumption (Peterson and Kern 1996), and coupling it to Bourdieu's concepts, Coulangeon (2003) refers to this type of omnivorousness as 'enlightened eclecticism', while Ollivier (2008) calls it 'humanist openness' and elsewhere argues that conspicuous openness has become a major ingredient in the behaviour of the upper middle classes, a way of demonstrating and performing distinction (Ollivier 2004). Finally, Kendall *et al.* (2009) assert that 'cosmopolitan omnivorousness becomes a symbol of social status and moral worth. More broadly, it is a particular type of cultural capital that demonstrates one is able to appreciate the cultural products and practices of others, suggesting openness and flexibility' (p. 145).

At a practical level, fulfilment of the cultural interests of cosmopolitan omnivores requires organizational settings of enablement. This refers to organizational bodies that, on the one hand, enable audiences in countries worldwide to be informed about and acquire first-hand acquaintance with works and recent stylistic trends from all over the world, and, on the other, enable local artists from different countries to perform and present their own works to worldwide audiences. Moreover, the interest in legitimizing these practices and the identity of the collective actors associated with them propels the creation of symbolic events and celebrations where these identities and practices are assessed. In addition, beyond actual consumption and production of art works and cultural goods, an interest emerges among such actors in placing local national culture at the frontiers of modernity and in demonstrating this as an accomplishment, and thus asserting their own status as worthy participants in those frontiers, on a par with actors from metropolitan centres or other peripheral countries. This is where the mechanism of international festivals comes in.

Rituals of valorization

In this respect, international festivals are a ritualized component in the set of organizational tools through which the international flow of cultural products is realized. Unlike the routine, steady and yet sporadic influx of art and cultural products that is offered all year round by the cultural industries, international festivals form occasions for concentrated activity that not only offer first-hand acquaintance with works and trends, but in fact assess and celebrate the collective quest for the cosmopolitan distinction of artists and audiences. Typically non-profit 'minimal organizations' (DiMaggio 2006), international festivals in 'small countries' are designed to serve the interests outlined above. Following the definition of festivals, Falassi goes on to offer a morphology of festivals, which consists of basic units, most of them consisting of one or another type of rite. Thus, for example, 'the framing ritual that opens the festival is one of *valorization*' (Falassi 1987: 4). The structure of the performing arts festivals, composed of the orchestrated function of such units, is clearly devised to celebrate the omnivore expectations of its typical publics in several dimensions.

In order to illustrate all the points above, the following section will describe four international festivals held in Israel. Excerpts from their self-presentation in brochures and websites will be quoted at some length as a way of demonstrating the valorization implied. Then some of their features will be discussed as rites of the type mentioned by Falassi.

Festivals in Israel

The fulfilment of cosmopolitan omnivore interests in a small country like Israel is routinely maintained through a scattered and yet constant influx of art products from various countries and by occasional international successes of art works from Israel. Dance and theatre companies, symphonic orchestras, jazz and pop–rock musicians from various countries visit Israel regularly to hold performances. European and East Asian films and, obviously, Hollywood movies are constants in Israeli movie theatres and cinematheques. Exhibitions by noteworthy foreign visual artists are often shown in local museums and galleries. Concurrently, Israeli artists regularly perform at venues in metropolitan as well as peripheral countries, and Israeli films are shown in festivals and in movie theatres around the world, with varying degrees of artistic and commercial success. Visual artists from Israel also exhibit work in galleries and museums in various cities. On a daily basis, then, actors in Israeli fields of cultural production find sufficient fulfilment of their quest for equal participation in the frontiers of modernity. They are given ample opportunities for first-hand acquaintance with works and products from many countries, and thus feel relatively up to date. This sense of being 'on top' of cultural innovations is complemented by the knowledge of, and even pride in, occasional successes by Israeli art works and cultural products abroad.

However, the scattered, unfocused nature of this routine hardly offers opportunities for celebrating cosmopolitan omnivorousness as a collective taste culture, or for assessing its legitimacy within national culture. Through the routine, cosmopolitan omnivorousness appears as an occasional, unfocused pattern of cultural consumption or production. The interest of cosmopolitan omnivores in symbolically assessing and celebrating, in collective fashion, the existence of aesthetic cosmopolitanism as a legitimate component of national cultural reality is not truly fulfilled by such scattered and un-orchestrated events. That aspect is instead covered by various international festivals of film and the performing arts. The four most prominent of these are presented here: the Israel Festival Jerusalem, a general performing arts festival; two film festivals, the International Film Festival Jerusalem and the International Film Festival Haifa; and the Red Sea Jazz Festival in Eilat.

It should be stressed that none of the cities in which the festivals are held has by itself the demographic or sociological infrastructure needed to support full attendance at all the events. The general motive for holding the festivals is coupled with the economic and tourist interests of these cities to draw business and visitors. It is also important to note that Tel Aviv–Yafo, the cultural centre of the country, has no prominent international festival. Consequently, the cities in which the festivals are held act during festival times as sites of cultural pilgrimage, a practice that emphasizes the functioning of festivals as collective gatherings of people sharing a common creed.

The Israel Festival Jerusalem

Probably the major international festival in Israel, this event is primarily concerned with art music: classical, early/ancient, jazz and world music. Popular music is occasionally present, but it is never salient. In 2008, for example, the festival featured orchestras and small ensembles from Spain, Italy, the USA, Poland, France, Romania and Scotland – in addition to local symphony orchestras and other Israeli ensembles – who represented a range of genres from medieval music (on original instruments), through classical music (a Franz Schubert 'marathon') to world music. In addition, there were several jazz ensembles, from Israel, Poland, Brazil and the USA. The festival also featured theatre productions from Israel, Poland, South Korea, France and Russia, and dance performances from France, Brazil and England, as well as a company billed as an Israeli–Japanese–Swiss collaboration. In 2009, in the realm of dance, the festival hosted Alarmel Valli, a dancer in the Bharatanatyam style from India, the National Dance Company of Spain, a ballet troupe from Montreal, Alonzo King's Line Ballet from the USA, and the Israeli dance company Mayumana. It also featured four shows for children: two from Israel, one from Spain and one from Georgia. In 2009 art music performances included concerts by the Israeli Philharmonic Orchestra, the Keller Quartet (with members from

Hungary and Israel), Ensemble Fretwork from England, the pianist Maurizio Baglini from Italy and the vocal group Cantus Köln. The festival also presented several 'world music' concerts, by musicians from Portugal, Israel, India and Switzerland, as well as three acts of Israeli pop–rock music. On its website the Israel Festival Jerusalem presents itself as follows.

> The Israel Festival was founded in 1961 by Aaron Zvi Propes as a summer music festival taking place in the ancient Roman theatre in Caesarea. The program was later broadened to include all the performing arts, and the location was enlarged to include venues all over the country. It was not until 1982 that the country's capital decided to adopt the Festival as its own, and since then the majority of performances are held in Jerusalem. The Festival takes place annually for a few weeks in the spring. Throughout the festival, audiences are able to enjoy performances by artists from all over the world, as well as premieres of Israeli works and tributes to leading Israeli artists. The public can also attend a large selection of free performances, including street theatre, children's shows and a nightly jazz club. The festival's staff and all those involved in its production view the festival as a means to promote artistic encounters crossing all political and national boundaries, to encourage collaborations between Israeli artists and their colleagues from abroad, and to introduce the public to emerging forms of art.

> The Festival is a non-profit organization headed by a public board ... [T]he festival runs on a small staff of five, which is supplemented during the festival period by extra production staff. The Israel Festival is a member of the European Festivals' Association.
>
> (http://www.israel-festival.org.il/2008/home_e.html)

Although it is the largest city in Israel in terms of population, Jerusalem is sharply divided along ethnic, national and religious lines. In terms of socio-economic status, it is one of the poorest cities in the country. The typical class groups the festival programme caters to, i.e. the educated, professional middle and upper middle classes, make up a relatively small section of the city's population (these assertions are based on Choshen *et al.* 2009). For audience attendance at all its shows and events, the festival has to rely on these sections of the population from all over the country. Indeed, during the festival Jerusalem is packed with visitors from other parts of the country who come to watch the shows and participate in various events. Thus, the festival becomes a site and occasion of artistic pilgrimage, in which the collective entity of cosmopolitan omnivores in Israel celebrates its existence and valorizes its aesthetic values.

The Red Sea Jazz Festival

Eilat, at the southernmost tip of Israel, is primarily a tourist resort. Filled with holiday hotels and adjacent to the shores of the Red Sea, it offers Israeli and foreign tourists sandy as well as coral beaches and the idyllic scenery of desert mountains and a deep blue sea. One hour's flight from Tel Aviv or four to five hours' drive across the desert, it is visited by Israelis primarily for vacation and leisure purposes. More than visiting Jerusalem or Haifa, then, coming to Eilat for several days, especially to attend the jazz festival, takes on the character of a pilgrimage – of a ritual congregation of individuals sharing a common interest and belief in a purpose. In 2008 the festival hosted twelve local jazz bands, eight ensembles and musicians from the USA (including Carla Bley and Oregon) and also musicians from Poland and Cuba. All of these played a range of styles from free jazz to traditional standards and salsa, and they included singers. This festival presents itself on its website as follows.

> The Red Sea Jazz Festival was launched in 1987 as a four-day international jazz festival with 9–10 concerts per evening, 6 clinics with guest artists and nightly Jam sessions. The festival is held yearly in the last week of August, between Monday to Thursday. The Red Sea Jazz Festival strives to introduce to the public the broadest possible musical spectrum, from New Orleans jazz to the contemporary, including Latin and World music. The festival presents guest groups from all around the globe plus Israeli top groups. The festival is also active in the jazz education field in Israel, promoting original jazz compositions and youth jazz bands.
>
> (http://www.redseajazzeilat.com/en/)

The website goes on to say that the festival concerts are held within the area of the sea port of Eilat. The venue includes four open-air concert halls, with capacities ranging from 1,500 to 3,000 seats. In addition, each evening there are jam sessions at the pool court of one of Eilat's hotels. Finally, the website also gives some attendance figures: the average audience comes to around 2,500, peaking at 3,500. Excluding the 2009 season, the Red Sea Jazz Festival sold some 75,000 tickets in its first 20 years. The general description goes on and proudly presents a very long list of all the musicians who have played at the festival since its inauguration, including a list of all the 'special events'.

The Haifa International Film Festival

Haifa is the third-largest city in Israel and one of its two ports on the Mediterranean. Although it has two universities and a local theatre company as well as other cultural activities and nightlife, the city's image among the Israeli public is of a cultural desert – especially when it is compared with Tel Aviv. Having a film festival is obviously an instrument to draw visitors and boost the domestic tourist industry. Once a year, then, Haifa becomes a site where cinephiles congregate to celebrate their tastes and explore past and present cinematic experiences. Altogether, with the audience attending films from different countries and genres, the festival becomes a rite of valorization, not only of the art of film, but of the omnivore public and aesthetic cosmopolitanism. In the words of the official website:

> The Haifa International Film Festival is held each year during the holiday of Succoth [late September or early October] on the ridge of Mount Carmel overlooking the Mediterranean Sea. The Festival was founded in 1983 and was the first of its kind in Israel. Over the years, the Festival became the biggest and most important film celebration in Israel. The Haifa International Film Festival brings together each year an ever-growing audience of 60,000 spectators along with hundreds of Israeli and foreign professionals from the film and television industries. 180,000 people in total take part in the activities of the festival, including the outdoor events, screenings, workshops and more, and dozens of journalists from both the print and broadcast media, from Israel and abroad, cover the event. During its eight days of celebration, the Festival proudly premieres 150 new films from the best and most recent international productions and holds 220 screenings in seven theaters and under the sky: feature films, documentaries, animation, short films, retrospectives and tributes.
>
> (http://www.haifaff.co.il/index.php)

The festival programme is divided into several categories. One is 'gala screenings', consisting of premiere screenings of what the organizers call 'the biggest film productions from Hollywood and Europe'. Another category, 'panorama', is devoted to world cinema, i.e. films from African, Asian, Latin American, Middle-Eastern and Eastern European countries. Two competitions that are a regular feature of the festival are the Israeli film competition – in which new Israeli films compete for awards in categories such as feature films, documentary films, TV dramas, animated and student films – and the Golden Anchor Competition for Mediterranean Cinema, a 'competition of quality productions from Mediterranean countries'. Finally, there is the category of 'retrospectives and tributes' that 'promotes filmmakers and themes that celebrate the history of filmmaking and its milestones'. In addition, every year the festival produces special events concerning particular themes, such as New German Cinema in 2008.

The Haifa Film Festival of 2008 showed films from about 40 countries, in addition to several Israeli productions. The festival opened with an Israeli premiere of Woody Allen's *Vicky Cristina Barcelona*, included an award-wining film, Laurent Cantet's *Entre les murs*, and closed with a screening of Saul Dibb's *The Duchess*. In addition, it offered numerous new films that would never be commercially distributed in Israel, especially ones from African and Asian countries.

The Jerusalem International Film Festival

Although one year younger than the Haifa Film Festival, the Jerusalem Film Festival has grown into an event drawing more public attention. This may be attributed to its larger budget, the location, or the salience of the Wolgin competition for Israeli films. During the festival, the Jerusalem cinematheque is packed by cinephiles from all over the country, and the crowded corridors between screenings often have the atmosphere of parties. Here, too, the official website tells the history of the festival and proudly highlights various aspects that together convey an impression of diversity, variety and openness, as well as assessing the quality of Israeli cinema.

> On May 17, 1984, *Le Bal*, directed by Ettore Scola, opened the first Jerusalem International Film Festival. Over the course of three weeks, about one-hundred films were screened, including Israeli premieres, alongside the year's best selection of international films. In addition, a distinguished group of guests honored the first festival, among them, the First Lady of Silent Film, Lillian Gish, as well as Jeanne Moreau and Warren Beaty, John Schlesinger, and Andre Delvaux ... From its inception, the festival has dedicated a central and unique space to Israeli film, premiering features, documentaries, and shorts. In 1989, the festival granted an official stamp of validity to Israeli film with the introduction of the Wolgin Competition ... Today, the Wolgin Competition grants a yearly award to a full-length feature, a documentary, and a short. The Wolgin Competition became the first stage to showcase the majority of the most important Israeli films of the past two decades ... This competition placed Israeli film in the limelight and turned the Festival into an esteemed stage for local cinema. Beyond its contribution to Israeli film, the Jerusalem International Film Festival remains one of the few platforms that present the world's finest contemporary cinematic trends to its local audiences.
>
> (http://www.jff.org.il/?cl=en)

During the 1980s the festival evolved into a ten-day event, during which 150–200 films are screened. Here, as in Haifa, the category of international films is called 'panorama'. The Jerusalem Film Festival also features a section called 'The Jewish Experience', dedicated to films dealing with Jewish identity and history. For some of its special productions – premieres or retrospectives – this festival takes advantage of the open-air venue located at the historical site known as 'The Sultan's Pool'. Here, contiguous to the Jerusalem cinematheque and below the ancient wall of the old city, the festival can offer spectacular screenings to an audience of thousands. The festival prides itself on being 'the most important cinematic gathering in Israel' and on screening debut films by directors such as Wong Kar Wai, Tsai Ming-liang, John Sayles, Jim Jarmusch, Stephen Frears, Spike Lee, Quentin Tarantino, Neil Jordan, John Lasseter and other names 'that have turned into the masters of our time'. As on other festival websites, here, too, a long list of names is presented as a sign of stylistic variety and wide-ranging international representation. In 2008 the festival had approximately 220 feature films, including 20 films under the category of 'new directors'.

Additional categories included the screening of new Israeli television dramas, over 30 documentaries and animated films.

Isomorphic rites

In his morphology of festivals, Falassi points out several rites that compose the score of festivals. In his view, festivals typically include at least some of the following: rites of purification, rites of passage, rites of reversal, rites of conspicuous display, rites of conspicuous consumption, ritual dramas, rites of exchange and rites of competition (Falassi 1987: 4–5). International performing arts festivals obviously do not include all of these rites but they certainly incorporate several of them, and these will be discussed below. The rites are in fact units, or components, in the organizational structure of the festivals. This structure, in turn, is isomorphically duplicated across festivals and countries. In other words, from an institutional perspective the festivals manifest an organizational isomorphism that stems not only from professional managerial knowledge about directing festivals but also from the similarities it evokes in the service of the cultural and symbolic interests of the festivals' participants – audiences and artists alike.

The organizational structure is basically a mechanism of concentration and juxtaposition. This means concentrating a large number of works in one space over a short period of time, and juxtaposing works by local artists with those by foreign ones, works regarded as avant-garde, experimental or canonical with works classified as popular and mundane, and works of various genres and styles with one another. In addition, the festivals' syntax allocates space, time and attention to so-called 'special events', in which attention is given to particular individuals, specific bodies of works or groups of works associated with certain themes. In the following section, each of these practices will be examined as a rite serving the general symbolic and ritual purpose of the festivals discussed here, i.e. that of performing arts festivals catering to the interests of the cosmopolitan omnivore.

Rites of conspicuous display

The first and most obvious component of the festivals that functions as a rite is the sheer quantity and stylistic spectrum of works shown and performed over a short period of time. Displaying this quantity and variety in all possible forms is a key element in the publicity of the festivals. It comes to demonstrate the wide horizons of the organizers and potential audiences, their acquaintance with and knowledge of the field(s) of art, and the openness of their evaluative criteria. The long list of performers, artists and names of shows, past and present, is on display in official brochures of the festivals, websites, street postings and journalistic coverage of the programmes. As a rite of conspicuous display, this practice serves the interest of the organizers in presenting their stock of cultural goods and art works as encompassing a wide range of styles and aesthetic idioms, or, in short, in demonstrating cosmopolitan omnivorousness.

Thus, the 2008 Israel Festival Jerusalem featured 15 theatrical plays, 4 dance shows, 15 concerts of art music, 19 events of world music, popular music and jazz, and 8 'special events', some of them designed especially for children. The Red Sea Jazz Festival featured 24 concerts, and the Haifa Film Festival showed 147 films and the Jerusalem Film Festival 221 (excluding short films and animated ones).

Rites of conspicuous consumption

Given the sheer volume of shows or screenings at every festival, organizers look for ways to ensure audience attendance at each and every show or screening. As well as producing publicity and advertising, they also offer the public packages of tickets at reduced prices. That is, the more tickets one buys, the cheaper the price is for an individual show or screening. This, of course, encourages many participants to purchase numerous tickets, in an act that also allows them to manifest a sense of omnivorous taste. Buying many tickets inevitably means attending presentations in a wide range of genres and styles from different countries. In other words, for many, attending the festival becomes a rite of conspicuous consumption of art. It is a rite that mirrors the rite of conspicuous display. On the side of demand, it allows consumers to exhibit their tastes and their willingness to experience and become acquainted with new styles or aesthetic idioms, thus intensively proclaiming and celebrating their identity as cosmopolitan omnivores. The festivals provide an occasion for condensed and intensive demonstration of conspicuous openness to diversity. Over a short period of time many individuals consume a large number of shows or film screenings. Some individuals may watch several films per day, or attend more then one musical show on one day. This is certainly much more then the average cultural consumption during the year, even among aficionados.

The 2007 Red Sea Jazz Festival, for example, reported that during the four days of the festival there were over 70,000 entries to its premises, where the 36 shows of that year, and other festival events, took place. Moreover, as mentioned above, the Haifa Film Festival proudly declares that 180,000 people visited the films and other festival activities in seven days. By any account, these numbers reflect the intensity of consumption on the part of visitors and audience.

Ritual dramas

A salient element in almost all the festivals' programmes is the category of 'special event'. Under this heading are found different productions, designed especially for the occasion of the festival, usually by its organizers. This means that whereas most shows and screenings are of acts and works for which the festival is simply one stop in an ongoing tour, or one screening in the circuit of international distribution, the 'special events' consist of an amalgamation of shows or screenings of films that occurs exclusively at the festival. Here one may find, in the case of film festivals, a retrospective screening devoted to one prominent director, actor, screenwriter or any other creative figure in film history (sometimes in conjunction with the presence of the individual as an honoured guest), a selection of films from one national cinema, or any other general theme. In the case of a general performing arts festival, the special event may include collaborations between dance or theatrical companies from different countries, a series of concerts all devoted to works by one composer, or a mixture of shows of different arts (theatre, dance, film, music) devoted to one theme or country. Although such 'special events' are not staged as 'dramas' in a strict sense of the word, they still provide focal points within the festivals' programmes in which the ritual purpose is dramatized. They are focal points in which the meaning of the festival as a site and occasion for celebrating and assessing past achievements of the art form in question, international parity and collaboration, and multiple stylistic diversity, is orchestrated in a condensed manner.

In 2008 the Israel Festival Jerusalem featured, for example, a show that was called *peepdance*, a collaboration between Israeli and Japanese dance companies, in which the audience could move between booths (like peep-shows) and 'peep' at dancers performing two totally different choreographies to the same music. International collaboration and equivalence as well as stylistic variety were thus dramatized in one event. Another example comes from the Haifa Film Festival, where one of its special events in 2008 was labelled 'a homage to Hollywood of the 1970s'. Screening films such as Arthur Penn's *Night Moves*, Robert Altman's *McCabe and Mrs. Miller*, Hal Ashbey's *The Last Detail* or Martin Scorsese's *Mean Streets*, the festival offered an opportunity to omnivorous cinephiles to exercise their historical knowledge and reassess their expertise and enthusiasm.

Rites of exchange and reversal

Artistic fields are, as a rule, hierarchical structures in which certain genres and styles occupy dominant positions whilst others struggle to gain legitimacy, recognition and, ultimately, become part of the canon (Bourdieu 1993). In addition to the artistic hierarchy based on the imposed criteria of evaluation, hierarchies are also grounded on divisions along notions of metropolitan versus periphery, veteran versus novice and other criteria. Indeed, one component that gives festival organizers and participants a sense of pride and importance is the inclusion in the programme of works and shows by artists associated with such consecrated or dominant positions in artistic fields. However, during the festival, by juxtaposing shows or films associated with names high on artistic hierarchies with other works and artists, the festival evokes rites of exchange and reversal. It projects an atmosphere of equality and parity between styles, works and artists. It constructs an aura of artistic equivalence between the peripheral and the metropolitan, those aspiring for recognition and the already recognized and canonized. Festival days offer a period during which all works and artists participating in the festival are perceived as equal members in the art worlds to which the festival is devoted.

Hosting individuals whose work and reputation pertain to well established and appraised positions in the field, and having them participate in the festival in various capacities, is a typical form of exchange and reversal rite. In 2008 the Jerusalem Film Festival, for example, held retrospective screenings in honour of director Michael Winterbottom and actor John Malkovich, and gave each of them an 'Achievement Award'. In exchange both individuals held open encounters of free conversation with the public, immediately following the screenings of their films. Thus, on the one hand, these two celebrities in the film art world shared their aura, in an egalitarian manner, with cinephiles and spectators in Israel, acknowledging the importance of this festival. On the other hand, by bestowing these awards, the festival in a way reversed the hierarchy, placing itself in the position of granting honours.

In a different spirit, apart the official shows the Red Sea Jazz Festival in Eilat traditionally holds a framework of performance that allows intimate acquaintance and exchange between famous international musicians, Israeli musicians (some already well known, others still in early career stages) and the audience. These are the jam sessions, held in one of Eilat's hotels after the official shows every night of the festival. The jams provide a setting in which highly regarded international and national musicians perform spontaneously together with young and aspiring local musicians, in front of a relatively small audience composed of adoring individuals. The situation thus projects an aura of intimacy and parity between consecrated individuals, artists aspiring for recognition, and worshippers, where hierarchies and national differences are cast aside, and where a communal experience of aficionados is created.

Rites of competition

Some of the festivals feature competitions and prizes as a rite signalling the existence of evaluative criteria and also as a way of giving the festival some sort of authority in the field. By holding competitions and awarding prizes, a festival aims at declaring itself as an event having the power to bestow honour on artists and their works. If successful the festival thus becomes an event to which artists want to bring their works, and the public congregates not just to celebrate and valorize their aesthetic cosmopolitanism in general, but also possibly to witness acts of consecration of works of art.

Of the four festivals discussed here, the most successful in this respect is the Jerusalem International Film Festival. The Wolgin competition, held for the first time in 1989, has become an authoritative event in Israeli film culture over the years. The Wolgin competition for Israeli full-length feature films has succeeded in establishing itself as a mechanism of consecration in the field. Every year the award ceremony is an event that draws much media attention, and it becomes a focal point of the festival, a major ceremony that projects an aura of artistic authority on the festival as a whole. In addition, this rite of competition is commingled with a rite of exchange by regularly inviting individuals from other countries to be members of the jury.

Conclusion

International film and performing arts festivals have proliferated in recent decades. A sociological understanding of this phenomenon with respect to current theoretical perspectives on world culture is long due. Two fruitful ways of examining festivals sociologically have already been pointed out in the case of film festivals. In an illuminating short analysis of a film festival (the Sundance Film Festival), Dayan has demonstrated how the festival framework means different things to different categories of participants. Not exactly one coherent and solid event, the festival fulfils various functions for a variety of groups. Each of these mines the festival for its specific purposes and interests (Dayan 2000). In a more recent study of film festivals, De Valck examines them not as isolated events but as nodes in a network that sustains in multiple ways the existence of different bodies within the film art world, and film as an international cultural institution in general (De Valck 2007). Using four festivals in Israel as an illustration, this chapter offers another sociological perspective, placing international performing arts and film festivals in the context of current theoretical discourse on cosmopolitanism and omnivorousness.

By way of conclusion, then, this perspective will be reiterated and reassessed. Festivals of the type described in this article should be understood as rituals in which class segments of cosmopolitan omnivores assess and celebrate their existence as a taste culture. Festivals function as rituals that valorize the objects of taste and appreciation around which such class segments organize their sense of distinction. Festivals are designed as celebrations of cultural diversity and openness, thus constituting venues and occasions for cultural pilgrimage in which cosmopolitan omnivores can congregate as peers, and appraise and reconfirm conspicuous openness as habitus. In the case of 'small countries', they do so in order to claim recognition for the equal status of local culture in the global frontiers of cultural and artistic innovation. By mixing local performers and works with those of metropolitan countries and initiating collaborations between local and foreign artists, the programmes of festivals in small countries design sequences of performances in which works and aesthetic textures representing national cultural uniqueness are intertwined with those from other countries. Festivals thus provide a setting in which cultural producers and consumers can experience a sense of parity between cultural products from their own countries and those from metropolitan centres, an experience that encourages self-perception as equal participants in world culture.

Performing arts festivals are thus clearly a component of the cultural public sphere, which, 'in the late-modern world' – as McGuigan writes (2005) – 'is not confined to a republic of letters ... and "serious" art, classical, modern or, for that matter, postmodern. It includes the various channels and circuits of mass-popular culture and entertainment' (p. 435). It is a site for the 'articulation of politics, public and personal, as a contested terrain through affective (aesthetic and emotional) modes of communication' (p. 435). Mixing in one event, over a short period of time and in a condensed manner, 'high-brow' and popular, traditional and avant-garde, and especially local and foreign forms of affective expression, festivals contest the nature of national culture. Through their various rites they declare, manifest and advocate aesthetic cosmopolitanism as a major cultural force.

References

Billig, M. (1995) *Banal Nationalism.* London: Sage.

Bourdieu, P. (1993) *The Field of Cultural Production.* Cambridge: Polity.

Choshen, M., Korach, M. and Kaufman, D. (2009) *Jerusalem: Facts and Trends 2007/2008.* Jerusalem: The Jerusalem Institute for Israel Studies (in Hebrew).

Coulangeon, P. (2003) La stratification sociale des goûts musicaux: Le modèle de la légitimité culturelle en question. *Revue française de sociologie* 44(1): 3–33.

Dayan, Daniel (2000) Looking for Sundance: The Social Construction of a Film Festival. In Bondebjerg, I. (ed.) *Moving Images, Culture and the Mind,* pp. 43–52. Luton: University of Luton Press.

De Valck, Marijke (2007) *Film Festivals: From European Geopolitics to Global Cinephilia.* Amsterdam: Amsterdam University Press.

DiMaggio, Paul (2006) Nonprofit Organizations and the Intersectoral Division of Labor in the Arts. In Powell, W. W. and Steinberg, R. (eds.) *The Nonprofit Sector: A Research Handbook,* pp. 432–461. New Haven: Yale University Press.

Falassi, A. (1987) Festival: Definition and Morphology. In Falassi, A. (ed.) *Time out of Time: Essays on the Festival,* pp. 1–12. Albuquerque: University of New Mexico Press.

Fraser, N. (2002) Recognition without Ethics? *Theory, Culture and Society* 18: 21–42.

Hebdige, D. (1990) Fax to the Future. *Marxism Today.* January: 18–23.

Kendall, G., Woodward, I. and Skribs, Z. (2009) *The Sociology of Cosmopolitanism.* London: Palgrave Macmillan.

Lamont, M. and Aksartova, S. (2002) Ordinary Cosmopolitanisms: Strategies for Bridging Racial Boundaries among Working-Class Men. *Theory Culture Society* 19: 1–25.

McGuigan, J. (2005) The Cultural Public Sphere. *European Journal of Cultural Studies* 8: 427–443.

Ollivier, M. (2004) Towards a Structural Theory of Status Inequality: Structures and Tents in Popular Music and Tastes. *Research in Social Stratification and Mobility* 21: 187–213.

Ollivier, M. (2008) Modes of Openness to Cultural Diversity: Humanist, Populist, Practical, and Indifferent. *Poetics* 36: 120–147.

Peterson, R. A. (1992) Understanding audience segmentation: from elite and mass to omnivore and univore. *Poetics* 21: 243–258.

Peterson, R. A. and Kern, R. (1996) Changing Highbrow Taste: From Snob to Omnivore. *American Sociological Review* 61: 900–907.

Regev, M. (2007) Cultural Uniqueness and Aesthetic Cosmopolitanism. *European Journal of Social Theory* 10: 123–138.

Turner, V. (1982) *Celebration: Studies in Festivity and Rituals.* Washington, D.C.: Smithsonian Institution Press.

8 Festivalization, cosmopolitanism and European culture

On the sociocultural significance of mega-events

Maurice Roche

This chapter focuses on 'mega-events', in particular international Expos or World Fairs, in a European context. It interprets their historical growth, institutionalization and contemporary social significance as aspects of cultural modernization and as processes involving the 'festivalization' of European national and international public cultures in the modern era. The discussion builds on the sociology and socio-history of 'mega-event' genres (including, besides Expos, also international sports events, such as the Olympic Games) (Roche 2000; see also references cited in Note 5). Its conceptual framework and terms of reference derive from socio-historical and sociological inquiries into analytic and normative 'cosmopolitan' aspects of European public culture and society (Roche 2007, 2010: ch. 9).

The chapter aims to open up and explore the following key questions. What are 'mega-events', and how do they help us understand the festivalization of European public cultures? How might the understanding of such mega-event-centred processes of festivalization contribute to the understanding of European public culture and society more generally in cosmopolitan terms? These expansive questions can be explored but not comprehensively resolved within the limited compass available here, so the conclusion of the chapter offers some suggestions as to the terrain that remains to be mapped and researched. Guided by the key questions, the chapter is organized into two sections, and it uses both social-theoretical and socio-historical perspectives in the two stages of the discussion. The first section addresses the socio-historical nature and significance of festivals and festive culture in Europe by focussing on mega-events. It discusses their socio-history, and aspects of festivalization related to them in Europe, from the nineteenth century until the present day. The second section considers the implications of these socio-historical discussions of mega-events and their future in relation to the sociological and policy-oriented analysis of contemporary European society. It focuses on the implications of mega-events for cosmopolitan topics in this context.

Europe's histories of nationalism, xenophobia and war provide an unpromising and non-cosmopolitan field for the exploration of cosmopolitan themes (Roche 2010: Chs. 3–5). However, these histories have developed in parallel with complex and communicative histories of trade, cultural exchange and international co-operation, of which the international and supra-national organization of the European Union is the pre-eminent example in the contemporary period. Europe's modern history all too readily presents itself as the non-cosmopolitan process of the organization of discrete nation-states, each with its elites and peoples organizing themselves into distinct 'nations' and 'nationalities' over the course of early and later phases of modernity. Nevertheless, in contrast, Europe has always also retained contrapuntal forms of international and cross-national collective memory, cultural tradition and self-understanding, which we can refer to, in analytical terms, as being 'proto-cosmopolitan' traditions and indeed 'heritages'. Thus, an *analytical* socio-historical issue for the chapter is the following one. How could Europe's mega-event-related processes of festivalization be said to have contributed to the maintenance and renewal of these contrapuntal proto-cosmopolitan traditions? This will be considered mainly in the first section of the chapter. Apart from this analytical issue, there is also the *normative* aspect of cosmopolitanism. This will be touched on in the second section of the chapter. There it will be argued that, in normative terms, a minimal or negative conception of cosmopolitanism is the most appropriate version of it to use in critical review and assessment of aspects of European public culture and society, including festive aspects such as those connected with mega-events.

Overall, taking the analytical and normative themes together, the chapter suggests that mega-event-based festivalization processes can be provisionally assessed to have contributed positively to the development of a proto-cosmopolitan European civil society and can continue to contribute to this in the contemporary period. In this chapter these types of festivalization process are understood to have characteristics and implications both at the structural and at the interpersonal and lifeworld levels. At a structural level, it is suggested that they contribute to the production, dissemination and reproduction of recognizable, trustworthy and potentially enjoyable place identities and to sociocultural space and mobility across Europe. At the lifeworld level, it is suggested that they offer normatively valuable and ontologically significant experiences of hospitality, celebratory co-presence and peaceful coexistence in contemporary European culture and society.[1]

It is a commonplace that festivals and festivalization processes have a very deep history in pre-modern Europe. The existence of religious festive and ritual sites and practices across Europe in prehistoric times has long been the meat and drink of European archaeology. In historical times their social characteristics and societal significance have been well documented and analyzed, particularly for pre-modern classical and medieval periods. However, in contrast to the line of argument in this chapter, the situation might be argued to be more ambiguous with respect to the modern era, whether in relation to Europe or to the West more broadly.

In a challenging study of 'the history of collective joy', for instance, Barbara Ehrenreich has recently argued that festive traditions flourished notably in particular pre-modern periods, particularly in Europe (Ehrenreich 2007). They involved what she refers to as the development and use of 'techniques of ecstasy' in popular festive and carnival-type events. These particularly included the use of such things as rhythmic music, dancing and singing; feasting and drinking to excess; the use of masking or face decoration and costume to change appearance; playing 'the fool', inverting social roles and mocking hierarchy; and generally active and significantly spontaneous participation by audiences and participants en masse. She charts their social and cultural occurrence and importance in the calendars of cultural events across European pre-modern history from classical Greek Dionysian ritual and Roman Saturnalia, through medieval, early-modern and colonial forms of carnival. No doubt Ehrenreich's overall analysis has its internal weaknesses. Arguably, its categories are too capacious and contain too many topics that should be better differentiated, and its historical and onto-logical reach too often threatens to exceed its grasp.

Nonetheless, Ehrenreich's discussion is original and challenging, and it gen-erally provides some support for giving due weight in socio-historical analysis to festive culture and related festivalization processes, particularly in relation to pre-modern society. However, from my perspective and in the interests of this chapter, it is possible to take issue with and to criticize one of Ehrenreich's main theses concerning the role of festival and festive culture in modernity. She argues that festive and carnival-type event forms and their uses of the 'techniques of ecstasy' substantially declined over the long course of recorded history, and particularly into the modern era. Her diagnosis of our contempo-rary period, in Europe or in the West more generally, is that, with some excep-tions, we are in a 'post-festive' era (Ibid.: p. 206).

This 'declinist' analysis of the festive in modern culture and society might be said to carry some echoes of comparable cultural declinist theses associated, on the one hand, with conservative critics of the secularization process and of modernity's alleged impacts on the popularity of religion, and, on the other hand, with Critical Theory and its disdain of the rise of mass and consumer culture. Ehrenreich's 'declinism' in relation to the alleged 'post-festive' character of modern public culture might also be compared with a rather different version of cultural decline in modernity. In his early work, Jürgen Habermas, drawing on British, French and German social history, provided an analysis of the rise and fall of the 'public sphere' in the modern era. The civil society of the new middle class in the late eighteenth and early nineteenth centuries was seen to have created a social space in modern society outside the state and tradition that enabled a distinctive quality of individualistic, liberal and critical communica-tion across both the political and the cultural dimensions of the public sphere. However, as with Ehrenreich's view of the decline in modernity of the Dionysian aspects of public culture on which she focussed, Habermas saw the more Apollonian aspects of the political and cultural 'public sphere' declining under the conditions of the late-nineteenth- and twentieth-century rise of organ-ized capitalism, the mass media and instrumentally rational social systems.[2]

The socio-history of festivalization in the case of mega-events, and of Expos in particular, to be explored in this chapter enables us to develop a critical dialogue with these and other related versions of cultural declinism in modernity. Ehrenreich's claims about the 'post-festive' character of contemporary culture sit awkwardly with her grudging recognition of the otherwise unexplained fact that aspects of contemporary pop music culture and sport culture have a festive character and continue to provide event-based opportunities for engagement in collective joy. In general, over the course of its various phases through to the present, modernity has been marked not by the decline of the festive but rather by the occurrence and recurrence of periods of cultural innovation, and these have involved the creation of new forms of festival.[3]

Habermas's early version of the cultural decline thesis can be judged in retrospect to have generally foundered on the realities of socio-historical development in modernity. The concept of an original middle-class public sphere is an idealization that neglects both the historical particularity of nation-state societies and also their *mixes* of classes, genders and forms of state–people communication. The socio-history of Expos in particular, which we consider in this chapter, attests to the growth and persistence of cultural genres in modernity that provide undoubtedly limited and flawed, but nonetheless real and distinctive, 'public' spaces for popular forms of inter-class and inter-gender, as well as international and cosmopolitan, experience and communication (see Notes 1 and 4). In addition, it points us to the issue of the degree to which, and the ways in which, publics can be convened by cultural events at a transnational level. Perhaps understandably, this is a muted issue in Habermas's original idealization. But evidently it is of major importance for understanding national societies and public cultures in the contemporary period, both in their unavoidable external openness to global influences and their explicitly multi-cultural complexity. The overview and interpretation of mega-events and festivalization processes undertaken in this chapter can help to remind us of this issue.

Europe, modernity and festivalization – mega-events and festive cosmopolitanism

'Festivalization' can be taken to refer to the role and influence of festivals on the societies that host and stage them – both direct and indirect, and in both the short and the longer term. Festivalization processes can be understood as traditions, institutions and genres of cultural performance. These processes operate within social formations and their professional and community networks, and have both historical and contemporary aspects. They do so in relation, in particular, to collective understandings and practices of space, time and agency. That is, festivals can firstly be said to influence societies' collective orientations towards and understandings of social space through their transient celebratory animation of particular locations and thus their influence on collective place identities. Secondly, festivals can be said to influence societies' collective orientations towards and understandings of social time and time-consciousness through the standing and active recognition of their calendars and through the links these calendars offer with memorable and narratable pasts, with the sociocultural rhythm of life in the present, and with anticipated futures. Finally, there is the issue of agency. Of course, festivalization in modernity can be reasonably interpreted as having mainly culturally hegemonic and ideological features and impacts.[4] However, festivals and mega-events can also be interpreted from alternative perspectives, as in the discussion in this particular chapter, emphasizing their positive implications for personal and social agency (e.g. Roche 2000: Chs. 1 and 8; Picard and Robinson 2006). That is, they can be said both to embody and to reanimate the social agency both of those who produce and of those who participate in them, making a sense of theatrical, dramatic and expressive power tangibly available to their engrossed and active audiences as much as to their leading performers.

In this section, then, we consider three questions. Firstly, what are mega-events, and how do Expos in particular illustrate some key features of the 'modern', 'proto-cosmopolitan' forms of festive culture that developed both nationally and internationally in Europe from the mid nineteenth century onwards? Secondly, given the longevity of the Expo genre of international festive culture from the mid nineteenth century to the contemporary period, why was there a generation-long loss of interest in staging them in the immediate aftermath of the Second World War in Europe? Thirdly, why has interest in staging them revived in the contemporary period in Europe?

In relation to the first of our questions, 'mega-events' refers to international public and popular cultural events, particularly the two main genres of international exhibitions or World Fairs (which I will refer to here as Expos) and international sports events (of which the first and still the biggest is the Olympic Games). These cultural event genres were 'invented' in the mid nineteenth century (Expos) and the late nineteenth century (the Olympic Games). Although these genres were ideologically flexible and institutionally relatively frail, they were only abandoned during the years of world war in the twentieth century. Otherwise, they have retained their presence in international and global culture over the course of the major period of modernization and through to the contemporary world. However, occasionally there have been some interesting gaps of one or more decades in this record, the reasons for which will be considered later. They were (and remain) 'modern' international events on a scale that (at least in the West) was historically unprecedented in terms of visitor attendance. Typically running for six months or so, Expos have reliably proved capable of attracting crowds accumulating into the tens of millions over this period. Whilst most visitors would be citizens of the host nation, their international and proto-cosmopolitan character would be evidenced by the fact that a certain proportion of attendees – both people associated with the visiting national exhibitions and international tourists – would also hail from other countries.

Events of these kinds have occurred according to a more-or-less formalized calendar in most of the leading modernizing societies, particularly Britain, France and the USA, since the late nineteenth century, but the list also includes many other nations.[5] Given the concerns of this chapter with the festive and festivalization in modern public culture, it is important to recognize at this stage in the discussion that, whether their appearances suggest this or not, these events and event genres *are* properly characterized as involving *significant* festive elements. That said, it is also fair to say that their particular forms of festive culture were always distinctive to them (and in the terms of this chapter could be said to be 'proto-cosmopolitan') and were not immediately comparable with or reducible to national-level or urban/community-level festivals and carnivals. This is clear enough in relation to the *international* sports genre and sports culture in general, and it has long been evident that international sports events can carry significant political and ideological, as well as cultural, meanings, values and communications. Sports events are structured as dramas with unpredictable outcomes. Sports spectators participate in this public and symbolic drama in proactive and often inexplicably passionate ways – ways peculiar to sports culture that derive from the nature of being 'patriots', being 'fans', being gamblers or taking on a mixture of these roles and identities. Sport is at least a highly visible, and arguably an important, aspect of contemporary public culture. I focus more on the Expo genre and its festive public cultural character, rather than on that of sport, in this chapter – purely for reasons of space.[6]

The festive attraction of Expos for the mass publics that typically attended them was always what we can call their 'infotainment' character. From my perspective, this characteristic can be interpreted as a popular version of elements of the 'cultural public sphere' role to which Expos aspired. So, on the 'information' front, visitors would get to see and celebrate impressive exhibitions of the promise of 'modernity', i.e. power and 'progress', and to some extent or another would experience the drama of being made to feel as if they were 'witnesses to history'. On the one hand, they would experience, interact with and communicate about new developments in the progress of the human technological 'mastery of nature' and the taming of natural forces. On the other, they would experience new technological applications that were perceived as being likely, sooner or later, to change and presumably 'improve' the material living conditions of the mass of the people, people 'like them', middle- and working-class people, 'citizens' even, visiting the Expo. Key examples are, in the nineteenth century, those of electric light, electrification in general and engineering-based architecture (e.g. the Crystal Palace and the Eiffel Tower at the London Expo in 1851 and the Paris Expo in 1889) and, in the twentieth century, the peaceful uses of nuclear power (Brussels 1958). In the field of communications technologies examples are the successive new developments from the telephone to film, to radio and to television.

This kind of informative and educational experience would be presented and received as if it were intrinsically 'fun', a dramatic, festive and celebratory experience in its own right. However, in addition there would be more conventional forms of 'fun' available in the form of fairgrounds and other types of popular entertainment. These were initially located outside, but close to, Expo sites, and Expo visitors could take them in en route to the Expo. However, increasingly they came to be integrated into the Expo concept and into Expo sites. This was particularly so from the late 1880s and 1890s on. At the 1889

Paris Expo commemorating the French Revolution and the founding of the First Republic, the organizers produced a unique and exciting new visitor experience in the form of the vertigo-inducing trip up the newly created Eiffel Tower and the unprecedented views of the great city from the tallest structure humans had ever built. They created an entertaining programme of 'exotic' shows and exhibitions from France's colonies. In addition, it is worth mentioning that the spectacular exoticism of this Expo and its host city was augmented by the fact that William Cody's 'Buffalo Bill Wild West' show also played in Paris at the time of the Expo to mass audiences that included the French president.[7]

The American organizers of the subsequent 1893 Chicago Expo took heed of some of these festive aspects of the Paris Expo in developing their own programme. They also encouraged Cody to stage performances of his great show outside, but alongside, the Expo. The Chicago Expo featured a new 'midway' zone (the 'Midway Plaisance'), incorporated within the Expo site, but distinct from the main national and technological display area (the 'White City'). This zone consisted of a conventional fairground, albeit one on a very large scale. To compete with, but also offer an alternative to, the Eiffel Tower type of experience, the zone also incorporated Thomas Ferris's newly created giant mechanically operated viewing 'wheel' (Rydell 1984). This giant viewing wheel concept, which was rapidly copied across America and Europe, came to characterize the festive culture of modern fairgrounds from the 1890s on (including notably Vienna's Prater Park wheel) and throughout the twentieth century and into the twenty-first as fairgrounds and city centres evolved into Expo-influenced theme parks and tourist zones.[8]

The modern mega-event genres were launched in the mid and late nineteenth century and established themselves as key new elements in the international cultural calendar relatively rapidly through processes of cross-national competition and emulation, copy-catting and leap-frogging. The first international Expo was staged by the British in London in 1851 and prompted the Americans and the French to follow suit in staging Expos in 1853 and 1855 respectively. Expos were staged on a relatively frequent but irregular calendar from that time on. A generation or so later the French-inspired Olympic Movement staged the first of the modern Olympic Games in Athens in 1896. The Movement established a regular four-year calendar for the staging of the Games, and, apart from the uncertainties of the early Olympics, which were staged as parts of Expos (Paris 1900, St. Louis 1904 and London 1908), and the intervention of the world wars, this has operated through to the contemporary period.

The European 'imperial Expos' of the late nineteenth century and interwar period often included spectacular mythologizing pageant-type elements and historical re-enactments. While these may have been influenced by the great example of Cody's American pageant (mentioned above), their contexts were typically national, imperial and European, and not American. In addition, they often included new European cultural innovations. Around the turn of the century, for instance, there were the influential architectural, sculptural and artistic currents associated with European 'Art Nouveau' and 'Modern Art' movements. These found various kinds of expression and presence in European Expos, for instance at the massive French Expo of 1900 in Paris. They also included, from the mid 1920s onwards, Europe's later distinctive artistic and stylistic contributions to Expos deriving from the 'Art Deco' movement, albeit this time alongside comparable, although distinctive, American influences in this tradition.[9]

Having been significantly convergent and even interactive in their mega-event experiences in the late nineteenth century, early twentieth century and inter-war period, European and American experiences noticeably diverged after the Second World War. On the one hand, Europe has staged half as many Expos as has America, and, on the other, it has staged over twice the number of world-level international sports mega-events (Olympics and World Cup soccer competitions). These differences have been particularly significant in relation to Expos. Compared with the irregular periodicity of roughly four to five years between the main Expo events that characterizes European experience in the late nineteenth century and much of the first half of the twentieth century, this periodicity is subject to a major thirty-year, generation-long interruption from *c.*1960 to 1990, before being resumed from the 1990s through to the present. As against this, although the Americans were slow to resume the staging of Expos in the post-war period, they did take it up again during the very period in which the Europeans dropped it, from *c.*1960 to 1990. And, as if to complete the contrast, they then dropped it from the 1990s to the present, the very period in which the Europeans have picked it up again.

The genre has continued to exist and adapt into the twenty-first century and it still appears (with some caveats that we shall consider in a moment) to be a viable one. However, at present this might be more true of developing countries than of developed ones. Indeed it is anticipated (at least it was anticipated before the current global economic recession) that the current Expo, which is being staged in Shanghai in 2010, will attract the greatest number of visitors of any such event in the long history of the genre; the estimate is of around 70 million visits (see Shanghai Expo 2010 in the references list). European and American societies have maintained a consistent and growing interest in staging international sports events over the post-war period and in our times in particular. However, as noted earlier, interest in staging Expos in these societies has periodically dried up for long periods on both continents since the end of the Second World War. Europe's Expo heritage includes its leading role in the initial invention and development of the genre. It also remains the base for the international governing body, the *Bureau International des Expositions* (BIE) in Paris, which categorizes and licenses international Expo events worldwide. However, after effectively only one major international Expo in the early post-war period, that in Brussels in 1958, Europeans appeared to have given up Expos for over 30 years, until one was held in Seville in 1992. Since that time the Expo mega-event genre has reappeared in Europe: in Lisbon in 1998, in Hannover in 2000 and in Zaragosa in 2008, together with the planned Milan Expo in 2015.

We can now turn to the second and third of the questions guiding the discussion in this section. What might help to explain both the initial post-war generation-long Expo gap in Europe and also the more recent return of European enthusiasm for staging Expos? Some provisional factors are connected with dynamics in post-war and contemporary festive public culture and festivalization processes in Europe, linked with what we can refer to (albeit somewhat awkwardly) as 'mediatization' and 'mobilization'. 'Mediatization' denotes in particular the phenomenon readily visible since the 1960s of the growth and universal dissemination of television as a mass medium across Europe, and its sociocultural impacts. In addition, it counsels us to keep a watching brief in relation to the continuing potential of media technologies and their changes to have major sociocultural impacts, a brief we currently need to exercise in relation to the internet and digital media in general. On the other hand, 'mobilization' refers to the phenomenon visible since the 1970s, but growing particularly since the 1990s, of mass international tourism and travel. In Europe this has been made possible by radical changes in travel infrastructures and systems at national, but particularly international, levels. These include almost universal car ownership, the extension of high-speed road networks, the creation of low-cost air carriers and new airports, and the building of long-distance, high-speed train networks. The existence and structural change in such media and transport technologies and infrastructures underpin the initial shift towards a 'mass' consumer culture in Europe from the 1960s to the 1980s, and subsequently the addition of a layer of a more individualized (de-massified) consumer culture overlaying the mass versions and forms since the 1990s. These observations are relevant to understanding Europeans' changing attitudes to the festive culture of Expos in the following ways.

The process of mediatization, which put a television into every household and into the daily lives of every man, woman and child in Europe from the 1960s on, could be said to have rapidly and radically undermined publics' interests in Expos (Roche 2000: Ch. 6). Expos had traditionally offered the masses in modernity unique opportunities to understand their world, and the world being changed around them by industry, technology, science and art, in contexts that were also festive and 'fun'. Television rapidly developed to be able to out-compete Expos on this sort of 'infotainment' territory. It came to offer a daily diet of addictive combinations of information (e.g. news and documentary genres) and entertainment (e.g. soap opera, and varieties of dramatic, comedic and other such genres). The inexorable growth in the inexhaustible daily flow of television culture, together with other social developments in the post-war period, such as the continued expansion of further and higher education, conspired fatally to undermine the rationale for Expos. They could no longer credibly offer the masses in advanced societies critically important arenas for infotainment experiences relating to such things as new and potentially life-changing new technologies, and new and potentially culture-changing art and communication technologies.

On the other hand, sports culture continued to grow in sociocultural significance in terms of what it could offer in the form of dramatic and emotional reassertions of local and national identities. In the new televisual media environment, sports culture and its high-profile mega-events were set to thrive, providing the masses with a new mediated-spectator form of presence at 'live' sports events (Roche 2000: Ch. 6). Add this to Europeans' distinctive sports heritage and interests in international sports, and the balance that had previously held between the two main mega-event genres in the interwar years was set to change dramatically in the early post-war years. The years 1958 and 1960 present something of a turning point in this respect. In 1958 the Brussels Expo presented what could be argued to have been one of the last opportunities to present a radical new technology, i.e. the peaceful uses of nuclear energy, to a mass European public still relatively unconnected with televisual culture. Although this disconnection did not much change until the early 1960s in most countries, nevertheless the televising of the Rome Olympics 'live' in European time zones first revealed the potential power of the new medium to provide mass access to and participation in great international sports events that had previously effectively been the preserve of elites. Overall, then, the coming of the television age effectively wounded and disempowered the Expo genre at the same time that it provided a radical new empowerment to the international sports event genre. The result of this was that a whole generation passed after the 1958 Brussels Expo before another one was staged in Europe.

We can now turn to the third question guiding the discussion in this section. Why did this long gap come to an end, to be replaced in the contemporary period by a considerable interest on the part of European societies and cities in staging Expos? Arguably, this has something do with the second of the factors noted earlier, that connected with the growth of tourism and the touristic mobilization of contemporary culture (Roche 2000: Ch. 5; see also 2009a). Expos may no longer be uniquely compelling arenas for world-changing technologies and thus able to claim the attention of 'the world' and its publics in the way that they once believed they could. Indeed, recent Expos within Europe such as those in Hannover in 2000 and Zaragosa in 2008, whatever the success of their international marketing, seemed to receive very little news coverage outside their host nations. However, they retain their capacity to hold the attention at least of the national publics of the nations that stage them, which in any case have always been the main source of visitors to Expos. In addition, there is the long-term growth of international tourism across the world, particularly in Europe, and the relevance of Expos in this context. National governments and the political leaderships in their major cities attach great importance not only to attracting international investment, but also to adding to the attractions they can offer to international tourists. In the contemporary world, international Expos are useful elements in the repertoire of techniques for upgrading the international marketing and branding of host cities and nations so as to make them appear attractive both to inward investment and to international tourists and their spending power.

This more limited and instrumental role for Expos in Europe in the contemporary period in the light of the promotion of tourism could also be argued to have a side-effect of some use and relevance to the cosmopolitan theme of this chapter. The cosmopolitan theme is less troubling for contemporary international sports events, in which, as we have suggested, Europe has a particular heritage and tradition of interest. The extent and depth of participation in contemporary sports culture in European societies implies that fans of national teams expect to make the effort to travel to provide their support for their team in international competitions – to become sports tourists, particularly if the events take place in Europe. The proto-cosmopolitanism that this involves in terms of the possibilities for peaceful and festive coexistence among people from different nations was well attested to in recent times in the case of the World Cup staged in Germany in 2006. In addition, it would seem that contemporary Expos, even with their instrumental orientations towards attracting tourists, thereby at least offer the prospect of reanimating and enabling versions of a festive proto-cosmopolitan experience. Such versions have at least a family resemblance to the cosmopolitan aspirations and self-images of earlier generations of Expos in North America and elsewhere, but particularly in the European tradition. We now need to broaden the discussion to consider more directly the theme of cosmopolitanism in a European context, together with the relevance of festivalization processes for this theme.

Cosmopolitanism, Europe and mega-events

Cosmopolitanism as a perspective – or, better, a problematic – in social theory and sociology, both in general and in its application to understanding European society and culture,[10] has two aspects. On the one hand there is an analytical aspect, oriented to the understanding of social realities and what *is*. On the other there is a normative aspect, oriented to envisaging a better social world that *ought* to be made real (Roche 2007). The two aspects can be addressed separately or in a connected way. For the purposes of this discussion we shall consider the analytical aspect first and the normative aspect second, emphasizing their connections.

From an analytical perspective, this chapter's review of the mega-event wing of European modern festive public culture suggests that such events can be seen as embodying not only nationalistic and non-cosmopolitan histories, attitudes and practices, but also proto-cosmopolitan ones. In what follows we also need to note how changes in the contemporary period pose new problems of understanding and call for a new generation of inquiries into the nature, dynamics and future of those aspects of European festive culture connected with mega-events. From a normative perspective, we shall focus on what the significance of mega-events might be, particularly for minimalistic interpretations of cosmopolitanism in a European context.

The socio-history of mega-events makes clear how much they are altered by and adapted to their changing social contexts. Of course, 'rust never sleeps'; social change is ongoing in our time and will influence the nature and production of mega-events as we move forward into the twenty-first century. No doubt they will have new implications for the festivalization processes and forms of public culture and cosmopolitanism associated with mega-events. In principle there are many such social structural changes that could reasonably be considered here. These include the geopolitics of the new, multi-polar world order that is emerging in the twenty-first century, particularly with the rise of China, and also the gathering storm of the planet's ecological crisis. However, at this point we should restrict the discussion to the two changes that were touched upon in the second section, i.e. mediatization and touristic mobilization.

For all sorts of cultural, economic and political reasons, people's mobility – whether in the developed world or increasingly also in the developing world, and whether for work or for consumption (tourism) – is highly likely to continue to grow in the twenty-first century, and not least in Europe. In world-regional terms, Europe has long been and remains the world's leading international destination for tourism. Moreover, within its world region Europe's national and cultural diversity, combined with the accessibility of that diversity, sustains high levels of cross-European tourism. These phenomena and tendencies imply that, on the one hand, there is a dynamic felt by national governments, cities and localities, as well as by mega-event producers – to continue to create and invest in festive events as part of their repertoire of tourist attractions. On the other hand, they imply that such strategies are likely to pay off. International tourists will be attracted and events will thus have some basic proto-cosmopolitan character in terms of the composition of their audiences and participants (Roche 2009a, 2009b; Picard and Robinson (eds.) 2006).

The nature of contemporary mediatization involves 'revolutionary' changes towards a digital public culture: a digital information and communication environment, centring on the (now mobile, ubiquitous and increasingly culturally pervasive) internet. The opportunities and challenges that this offers to the production and consumption of mega-events and their associated festive and cosmopolitan aspects present a complicated picture. In relation to the post-war period we pointed out the role of mediatization, in the form of mass television, in transforming the cultural conditions for mega-events. We noted that, at least in Europe, this led to a decline in the staging of Expos and an ascendancy of sports culture and international sports events in the continent's festive culture and calendars. Changes in the dynamics of mediatization continue to present new challenges to the organization of mega-events and their festive culture and influences. The rise of the internet and, within this, of person-to-person and video-streaming services, has the potential to provide a certain limited amount of reanimation to festive events such as Expos. The powerful public cultural hybrid of media-sport emerged in, and resulted from, the mass television era. Governing bodies in the major popular sports took a lead in creating this symbiosis between mass sport and mass television. Their gambles paid off in most cases. They have generally thrived and thus been able to invest heavily in the production of national and international sports events and their festive culture. They have been able to charge premium prices to media companies for the sale of television sports rights and associated intellectual property rights on an exclusive basis. However, the media tide may now be turning.

The contemporary development of the internet, noted above, has also been associated with a rise in 'internet piracy'. This has led to a potentially fatal leaking away of commercial control and rationale in notable cultural fields and industries such as music and film. As the second decade of the twenty-first century opens, it is probable that internet piracy will also, in a similar way, begin to undermine the exclusivity of the television rights to national- and international-level sport and its events, which have traditionally been purchased at such high cost by media companies. The prices achievable for what might become effectively non-exclusive programming content, and therefore the income available for the sports event producers, could decline substantially. The effects of the new dynamics of mediatization, the sharing of festive culture through the internet equivalent of 'word of mouth' communication, could have two divergent impacts on mega-events. On the one hand, Expos might begin to recover in advanced societies, albeit at a lower level than previously. On the other, international sports events, as mass mediated and widely sharable events, could begin to stumble in the new twenty-first-century media environment, which is potentially a hostile one for their organizers.

Finally, there is the explicitly normative dimension of cosmopolitanism and its implications for European public and cultural policy. As we noted earlier in this chapter, European history, society and collective experience have many non- or even anti-cosmopolitan vectors of nationalism, xenophobia and violence running through them as well as contrapuntal proto-cosmopolitan vectors of the kind we have discussed in relation to mega-events. Generally, we need to know more about, as well as to value more, everyday forms of life in Europe involving routine co-presence and mundane forms of civility in the 'actually existing' versions of cosmopolitanism that characterize individualized and culturally fragmented populations, particularly in cities. These include those involved in life in local city-neighbourhoods, the use of public transport and everyday consumer practices. But they also include participation in the public cultural fields of leisure, tourism and sport. Such participation involves sharable public and popular events and event calendars, whether of a political, commemorative, festive or sporting kind, and the reconstruction and evolution of such calendars either within European nations (in order to reflect their multinational, multi-ethnic or multi-religious composition) or beyond the level of the nation and at international European or EU levels. In this chapter I have tried to indicate why the staging of festive mega-events should also be part of this research field.

Each of the main genres of mega-event discussed in this chapter developed traditions of normative public cultural discourse connected with notions such as 'progress', 'civilization' and 'humanity', 'human communication' and 'human co-operation'. These were codified into formal aspirations and ideologies by event-organizing institutions such as the International Olympic Committee (IOC) and the BIE, and by their associated movements. These discourses and ideologies typically have strong cosmopolitan themes running through them, including reference to such concepts as human rights. This is readily visible, for instance, in the elements of 'Olympism' that are typically built into the rituals of opening ceremonies of the Olympic Games. We can refer to these versions of normative cosmopolitanism as being positive, maximalist and utopian. In contrast, it was suggested in the first section that it would be more useful to interpret normative cosmopolitanism in minimalist or negativist terms. This holds in general, and also in terms of the kind of cosmopolitanism we might aspire to seeing mega-events encouraging.

Mega-events and their festivalization processes may or may not have achieved the maximalist cosmopolitan goals they have often claimed to aspire to, whether in Europe or other parts of the world. But the suggestion from the review undertaken in this chapter is that, given Europe's histories of war, oppression and genocide, it would be better and more relevant to investigate and interpret the social roles and influences of such events and processes in minimal or negative cosmopolitan terms. These terms focus on the principle of peaceful coexistence. This requires moral agents to tolerate the actual or potential embodied co-presence of non-threatening others and their participation in a sharable world. In addition, it is also connected with principles that value hospitality in terms of enabling the access of others to conditions of peaceful co-presence.

Conclusion

This chapter addressed the two main mega-event genres of Expos and international sports events, particularly Expos as key cases of the development of festive public culture in Western modernity in general and European modernity in particular. It was suggested that these genres could be understood as involving related processes of festivalization of the national public cultures of event hosts and of international public culture in respect to social space, social time and social agency. The chapter looked into what these cultural developments might be judged to have contributed to understanding European society in cosmopolitan terms. In conclusion we can take a brief look at the challenges implied by the discussion, particularly in the second section above: the research challenges first, and then the normative/policy challenges.

First, what are some elements of the new research agenda facing the study and understanding of contemporary and future mega-events and their associated festive and cosmopolitan influences, particularly in the European context? The chapter suggests that within any such research agenda an important focus needs to be assigned to various kinds of media studies. In the study of festivals, mega-events and festive culture in the twenty-first century, we need to recognize and explore the complex uses being made of various new media systems, both by event producers and by audiences, to enhance the audience experience of events. These include, among others, digital multi-channel television, city-based large-screen public viewing operations, and video-streaming to fixed and mobile internet platforms. Interwar and post-war forms of mediatization already created veneers of cosmopolitanism in the cultural experience of the most parochial members of advanced societies. It is reasonable to assume that the advent of the internet and related new media has radically deepened the penetration of mediated cosmopolitanism into people's everyday experiences of the world, and also that this will be expressed in various new ways in people's interest in, presence at and participation in the festive culture of mega-events. However, the studies that the sociological and related social-scientific community might consider in order to throw light on such assumptions remain to be undertaken; indeed, they remain even to be conceived.

Secondly, how might we understand the potential normative and public policy roles of mega-events and their festive culture in the socio-historical contexts and the contemporary contexts of European society? The chapter suggests that the concepts of European cosmopolitanism and European civil space, in both their analytical and their normative interpretations, can offer ways of helping to understand international mega-events in these terms (Roche 2010: Ch. 9). Such international mega-events, and the network of national and sub-national festive events that they overarch, can be interpreted as having helped to produce and reproduce European civil space in at least the minimally cosmopolitan sense of providing valuable instances and models of peaceful coexistence and co-presence. Such events tend to have some interactional and communicative experiential characteristics for participants. Moreover, they can be interpreted as typically having had normatively positive and celebratory characteristics for the varied publics who visited and participated in them. Such festive event histories, memories and models can provide a basis for popular reflexive and critical discourse about culture and politics. In addition, they can provide encouragement for cultural politics and cultural policy-making in contemporary Europe, both at national and at international or transnational EU levels, to pursue the production of further programmes of such major cultural events.

As Mark Mazower reminds us, Europe's history is as much that of a violent and 'dark continent' as it is that of an enlightened 'civilization'.[11] In the modern period, international mega-events at various stages in modernity have offered Europeans visions and experiences of what they deeply needed to know. This was that a non-threatening 'proto-cosmopolitan' and 'minimally cosmopolitan' European society and culture could be more than an idle wish; that, however transient, it could be a practical and lived reality. In the twenty-first century, Europe and the EU face many new political, economic and cultural challenges. In these uncertain times what is the social and political relevance of the festive culture of mega-event genres? Is its significance reducible to the escapist distractions that appear to characterize so much of contemporary popular culture? Or, in the twenty-first century, can it continue to offer the informed versions of the future and the models of practical proto-cosmopolitan experience that it has so often provided in the past? European citizens might reasonably hope for the latter, and European cultural policymakers could do worse than foster and service that hope.

Notes

1 I interpret the cultural aspects of concepts such as 'the public sphere' in terms of (i) 'public culture' (see Roche 2000: Part 1 *passim*) and (ii) the structural and life-world aspects of mega-events. For a relevant social-theoretical discussion of these latter aspects (see Roche 2000: Ch. 8).

2 See Habermas ([1962] 1991). His early-career 'public sphere' analysis contains a thesis about its historical 'decline' over the course of modernity. For a set of theo-retical and historical critiques of this, see Calhoun (ed.) (1992). The latter also contains some of Habermas's late-career responses to his critics in which he displays a less declinist and more positive perspective.

3 New festivals have been continuously created in modern societies throughout the post-war and contemporary periods, particularly in Europe. For contemporary studies of festival, see, for instance, Picard and Robinson (eds.) (2006) and also the studies in the rest of this book, and other products of the European Commission's Euro-Festival research project led by Gerard Delanty and Liana Giorgi and based at the ICCR, Vienna.

4 See for instance Rydell (1984, 1993); Bennett (1995); Ritzer (1996, 1999); see also Roche (2000 Chs. 2–4; 2001; 2006).

5 On the socio-history of Expos in particular, see Greenhalgh (1988); Roche (1998b, 2000, 2009b); Rydell (1984, 1993); Rydell and Gwinn (eds.) (1994); Rydell and Kroes (2005); Schroeder-Gudehus and Rasmussen (1992).

6 On the relevance of the sport form of public culture for cosmopolitanism in con-temporary Europe, see Roche (2007, 1998a).

7 Cody's highly popular show, while not officially part of the 1889 Paris Expo, none-theless interacted with it in various ways and added to the festive atmosphere in the city at the time. Indian tribesmen from the show, for instance, appeared in costume within the Expo site, and climbed the new Eiffel Tower (Rydell and Kroes 2005).

8 Kasson (1978); Roche (2000: Ch. 5). It is worth observing that this large-scale observational wheel concept, which, like the observational tower concept, was born in the fair aspect of the Expo genre, has recently been updated (initially in the case of London's 'Millennium Wheel' in 2000 and currently in plans for a 'Great Berlin Wheel', etc.) to help characterize the festive character of cities across the world and to brand them as festive destinations for international tourists, thus pro-moting them as potentially proto-cosmopolitan spatio–temporal hubs.

9 For relevant studies of Art Nouveau, see e.g. Greenhalgh (ed.) (2000), and of Art Deco, see e.g. Benton *et al.* (eds.) (2003).

10 On cosmopolitanism in social theory and sociological analysis, particularly in rela-tion to the understanding of European society, see Beck and Grande (2007); Fine (2006, 2007); Roche (2007, 2010: Ch. 9); Rumford (ed.) (2007).

11 Mazower (1998); see also Roche (2010: Chs. 3–5).

References

Beck, U. and Grande, E. (2007) *Cosmopolitan Europe*. Cambridge: Polity.

Bennett, T. (1995) The exhibitionary complex. In his *The Birth of the Museum: History, Theory and Politics*. London: Routledge.

Benton, C., Benton, T. and Wood, G. (eds.) (2003) *Art Deco 1910–1939*. London: V&A Publications.

Calhoun, C. (ed.) (1992) *Habermas and the Public Sphere*. London: MIT Press.

Ehrenreich, B. (2007) *Dancing in the Streets: A History of Collective Joy*. London: Granta.

Fine, R. (2006) Cosmopolitanism and violence: difficulties of judgement. *British Journal of Sociology* 57(1): 49–67.

Fine, R. (2007) *Cosmopolitanism*. London: Routledge.

Greenhalgh, P. (1988) *Ephemeral Vistas: The Expositions Universelles; Great Exhibitions and World's Fairs*. Manchester: Manchester University Press.

Greenhalgh, P. (ed.) (2000) *Art Nouveau 1890–1914*. London: V&A Publications.

Habermas, J. ([1962] 1991) *The Structural Transformation of the Public Sphere*. Cambridge: Polity.

Kasson, J. (1978) *Amusing the Million: Coney Island at the Turn of the Century*. New York: Hill & Wang.

Mazower, M. (1998) *Dark Continent: Europe's Twentieth Century*. London: Penguin.

Picard, D. and Robinson, M. (eds.) (2006) *Festivals, Tourism and Social Change*. Clevedon: Channel View Publications.

Ritzer, G. (1996) *The McDonaldization of Society*. London: Sage.

Ritzer, G. (1999) *Enchanting a Disenchanted World: Revolutionising the Means of Consumption*. London: Sage.

Roche, M. (1998a) Sport, Popular Culture and Identity: An Introduction. In Roche, M. (ed.) *Sport, Popular Culture and Identity*. Aachen: Meyer and Meyer Verlag.

Roche, M. (1998b) Mega-Events, Culture and Modernity: Expos and the origins of public culture. *International Journal of Cultural Policy* 5(1): 1–31.

Roche, M. (2000) *Mega-Events and Modernity: Olympics and Expos in the Growth of Global Culture*. Routledge: London.

Roche, M. (2001) Modernity, Cultural Events and the Construction of Charisma: Mass Cultural Events in the USSR in the Interwar Period. *Cultural Policy* 7(3): 493–520.

Roche, M. (2006) Nationalism, Mega-Events and International Culture. In Delanty, G. and Kumar, K. (eds.) *Handbook of Nations and Nationalism*. London: Sage.

Roche, M. (2007) Cultural Europeanisation and the 'Cosmopolitan Condition': EU regulation and European sport. In Rumford, C. (ed.) *Europe and Cosmopolitanism*. Liverpool: Liverpool University Press.

Roche, M. (2009a) Mega-Events and Micro-Modernization: On the sociology of the new urban tourism. In Page, S. and Connell, J. (eds.) *Event Tourism*. London: Routledge.

Roche, M. (2009b) Cosmopolitanism, Festivalisation and European culture: On the social significance of mega-events. Paper delivered at the 'Public Culture and festivals' international workshop, Euro-Festival Consortium, ICCR, Vienna.

Roche, M. (2010) *Exploring the Sociology of Europe: An Analysis of the European Social Complex*. London: Sage.

Rumford, C. (ed.) (2007) *Europe and Cosmopolitanism*. Liverpool: Liverpool University Press.

Rydell, R. (1984) *All the World's a Fair: Visions of Empire at American International Expositions 1876–1916*. Chicago: Chicago University Press.

Rydell, R. (1993) *World of Fairs: the Century-of-Progress Expositions*. Chicago: Chicago University Press.

Rydell, R. and Kroes, R. (2005) *Buffalo Bill in Bologna: The Americanisation of the World, 1869–1922*. Chicago: Chicago University Press.

Rydell, R. and Gwinn, N. (eds.) (1994) *Fair Representations: World Fairs and the Modern World*. Amsterdam: VU University Press.

Schroeder-Gudehus, B. and Rasmussen, A. (1992) *Les Fastes du Progress: Le guide des Expositions Universelles 1851–1992*. Paris: Flammarion.

Shanghai Expo (2010) World Expo 2010 Shanghai China: Communication & Promotion Plan. Shanghai: Shanghai 2010 World Expo Organising Committee. Available at: http://en.expo2010.cn/expo/expo_english/document/dc/userobject1ai48897/00000000.pdf.

9 Festival spaces, green sensibilities and youth culture

Joanne Cummings, Ian Woodward and Andy Bennett

This chapter examines the significance of contemporary music festivals as a means through which young people gain knowledge of eco-political issues. Beginning with a brief overview of how eco-politics has developed as an aspect of the contemporary music festival, early examples being Woodstock and Glastonbury, the chapter goes on to examine the increasing emphasis on ecological issues at festivals and the various means through which this is enacted. Drawing on aspects of music scene theory, it considers whether greenism within the festival scene is created through the boundary work of the organizers or manifests a developing, translocally dispersed, green ethos centred around alternative, indie and other fringe musics that feature at contemporary music festivals. It considers the possibility that festivals may function as a component of the cultural public sphere: as nodal points for the articulation of a series of developing youth sensibilities and practices centred around environmental awareness and neo-greenist ideology and practice. The chapter concludes by viewing the broader significance of the 'green' festival for youth as a type of cosmopolitan experience pertaining to the construction of sustainable lifestyles and a cosmopolitan outlook grounded in notions of responsible global citizenship.

The festival space as 'green space'

The connection between the music festival and greenist ideology is typically linked to the late 1960s and the emergence of the hippie counterculture (see e.g. Reich 1971). The counterculture, it is argued, became an inspiration for greenism and more eco-friendly youth cultures and festivals (McKay 1998, 1996, 2000) due to the hippie ideals of 'back to the land' communes, anti-urbanization politics and the sharing of available resources (see Webster 2006). The original Woodstock Festival, held on a green field site in Bethnal, upper New York State in August 1969, was widely believed at the time to constitute the consolidation of this hippie ideal. Clothed in the imagery of an alternative hippie community and helped along by songs such as Canned Heat's 'Going Up the Country' and Joni Mitchell's 'Woodstock', the popular representation of Woodstock was as a pastoral Utopia grounded in a wholesale rejection of urban values and lifestyle. Ironically, however, the filmic document *Woodstock: The Movie*, released a year later, suggested that the hippie ethos was not necessarily green or sustainable. During the film scene of Jimi Hendrix's headline performance, by the time of which many festivalgoers had already left, the camera sweeps over the dwindling audience, revealing as it does so huge amounts of rubbish strewn across the festival site (Bennett 2004). A similar contradiction was witnessed in the UK festival scene. Thus, festivals such as the 1974 Stonehenge free festival were allegedly based on eco-politics, the idea of returning to nature and the sun and reclaiming the land for an alternative community. As McKay notes, however, what was often ignored by the festival participants was the question of 'who cleared up the unrecycled glass and rubbish and burnt out cars afterwards' (McKay 2000: 174).

As examples such as these serve to illustrate, despite the interpretation read into festivals as pivotal elements in counterculture's rejection of mainstream society and technocratic rationale (Roszak 1969), in practice these early examples of 'green' festivals lacked both the infrastructure and the practical competence to provide an ecologically sustainable environment. Similarly, once the festivals were over, audiences returned, by and large, to domestic environments in which little or no awareness existed of the processes and principles of green living. Indeed, beyond the countercultural rural communes, very few of which were able to survive beyond a few years, environmental issues and sustainability were scarcely visible as aspects of public and political debate. In many ways, then, the 'back-to-the-land' rhetoric that informed Woodstock and its replicas operates largely at the level of popular myth (Street 2004): part of the repertoire of idealism and romanticization through which the Woodstock generation continues to represent itself as a 'golden age' of youth, music, politics and activism (Bennett 2001).

In the intervening years, focused attention on climate change has prompted greater stress on the need for more environmentally friendly energy forms and sustainable lifestyles (e.g. through the recycling of materials and products). In 1992 the United Nations Conference on Environment and Development (UNCED) put out 'a call for the development of national policies and strategies to encourage changes in consumption patterns' (Hobson 2001: 191). A way to achieve this was through the media promotion of sustainable lifestyles (the World Commission on Environment and Development (1987: 24) having defined sustainability as 'development that meets the needs of the present without compromising the ability of future generations to meet their needs'). The key, it was argued, involved changing consumers' attitudes in order to decrease the amount they consumed and alter the nature of the goods consumed. In the UK, action programmes were set up to encourage households to live sustainable lifestyles, e.g. the 'Action at Home' programme (Hobson 2001). The Action at Home programme is a six-month voluntary scheme endeavouring to change individual households' consumption practices through behavioural changes. Participants in the scheme receive monthly information packs and suggestions on ways to live more sustainable lifestyles. The impact of this programme of the late 1990s can be seen in recent television broadcasts such as *Wasted, Carbon Cops* (Australia), *Dumped* (UK) and *Outrageous Wasters* (UK).

In the current climate of 'environmental crisis' (Houston 2008) and concerns about 'environmental sustainability' (Giblett and Lester 2008), the music festival industry has moved somewhat beyond the utopian ideals of events such as Woodstock and Stonehenge. Armed with knowledge drawn from scientific reports and official policy documents, many contemporary music festivals now seek to stage 'environmentally friendly' and carbon-neutral events that promote the status and attraction of sustainable lifestyles. An important forerunner in this context is Glastonbury, an annual summer festival held in Wiltshire, UK. Established in 1970, over the last three decades Glastonbury has been involved with a range of socio-political causes including the Campaign for Nuclear Disarmament (CND) (1981–90), Greenpeace (1992 onwards) and Oxfam, as well as the establishment of the Green Fields, which is a regular and expanding eco-feature of the festival (from 1984 onwards) (see McKay 2000). Glastonbury's Green Fields are a green space set aside within the festival for presenting and exploring different ideas and solutions to environmental concerns. This space includes workshops, stone circles, experiments in low-impact living and sweat lodges (McKay 2000).

A critical audience base for Glastonbury, and for similar festivals in other national contexts, consists of young people between the ages of 18 and 26. On a global scale, young people have been targets of campaigns aimed at promoting green sensibilities and sustainable lifestyles. In 2004 a survey was conducted by the Australian-based National Youth Affairs Research Scheme (NYARS) into the relationship between sustainable consumption and young Australians (Bentley *et al.* 2004). Significantly, the study identified music festivals as a way of improving the status and attraction of sustainable lifestyles to young people, who were identified as 'agents of social change'. The rationale underpinning this claim by the NYARS was that musicians could play a key role in the symbolism and narrative around sustainable lifestyles and could be used as a means of promoting the status and attractiveness of such lifestyles to young people.

Brooks *et al.* (2007) argue that, while this process of engagement on the part of the music festival industry with environmental sustainability is clearly important, any positive effects continue to be outweighed by the social and ecological impacts of the music festival on the environment. For Brooks *et al.* such impacts are most clearly characterized by 'unsustainable flows of energy and materials between the event, society and the biosphere' (Ibid.: v). They go on to suggest five ways to move the organization of music festivals towards a basis of sustainability; each of these is centred around festival organizers, who play a crucial role in the boundary work of the festival (Dowd *et al.* 2004).

Firstly, argue Brooks *et al.*, festival organizers need to be educated about how strategically to plan for sustainability. Through education they will develop the capacity and confidence enthusiastically to share their vision, goals and actions with suppliers and artists, and will bring the message to the audience at large

(Brooks *et al.* 2007). Secondly, festival organizers will be required to act as the supply chain 'middle man', since they are the point of contact for the numerous and varied stakeholders involved in the festival event: the audience, artists and suppliers (including those of transport and energy systems). For the festival to become sustainable, its organizers depend on the co-operation and creativity of their supply chain. Education and capacity become particularly important in this context as the festival organizer conveys the sustainability message in a way that seems achievable in the short term and beneficial in the long one.

Thirdly, it is necessary for the festival organizer to form strategic alliances, since there is great potential for music festival organizers to join together to shift the attitudes of their key stakeholders and society at large. Festival organizers by combining might send a clear message to stakeholders that 'this is the direction the industry is going' (Brooks *et al.* 2007). Fourthly, it is essential that the festivals are profitable, with regulatory or financial signs supporting sustainable development; this could provide greater assurance that sustainability initiatives and modifications to supply chain practices will be supported and viable (Brooks *et al.* 2007). Finally, it is necessary for there to be a realization of potential through the resonance of messages promoted among the broader community at the festival. With music festivals at the cutting edge of social and artistic expression, there is great potential for stakeholders, particularly artists and audience, to receive and act on sustainable ideas and initiatives (Brooks *et al.* 2007).

Concerns about the sustainability and environmental impacts of festivals may often be short lived, as these issues usually only arise while the festival is running and are often overlooked afterwards. The music festival industry is, however, starting to adopt 'green' policies in all aspects of planning its events. In 2006, A Greener Festival was set up to promote sustainable events and environmentally friendly music and arts festivals. This not-for-profit organization promotes an annual awards scheme in collaboration with the UK festival awards. The awards are based on a seven-part questionnaire covering event management, travel and transport plans, CO_2 emissions, fair trade, waste management and recycling, water management and noise pollution. Points are awarded for festivals that can display an active plan to promote public transport, reduce on-site waste, recycle and compost wherever possible, reuse water and resort to sustainable power. Festivals are expected to have a coherent environmental policy, and A Greener Festival has environmental auditors who visit as many festival sites as possible to assess how festivals implement their plans (AGreenerFestival.com 2008).

Formulating green festivals' policy and practice

Although there has been vibrant discussion relating to the capacity of music festivals to promote issues pertaining to the environment and sustainability among young audiences, to date no research has comprehensively documented the effectiveness of music festivals in promoting eco-awareness and sustainable lifestyles among young people. However, formative research by one of the authors concerned with music festivals has begun to engage with this issue by focusing on a number of contemporary music festivals in Australia that promote a green ethos (Cummings 2006, 2007). The five examples considered in this research are Peat's Ridge Festival, Big Day Out, Splendour in the Grass, the Falls Festival and Homebake. Research conducted at these five festival sites indicates that the music festival industry is a front runner in experimenting with using 'sustainable' sources of energy and promoting the 'carbon neutral' cause as part of its narrativization of the festival experience for visitors. The research further suggests that the music festival industry is now actively beginning to promote corporate and community responsibility by improving the status and attraction of sustainable lifestyles for young people.

Each of these festivals will now be examined in turn, and it will be shown how each has adopted 'green' policies. The following section will cover each festival's goals, aspirations and actions towards making itself 'greener', based on the organizers' own advertising and public statements and the ethnographic fieldwork conducted by one of the authors. Later in the chapter, the function and meaning of such discursive formations about the green festival will be critically examined.

Peat's Ridge Festival

The Peat's Ridge Festival, held annually on a farm in Glenworth Valley, New South Wales, was established in 2004 and is an illustrative example of how to produce a sustainable festival. In 2006 an environmental audit of the festival was undertaken by the University of New South Wales's Eco Living Centre, which examined the way the festival approached sustainability and environmental management. The results of this audit were used for the first time at the 2008 festival. Peat's Ridge aims at becoming a 'model event' and a paradigm for other festivals. The 2009 website contained detailed information on how the festival implemented sustainable practices, including the types of intervention (e.g. composting toilets or solar power), costs, logistics, information and resources, tips and supplier details (Peat's Ridge Festival 2009). Some of the industry's leading initiatives in practice at the festival include:

> 100% bio-diesel generators, odour-free composting toilets, grey water management, container deposit system, organic waste composting, reclaimed materials for decoration, certified organic food at the stalls, bio-degradable cutlery, onsite bike couriers, natural ink printing, chemical-free cleaning product.
>
> (Peat's Ridge Festival 2008)

The Big Day Out

The Big Day Out (BDO) is an annual national touring festival first held in 1992. After conducting two energy audits of the show, in 2008, the organizers decided to go 'carbon neutral'. They planted 6,750 trees, which earned them carbon credit, and they aim to continue the event as 'carbon neutral' in the future. The BDO approach is different from that of Peat's Ridge, as they are not aiming for sustainability but rather 'carbon neutrality'. The BDO's 'Clean and Green' promotion used the catchphrase 'reduce, recycle and offset'. In 2009, BDO patrons were offered the opportunity to reduce their carbon emissions for the day by purchasing a Green ticket (this has been done successfully in the past by Splendour in the Grass and by festivals overseas). The carbon offset is achieved by planting native Mallee Eucalyptus trees (Big Day Out 2008a, 2008b). Additionally, in 2008 the BDO's Lilly World stage had a carbon offset/ climate change theme and encouraged festivalgoers to reduce their carbon consumption by purchasing a 'green' t-shirt. They also expanded the recycling programme to all cities on the tour with the aim of 80 per cent recyclability across all shows by 2010. The festival also encouraged festivalgoers to 'reduce, recycle and offset' in their everyday lives, urging them to:

[u]se less power, cut down on your car use, talk it up (vote/political action), buy less, compost all organic waste, support local, global and national environmental groups, and offset your personal emissions.

(Big Day Out 2008a, 2008b)

Splendour in the Grass

Splendour in the Grass is an annual winter festival held in Bryon Bay, New South Wales. In 2008 the Splendour in the Grass festival sold 4,091 (23 per cent of the audience) green tickets. The green ticket initiative was a result of the partnership between the festival and its sponsor 'Climate Friendly' (Splendour in the Grass 2008a). In addition, Climate Friendly hosted a 'green space' at the festival, which provided recycled beanbags, free cups of Fair Trade organic tea, the latest in sustainable gadgets, soaps, bags and information from influential climate change organizations such as Friends of the Earth, the Wilderness Society, Greenpeace, World Wildlife Fund and the Australian Conservation Foundation. Festivalgoers who missed out on green tickets were able to purchase a recycled, ethically made fabric 'I like my music loud and green' patch. The patch cost seven dollars and offset two days' worth of the festivalgoer's carbon emissions (Splendour in the Grass 2008a).

Like the other festivals, Splendour in the Grass operates a recycling initiative where festivalgoers are encouraged to recycle all beverage containers. For every five cans or bottles recycled the festivalgoer receives one drink ticket. Another green initiative at Splendour in the Grass is the presence of Eco Cops (similar to the Eco Cops at the Glastonbury festival), who patrol the festival grounds and encourage visitors to recycle. They provide the festivalgoers with information about the festival's green policies and promote the festival's 'Binyabutt' campaign, which encourages people not to litter with their cigarette butts by giving away free pocket-sized ashtrays made from recycled film canisters (Splendour in the Grass 2008b).

The Falls Festival

The Falls Festival is a dual-site festival held simultaneously in Lorne, Victoria and Marion Bay, Tasmania. It aims at creating a positive environmental impact by applying extensive environmental practices to a significant population over three days. The organizers aim to minimize the impact of the festival on the local environment and make improvements to existing conditions where possible. They also aim to reach beyond the festival by using it as an opportunity to pass on important information and ideas to the wider community (Falls Festival 2008).

Initiatives undertaken by the Falls Festival include developing a recycling programme similar to that of Splendour in the Grass, and their aims are also reflected in their policies for caterers and other stallholders (who must supply biodegradable cutlery and recyclable packaging) and the provision of composting/waterless toilets (which save well over 50 kl of fresh drinking water at each event). The festival supports ongoing enhancement and protection projects on its own and surrounding sites (including tree planting, fencing and track work). Surveys are carried out to identify threatened or protected wildlife and flora in the surrounding areas so that they can be monitored and protected from human disturbance. The festival also promotes educational activities for developing awareness, respect and the ongoing protection of both the local and the global environment. During the event the organizers aim to give festivalgoers as much information as they can via their website, the event guide available, signs, the super screen and specially trained staff (Falls Festival 2008).

Homebake

Homebake is a Sydney-based festival held annually in the Domain. The Homebake Festival runs a recycling initiative in partnership with its sponsor Slate Bourbon, which started in 2008. The scheme used at Homebake is different from that of Splendour in the Grass. When visitors buy a beverage served in an aluminium can or PET bottle, a $1 deposit is included in the price. When they recycle their containers, they each receive a drink voucher for $1. At the end of the night, when the festivalgoers return their last drink containers, the recycling staff return the original $1. Prior to this initiative Homebake had recycling bins scattered around the festival site, but this proved to be less effective than the drink ticket system due to cross-contamination of the bins (email to the author, 17 November 2008).

On the surface, at least, it appears that festivalgoers have welcomed the green changes to festival culture. A recent survey conducted by Buckinghamshire New University has shown that festivalgoers want green events. Researchers surveyed 1,407 festivalgoers across Europe (500 visitors in the UK, 600 in Finland and 330 in Germany and the Netherlands). When asked about environmental issues, over 80 per cent of the festivalgoers thought that noise, waste and traffic had negative impacts. Festivalgoers were also aware of a rise in CO_2 emissions, and 48 per cent of the visitors would pay more for greener events, whilst 36 per cent of them said that having a green policy was important to them when buying a ticket. Overall, the UK festivalgoers were found to be greener than European ones (AGreenerFestival.com 2008). This research provides a good starting point for further studies to be conducted on festivalgoers' reception of green issues and the eco-political content of festivals.

Green festival sites and global cosmopolitan awareness

Dowd *et al.* (2004) suggested that music festivals provide a unique social space within which to express oneself and to experience and experiment with different identities (see also Cummings 2008). At one level, then, the contemporary music festival could be regarded as a site of what Bakhtin (1984) refers to as carnival forms of behaviour. Freed from the routines of mundane everyday life and the embedded strictures of civil society, individuals are free to reinvent themselves in the context of the festival space. At the same time such carnival qualities of the festival space may lend themselves to the free flow of alternative discourses, practices and sensibilities. Peterson and Bennett (2004) have argued that music scenes, rather than defining specific, locally situated events, might better be theorized as linking spaces or nodal points for translocally dispersed audiences sharing similar musical tastes, political and/or aesthetic values. Viewed in this context, the green festival space may serve as a site in which a global consciousness of environmental issues and global awareness are manifested and further developed among a translocal young adult audience. The idea of an emergent, outward-looking and globally reflexive cosmopolitan form of citizenship might be a useful way of thinking about the nature of festivals in general, as well as the emergent practice of 'greening' festival scenes in particular. As sites for the diffusion of cultural ideas and goods, festivals become effective spaces for cultural exchange and learning as much as they are spaces of visceral celebration, performance and the carnivalesque. These types of learning can be cultural, in the sense of learning about new music, musical styles and aesthetic codes, or they can also relate to learning about social and environmental issues through informal processes, or via the design and infrastructure of the festival itself. Festivals, then, are an important contemporary vehicle of the cultural public sphere (McGuigan 2005). At their surface they are about entertainment, participation and pleasure, but they also offer opportunities to experience and reflect on crucial issues related to a variety of social and personal themes.

Cosmopolitanism is derived from an ancient Greek term meaning a 'citizen of the world'. In recent social and cultural theory the concept has been used in a variety of ways, but frequently it is used to refer to a growing trend of receptiveness and openness towards the other. It is an ethical stance – experienced through and stimulated by immersion in a variety of everyday cultural domains such as music, travel or food – in which the individual tries to empathize with and connect beyond those nearest to him or her and endeavours to see the value of difference, working towards the possibility of connection and dialogue with the cultural other. Cosmopolitanization also involves a dimension where local interests come to be seen in the context of regional and local needs. Though we often just think of other people as part of the cosmopolitan universe, the cosmopolitan frame can be extended to include the environment and other non-human elements that form the spatial settings for the performance of cosmopolitan ethics and values. In bracketing the appeal of the local and the familiar, cosmopolitans de-privilege their local situation and look outward to see differences as an opportunity for connection with diversity and difference as the basis for learning and reflection, rather than as a pretext for separation. As sites of collective, visceral aesthetic experience, festivals become social spaces for learning and experimentation, where the potential for cosmopolitan experiences is in part encouraged by the 'architecture' and design of the festival itself.

Cosmopolitanization processes are generally seen as a result, in part, of the globalization of ideas, objects and people, though this global dimension is not always a requirement for being cosmopolitan. In theory, at least, the increased global flows of these things create a hybridized world in which identification with the local and parochial becomes less valued and less necessary, and, in fact, among specific status groups, sole immersion in the local is a symbol of narrow mindedness, unless such local action can be reinterpreted through a global lens. Awareness of global issues such as human rights, environmental topics and economic inequality is one of the hallmarks of the cosmopolitan individual, so, in this sense, cosmopolitanization is often thought of simplistically as the 'good face' of globalization. More importantly, in the cosmopolitan model awareness translates into forms of ethically motivated action. Many spheres of life, not just institutional politics but also leisure, including a variety of consumption fields such as music, food and travel, come to reflect, and also serve to diffuse, a cosmopolitan ethic of openness and interest in cultural difference. An important component of this includes the way an individual feels connected to ecological processes. Cosmopolitan individuals are likely to interpret their everyday actions within a global frame and to have an understanding of the nature of person–environment interactions. This type of understanding is particularly important among young people, who are more likely to feel strongly about environmental impacts on a range of levels. Music festivals thus cater to the environmental concerns of these young people in order to provide a narrative frame for 'proper' and ethical ways to consume the festival, which itself could easily be susceptible to re-narrativization by visitors and society in general as an environmentally unfriendly mega-event. Through their management festivals also partly construct and define the nature of the environmental risk itself, and in doing so offer plans of action to alleviate personal and collective impacts, thereby reassuring festivalgoers that environmentally sound principles guide the planning and management of the festival they are attending.

The nature of the link between emergent forms of cosmopolitan citizenship and festival attendance raises the broader issue of how media, leisure and consumption experience relate to ethical action, particularly cosmopolitan action. Szerszynski and Urry (2006) point to the role of iconic events and media spectacles – globally presented and reported – which help to present cultural difference, while at the same time fostering a sense of global identification and belonging. Citing Anderson's (1983) work on collective belonging, they suggest that identifications of global citizenship can be fostered through the global imagery and narratives found in diverse media. Such representations point to the ways people can empathize with or become curious about culturally different experiences or about the suitable and necessary responsibilities of global citizenship. Global media spectacles, for example, are an important way of communicating such collective belonging by identifying the local as only one of multiple sites of belonging. In this sense, environmental awareness becomes an important dimension for identifying the links between the local and the global.

As one prominent iteration of contemporary affective media (McGuigan 2005), music festivals are more broadly associated with lifestyle and identity, community and ethical–political action, as well as simply being about the collective enjoyment of live music. For this reason we need to consider the relationship between consumptive and ethical forms of cosmopolitanism. Does consuming festivals, for example, become a pathway to fostering cosmopolitical ethics? On this general matter, Szerszynski and Urry (2002) suggest that the selling of mundane, commodified forms of cosmopolitan lifestyle may go hand in hand with more fundamental and progressive, social-structural changes. That is, rather than being merely superficial features and apparently trivial aspects of globalization, they do, in fact, have an important symbolic value and are the harbingers of wider social changes. On the side of leisure and lifestyle, we have middle-class lifestyle forms such as travel shows and newspapers based on food, adventure and dimensions of luxury and discovery; on the political and economic side, daily news devotes itself to international events, traumas and dramas that can either suggest to us that we need to cocoon and insulate ourselves further from the world or can encourage us to take action to confirm our own investment in the global meaning of social action.

The contemporary music festival could perform a role much like that of coffee houses, salons and *Tischgesellschaften* in the emergence of a public sphere during the seventeenth and eighteenth centuries, as an incubator for the articulation of ideas and movements related to the recognition of cultural and environmental equality (Habermas 1989). Likewise, as Nava (2002) shows in her study of Selfridge's department store in the nineteenth century, openness in these consumption settings was effectively performed through advertising, store facilities and layout and promotions. Although this was a deployment of cosmopolitanism related to the growth of modern consumer cultures, representations of luxury, hedonism and display and the presentation of conspicuous signifiers of identity, Nava argues that this does not necessarily diminish its critical or transformative efficacy as a cosmopolitan cultural text. Sociologists are often sceptical about the capacity of such experiences to engender critical and transformative capacities in consumers, though such an idea must be subjected to closer empirical study by researchers. By combining commercial and commodified cultural forms with celebratory and visceral forms of community pleasure, music festivals have much potential to be meaningful. As McGuigan comments in relation to the affective communications at the heart of the cultural public sphere:

> Affective communications help people to think reflexively about their own lifeworld situations and how to negotiate their way in and through systems that may seem beyond anyone's control on the terrain of everyday life. The cultural public sphere provides vehicles for thought and feeling, for imagination and disputatious argument, which are not necessarily of inherent merit but may be of some consequence.
>
> (McGuigan 2005: 435)

The sonic and visual cultural production at the heart of the music festival can be an effective carrier for the development of cosmopolitan viewpoints, insofar as it affords ideas of trans-national interconnectedness and global citizenship not just through the music but also through its design and facilities. At least it can possibly represent new ways of being with the cultural other or – through the pleasurable embodied practices of listening or dancing – engender a new respect for other cultures and lifestyles, and environmental responsibility. Furthermore, through the more rigorous environmental protocols festival promoters are now meeting (partly by observing legislative and environmental requirements, but also partly to convince the festivalgoer of their environmental credentials), festivals promote themselves as a small part of the response to global environmental problems.

But we also need to treat such claims with a degree of methodological reflexivity and have due regard for questions of the everyday reception and use of such imagery and objects. First, we need to countenance the possibility of moral indifference to these forms of representation (Stevenson 2003: 116). Stevenson summarizes these debates effectively. He points to Tester's (1999) argument that the world awash with sounds and images from 'elsewhere' and replete with the ethical agendas of others actually creates a blasé attitude amongst consuming audiences. In the case of news and visual media audiences may perceive images of environmental destruction, for example, but see them as an unpleasant window into other people's worlds, a window that can thankfully be quickly shut to protect one's comfort and emotional balance. Rather than being a cosmopolitan 'bridge', they are an ambivalent 'door', which can be closed to protect those offended (disgusted) by the consumption of visual unpleasantness. Using the example of global charities, Stevenson admits that such events putatively tap into latent cosmopolitan attitudes, potentially helping people to see their connections and responsibilities to others. Yet there is rarely a deep engagement with the systematic causes of inequality, of cultural difference, one's own moral responsibility and a deeper ethic of solidarity based upon a complex understanding of hospitality and responsibility. It is similar with the festival; engagements may be partial and temporary, failing to generate the deep emotional bonds necessary to effect change. On the other hand, they may not, and this is where sensitive and skilled ethnographic and observational research is required.

Conclusion

Further research needs to be undertaken to address the connection between music festivals and environmental sustainability. Though it represents an intriguing, topical empirical and theoretical question, sociological research into the issue of youth, music festivals and environmentalism has been lacking up to now. Further study is needed in order to investigate whether there is a connection between 'green' music festivals and young people's decision making when it comes to alternative consumption and sustainable lifestyles. That is, to what extent are a festival's green credentials an issue for visitors that might influence their attendance patterns? In line with recommendations from the NYARS report, further research also needs to explore the link between young people's consumption practices and sustainable lifestyles (Bentley *et al.* 2004: 86). Thus, the longer-term impact of the greening of festivals is a pertinent question in terms of its association with broader patterns of green and ethical consumption. How might the greening process affect the way festivals are managed and organized? Are the discourses and narratives associated with festivals, particularly youth festivals, changing to accommodate greening imperatives, and how might this alter the types of festivals to be run in the future? Finally, might it be that attendance at music festivals will become an important venue for generating an ethics of green consumption among young people?

Over the last decade, the post-subcultural turn in youth cultural research (see, e.g., Bennett 1999; Muggleton 2000; Bennett and Kahn-Harris 2004) has emphasized the increasing diversity and fluidity of youth cultural groups, in which aspects of musical taste and attendant aesthetically informed cultural practices provide platforms for sociality. In this context the contemporary music festival is becoming an important nodal site for the congregation of an audience drawn from diverse translocal and, increasingly, global locations. This critical transition in the ways that youth cultural practice is now understood currently lacks any clear political dimension in its mode of inquiry and explanation. The theoretical and empirical issues explored in this chapter offer a critical insight into how a post-subcultural politics of youth may begin to take shape – one in which a series of pertinent issues, relating to the environment, sustainability and global citizenship, is placed at the centre.

References

AGreenerFestival.com (2008) Music fans want green events. Press release, February 2008, from http://agreenerfestival.com/

Anderson, B. (1983) *Imagined Communities: Reflections on the Origin and Spread of Nationalism*. New York: Verso.

Bakhtin, M. (1984) *Rabelais and His World* (Trans. by Iswolsky, H.). Bloomington: Indiana University Press.

Bennett, A. (1999) Subcultures or Neo-Tribes?: Rethinking the Relationship Between Youth, Style and Musical Taste. *Sociology* 33(3): 599–617.

Bennett, A. (2001) *Cultures of Popular Music*. Buckingham: Open University Press.

Bennett, A. (ed.) (2004) *Remembering Woodstock*. Aldershot, Hampshire: Ashgate.

Bennett, A. and Kahn-Harris, K. (eds.) (2004) *After Subculture: Critical Studies in Contemporary Youth Culture*. London: Palgrave.

Bentley, M., Fien, J. and Weil, C. (2004) *Sustainable Consumption: Young Australians as Agents of Change*. National Youth Affairs Research Scheme.

Big Day Out (2008a) Ambience. Clean and green – what can you do? Retrieved 04/08/2008, from www.bigdayout.com/ambience/cleangreenwhatcanyoudo.php

Big Day Out (2008b) Ambience. Clean and green – BDO statement. Retrieved 04/08/2008, from www.bigdayout.com/ambience/cleangreenbdostatement.php

Brooks, S., O'Halloran, D. and Magnin, A. (2007) *Rock on!: Bringing Strategic Sustainable Development to Music Festivals*. Karlskrona, Sweden: Blekinge Institute of Technology.

Cummings, J. (2006) It's More than a T-Shirt: Neo-tribal Sociality and Linking Images at Australian Indie Music Festivals. *Perfect Beat* 8(1): 69–84.

Cummings, J. (2007) We're all in this Together. The Meanings Australian Festivalgoers Attribute to their Music Festival Participation. In Kallioniemi, K., Kärki, K., Mäkelä, J. and Salmi, H. (eds.) *History of Stardom Reconsidered: The Referred Proceedings of the Inaugural Conference of IIPC*. University of Turku, Turku: International Institute for Popular Culture.

Cummings, J. (2008) Trade mark registered: Sponsorship within the Australian Indie music festival scene. *Continuum: Journal of Media and Cultural Studies* 22: 675–685.

Dowd, T. J., Liddle, K. and Nelson, J. (2004) Music Festivals as Scenes: Examples from Serious Music, Womyn's Music and SkatePunk. In Bennett, A. and Kahn-Harris, K. (eds.) *Music Scenes: Local, Translocal and Virtual*. Nashville, TN: Vanderbilt University Press.

Falls Festival (2008) Environment. Retrieved 14/11/2008, from http://www.fallsfestival.com.au/htmlsite/environment.php?locCode=LO&pgCode=env

Giblett, R. and Lester, L. (2008) Environmental Sustainability. *Continuum* 22(2): 167–170.

Habermas, J. (1989) *The Structural Transformation of the Public Sphere: An Inquiry into a Category of Bourgeois Society*. Cambridge: Polity.

Hobson, K. (2001) Sustainable Lifestyle: rethinking barrier and behavioural change. In Cohen, M. and Murphy, C. (eds.) *Exploring Sustainable Consumption: Environmental Policy and the Social Sciences*. New York: Elsevier.

Houston, D. (2008) Crisis and Resilience: Cultural methodologies for environmental sustainability and justice. *Continuum* 22(2): 179–190.

McGuigan, J. (2005) The Cultural Public Sphere. *European Journal of Cultural Studies* 8(4): 427–443.

McKay, G. (1996) *Senseless Acts of Beauty*. London: Verso.

McKay, G. (1998) *DiY Culture. Party and Protest in Nineties Britain*. London: Verso.

McKay, G. (2000) *Glastonbury: A Very English Fair*. London: Victor Gollancz.

Muggleton, D. (2000) *Inside Subculture: The Postmodern Meaning of Style*. Oxford: Berg.

Nava, M. (2002) Cosmopolitan Modernity: Everyday Imaginaries and the Register of Difference. *Theory, Culture and Society* 19(1–2): 81–99.

Peat's Ridge Festival (2008) Sustainability. Retrieved 21/10/2008, from http://www.peatsridgefestival.com.au/home.asp?pageid=E7504F407896B639

Peat's Ridge Festival (2009) Sustainability. Retrieved 03/12/2009, from http://www.peatsridgefestival.com.au/index.php/sustainability

Reich, C. A. (1971) *The Greening of America*. Middlesex, England: Allen Lane.

Roszak, T. (1969) *The Making of a Counter Culture: Reflections on the Technocratic Society and its Youthful Opposition*. London: Faber and Faber.

Splendour in the Grass (2008a) Enviro Initiatives. Retrieved 12/11/2008, from http://www.splendourinthegrass.com/page.php?name=enviroinitiatives

Splendour in the Grass (2008b) Green Space. Retrieved 12/11/2008, from http://www.splendourinthegrass.com/page.php?name=greenspace

Stevenson, N. (2003) *Cultural Citizenship. Cosmopolitan Questions*. Buckingham: Open University Press.

Street, J. (2004) "This is your Woodstock": Popular Memories and Political Myths. In Bennett, A. (ed.) *Remembering Woodstock*. Aldershot: Ashgate.

Szerszynski, B. and Urry, J. (2002) Cultures of Cosmopolitanism. *Sociological Review* 50(4): 461–481.

Szerszynski, B. and Urry, J. (2006) Visuality, Mobility and the Cosmopolitan: Inhabiting the World from Afar. *The British Journal of Sociology* 57(1): 113–131.

Tester, K. (1999) The Moral Consequentiality of Television. *European Journal of Social Theory* 2(4): 469–483.

Webster, C. (2006) Communes. In Jefferson, T. and Hall, S. (eds.) *Resistance through Rituals. Youth Subcultures in Post War Britain* (2nd edn.). London: Routledge.

World Commission on Environment and Development (1987) *Our Common Future: The World Commission on Environment and Development*. Oxford: Oxford University Press.

10 Cannes

A French international festival

Jérôme Segal and Christine Blumauer

> The festival is an apolitical no-man's land, a microcosm of how the world
> would be if people could have direct contacts and speak the same language.
> (Jean Cocteau)

As an idealistic project for conflict resolution, it is said that the Cannes Film
Festival is part of the public sphere, as Jean Cocteau asserted in 1954. The
quotation remained on the front cover of the festival statutes until the mid
1980s. Yet the history of the festival does not entirely fit in with this idealistic
framework – neither at the time of its inception nor later. Instead, the Cannes
festival is exemplary of the way in which film and the arts more generally are
entangled with political and economic interests in addition to representing an
arena for debating the meaning and scope of cultural values within national and
international frameworks. Furthermore, these debates during a film festival
constitute a good example of affective modes of communication, both aesthetic and emotional, in the cultural public sphere (McGuigan 2005).

From the very outset, the Cannes Film Festival was an official event and
financed by state subsidies. Struggles for supremacy characterized the beginnings
of the festival: which city would host it? Where would the money come from?
What was it to stand for in comparison with other festivals such as Venice?
How was it to be organized in a way to foreground French interests without
vexing other participants, especially the United States? The festival faced many
challenges, and its foundation was the result of a subtle and patient diplomatic
tightrope act. In the context of the Cold War especially, Cannes was used as a
framework for informal confidence-building meetings between representatives
from both sides of the Iron Curtain or, at least, from both Superpowers, the
USSR and the USA.

Over time, diplomatic and state priorities gave way to cultural and economic
considerations. In the late 1950s and early 1960s new forms of film-making
emerged, chiefly the *Nouvelle Vague* and the '*cinéma d'auteur*', and these came
to compete with more traditional film styles that enjoyed greater state support
and were more likely to pass the official screening. Both the shifting identity
inherent in the concept of a festival and the celebration of an art form that
defines itself through movement and the contraction of space and time imbued

the Cannes Film Festival with a dynamism of its own. At the same time the festival was subjected to external influences such as socio-political changes and shifts in the perception of what cinema was intended to be and to do.

Jean Cocteau's ideal, as quoted above, may never be fully reached. Yet, over time, the festival has created a space for new generations of film directors from all over the world, and this has imparted to it a cosmopolitan atmosphere. Internationalism and multiculturalism coexist in Cannes. They centre on the '*cinéma d'auteur*', enabling movie productions to be screened that would have difficulties reaching an audience otherwise. The two pillars of the festival, the official selection and the parallel sections, illustrate this coexistence. The first pillar, the official selection, guarantees that stars will show up on the red carpet and provides the glamorous side of Cannes with its international reputation as a major official event. The parallel sections, on the other hand, facilitate the advent of new generations of film-makers from all over the world and give the public the opportunity to discover films from different countries. This second pillar guarantees intercultural dialogue, as it is the window to other film industries and hence other cultural arenas.

The main question is that of legitimacy between tradition and innovation. This very balance will be at the centre of the present analysis on a journey through the history of the Cannes Film Festival. The four stations of this journey will illustrate the importance of this festival for the cultural public sphere: first the role played by France in the map of world cinema, then the shift from films perceived as cultural objects to films regarded as having cultural value, after that the consequences of the unrest of 1968 and finally Cannes Film Festival's present role as a stage for world cinemas.

Putting France on the map of world cinema

The Cannes Film Festival was founded in reaction to the *Mostra*, the Venice Film Festival, which had come under Fascist control in the late 1930s. In Venice, cinema was added to the Biennale in 1932 and was the target of political intrigue from the very beginning. In 1937 Mussolini interfered to ensure that the pacifist film by Jean Renoir, *The Big Illusion*, would not receive an award. A year later, in September 1938, Hitler and Mussolini respectively overruled the jury's decisions in favour of an Italian film produced under the supervision of Mussolini's son, and Leni Riefenstahl's *Fest der Völker*, dealing with the 1936 Olympic Games in Berlin. These events deeply shocked American, British and French officials, and it was on the train journey back to Paris that the representative of the French government, Philippe Erlanger (1903–1987), started to think about creating an alternative festival (Erlanger 1974).[1] Erlanger, a well-known French historian, had just been put in charge of the French Agency for Artistic Activity (AFAA), the aim of which was to promote French cultural interests at home and abroad.

Identifying a suitable location for the new international festival was the next step. The promotion of Cannes as the venue for this international event is linked to middle-class and aristocratic tourism (Milliet-Mondon 1986; Monsigny and Meeks 2007). The city of Biarritz was Cannes's most serious competitor to host the festival. A kind of bidding took place between the two cities, and Cannes won when it offered important subsidies and free accommodation to all foreign journalists and stars – and the casino to stage the event.

The American film industry was hugely overrepresented at the first Cannes Film festival in 1939. Metro-Goldwyn-Mayer (MGM) rented a large transatlantic liner to ship stars such as Tyrone Power, Gary Cooper, Douglas Fairbanks, Jr, George Raft, Paul Muni, Norma Shearer and Mae West across the Atlantic. Ten American productions were scheduled for screening, reflecting great variety: fantasy represented by *The Wizard of Oz* but also a western, dramas, comedies and adventure and historical films. France had a selection of eleven films, mostly from the poetic realism movement but also showing the wealth of the country: France as an 'Empire' with its colonies in *L'homme du Niger*, a film on Corsica, *L'Ame de la Corse*, and a film on the city of Rouen, a symbol of French national history. The Soviet Union was equally well represented with eight films, mostly adulating the working class and Lenin but also introducing new cinematographic techniques, since they included the only film of the festival in colour. But most of these films could not be screened. On 31 August 1939 *The Hunchback of Notre Dame* was shown during a sumptuous reception, and on the very next day Germany invaded Poland. On 3 September France and Great Britain declared war on Germany and the festival was cancelled midway through.

Following the end of the war the provisional French government urged resuming the festival as early as possible despite the fact that the country was facing many other urgent problems. One of the goals was to relaunch Cannes before the *Mostra* could blossom once more. Erlanger managed to win over Robert Favre Le Bret (1905–1987), as the organizer of the festival. Even though Le Bret had no link to the world of cinema, he had very good connections in different ministries and this was thought useful at the time in view of general financial restrictions. Moreover, Le Bret had previously managed the prestigious Paris Opera House and thus was attuned to cultural diplomacy (Monsigny and Meeks 2007: 40).

The festival was relaunched in the name of peaceful competition. In his editorial to the special issue of the journal *Le Film Français*, dedicated to the first Cannes festival after the end of the war in 1946 and entitled '*Le festival de la liberté*', Maurice Bessy (1910–1993) wrote:

> International conferences, which have been taking place around the world for a few months, are still affected by the echoes of war. These conferences, which will decide on peace, are still discussing the outcomes of conflicts. And now it turns out that the first of these meetings really to be considered peaceful is taking place under the auspices of cinema ... Under the emblem of tolerance, of elegance without surrogate and under an indulgent sun, all those who like unblinkered talent and work in dignity

will prove to the world that joy and happiness are positive forces, active ones, indeed the essential foundations of invention and creation. There is no total liberty for nations, nor moral health, unless they communicate intensively with their friends. It is by knowing one another that we learn to love one another.

(Bessy 1946: 1)

This sense that the festival was intended to support peace and improve understanding among nations is also reflected in the statutes of the festival, printed in the same issue. The statutes' second article indicates that '[the] objective [of the festival] is to encourage the development of cinematographic art in all of its forms and to create among all film-producing countries a spirit of cooperation.'

Diplomacy was, however, not the sole driving force behind the festival. Next to the expected boost to tourism on the French Riviera, the festival was considered an important occasion for reinvigorating the war-torn French film industry in view of the growing economic and cultural hegemony of American film. This was especially the case after the 'Blum–Byrnes Agreement'[2] on the cancellation of the French debt to the United States after the Second World War. The agreement, which was signed in May 1946, had three main points: cancellation of French debt to the United States, a new loan with advantageous conditions and a requirement for the screening of American films – unlimited access to all movie theatres for 9 weeks out of 13 in each quarter (Gimello-Mesplomb 2006; Le Forestier 2004). During the war American companies had produced about 2,000 films, and the US government was correspondingly keen to secure their distribution in Europe.

Against this backdrop the Cannes Film Festival appeared a suitable channel for promoting American movies as well as French films. In June 1946 the French government set up a commission for previewing and selecting French films for the Cannes Film Festival. This was the predecessor to the National Centre for Cinema (*Centre National de la Cinematographie*, CNC), established in October of the same year. As Dubosclard has shown, 'although the French Government never referred to the cinema as a political tool prior to 1915, and despite the limited finances that it allocated to this domain, the filmic medium soon offered diplomacy a vast field for experimentation' (Dubosclard 2004: 57). The history of the two first events, in 1939 and 1946, exemplifies how international relations played a major role in the Cannes Film Festival.

During the post-war years both Cannes and Venice endeavoured to position themselves as the more cosmopolitan event. When the Cannes Film Festival was opened in 1946, just five days after the *Mostra*, the organizers made an important point of using flags from all the 19 countries that had sent films, to demonstrate the international nature of the festival. This was also highlighted in the newsreels of the time. The urban space was transformed to present Cannes as the capital of world cinema.

Soon government officials realized that coming to an arrangement with Venice would be a better policy than completely ignoring the Italian festival, which had turned out to be a success as soon as it was relaunched in the summer of 1946. Many internal reports confirm the impression that the French first tried to eliminate the *Mostra*. An inter-ministerial committee held arduous negotiations with the Italians, but the French were hindered by the fact that both the USA and the USSR supported Venice.

> The French committee, faced with precise suggestions from Italy, realized that it was not really possible, in the future, to make the Venice Festival simply disappear, and that it was better to take advantage of the circumstances to reach an agreement that, following the terms of 1946, would prevent an unfortunate rivalry in the future and the existence of a germ of discord on the cultural level between both countries.[3]

Venice was not the only festival with which Cannes maintained a rivalry. The late 1940s saw several other film festivals being created, following the recognition that film was not only a successful and growing industry but also a medium that could be used to influence public opinion. Examples include the Brussels Festival and the Locarno Festival and later that of Berlin (launched in 1951).

This 'threat' of international competition helped Cannes consolidate its economic basis through state subsidies in the early 1950s. Later on, when the huge impact of the festival on tourism became apparent, an arrangement was made with the local authorities to increase their share in the budget. This led to a fixed quota system for the first half of the 1950s with 72 per cent of the budget coming from the state, 16.5 per cent from the City of Cannes and 11.5 per cent from the regional council. This did not even change significantly later; in the 1990s the French state continued to support the Cannes Film Festival with subsidies, the latter making up 87.4 per cent of the budget in 1992.

From cultural fact to cultural value

The invention of cinema took place amidst the most heated nationalist discourses in Europe, and soon cinema became another arena in the race for national prestige. First, cinema was established as an industry and a way of generating national prosperity. Then its aesthetic and artistic dimensions came to be acknowledged. Only then did it also become obvious that films could serve the purposes of political propaganda. That is why, in the context of the First World War, France started to consider films as strategic tools in the game of international diplomacy.

In this process the contribution of cinema reviews and critics was crucial. Not only did they legitimize the artistic dimension of films; they also granted them the status of forming part of national cultural heritage.[4] Two good examples are Ricciotto Canudo (1879–1923), an Italian intellectual who lived in France, and George Dureau, editor in chief of the review *Ciné-Journal*. In 1911

Canudo published a book entitled *La naissance d'un sixième art – essai sur le cinématographe*, which equated the actual birth of the sixth art form with the advent of the cinema. Canudo considered that art in general and cinema in particular could only flourish within national contexts. In 1913 Canudo went on to found the review *Montjoie!*, which defined itself as the 'mouthpiece of French artistic imperialism', linking nationalist ideas to aesthetic innovation (Blumenkranz-Onimus 1971). Georges Dureau also gave depth to this idea of a national art of the cinema in an article entitled 'Let us give a national soul to films' (published on 12 April 1913).

> Instead of delineating the productions of directors by generalizing them, leave them entirely their individual or national character that makes them remarkable. Frenchmen, make films that – like the violin of patriotic romance – have the soul of France. [...] The theatrical film will be a national one or it will not be anything [...] because we are still far away from the time dreamed of by philosophers when all peoples will have the same soul.
>
> (Gauthier 2004: 60)

According to Gauthier, at the time it was taken for granted that film directors would contextualize their films within their own national culture:

> So if, as always, the thoughts of a poet bear his nationality, if the harmony and melody confirm the musician's race, film must logically have the nationality of the light that illuminated the sites captured by the lens which it stands in awe of.
>
> (Gauthier 2004: 63)

The idea of a *national cinema* expressing distinct *cultural values* was welcomed by politicians. This was explained by Paul Verneyras (1898–1996), a major supporter of the festival and a member of the French Christian Democratic Party (*Mouvement Républicain Populaire*) in the following way.

> It is in fact desirable that we let cinema fulfil its task of entertainment, which is usually pleasant and which we also hope to be healthy and optimistic. *We should also try as much as possible to attribute cultural value to films.* [...] Undoubtedly, a certain number of viewers seek artistic pleasure in cinema. But the vast majority, about 90 per cent, is interested above all in the story. Our forefathers were acquainted with troubadours and nocturnal revels; then theatre and the instalment novel came along. Now we have cinema, which is incomparably more powerful. In it, the majority of today's youth finds its literature; it is where they gather their experiences of life.
>
> (Authors' emphasis)[5]

Thus, the Cannes Film Festival became the guardian of those film genres extolling the intimate relationship between directors and their films, trying to enhance the critical and artistic sensibilities of viewers and, on this basis, enabling the depiction of national characteristics in an authentic way. Things would change in the 1950s with the emergence of the *Nouvelle Vague*.

A time of turmoil and new beginnings

The expression *Nouvelle Vague* first appeared when the editor in chief of *L'Express*, Françoise Giroud, announced a major survey concerning the generation aged between 18 and 30 on 23 August 1957.

> The results were published in the issues [of *L'Express*] from 3 October to 12 December 1957. The front cover of the first issue showed a young girl with the caption '*La Nouvelle Vague* is coming!' followed by a quotation from Péguy: 'We are the centre and the heart. The axis goes through us. It is from our watch that time will have to be read.' This quotation stresses the importance that the eldest attach to the new generation. Thus, '*Nouvelle Vague*' designated a sociological reality, and this was the way it would be first applied in relation to the cinema.
>
> (Frodon 1995: 142)

Hence, the term *Nouvelle Vague* came to refer to all *new* trends in French society in the late 1950s. In film it was soon associated with a young generation of directors linked to the new journal *Les Cahiers du Cinéma*. *Les Cahiers* were founded on 1 April 1951 in the spirit of *La Revue du Cinéma*, published between 1928 and 1949. Famous film directors such as Jean-Luc Godard, François Truffaut, Eric Rohmer, Jacques Rivette, Claude Chabrol and others wrote their first film criticism there, even before they started to make their own movies (Deforseau 2007).

André Bazin was the spiritual father of this new generation of film critics, who would soon be referred to as 'Young Turks'.[6] Bazin considered culture as a way of emancipating people, and assumed that if high-quality films were well explained to a broad public this public would become more demanding and discriminating. Bazin basically focused on films and the stories they told. Truffaut and the like-minded Jean-Luc Goddard and Claude Chabrol took these ideas one stage further and developed the approach of the '*cinéma d'auteurs*'. The principles of this 'author-driven cinema' were summarized by John Hess in 1974 as follows.

> [T]he most important determinant of an auteur was not so much the director's ability to express his personality, as usually has been claimed, but rather his desire and ability to express a certain world view. An auteur was a film director who expressed an optimistic image of human potentialities within an utterly corrupt society. By reaching out both emotionally and spiritually to other human beings and/or to God, one could transcend the isolation imposed on one by a corrupt world. Thus the characters in

the movies of auteur directors are larger-than-life figures who rise above the ordinary.

(Hess 1974: 20)

In addition, the *'politique des auteurs'*, a mode of film criticism, was developed. This aimed at putting directors and their films at the focus of critics' attention instead, of using the approach of relating directors to film genres. Films became the road map for comprehending a specific director's work. According to this approach, understanding directors implied establishing an intimate relationship with their biographies and origins. Only this enabled an understanding of their oeuvre and the means they used to depict certain worldviews.

This new generation of critics and film directors applied these new theories to their own films, as they wanted to emphasize the opposition between the *'cinéma d'auteurs'* – films as art – and commercial productions – films as entertainment – and explore the possibilities provided by film to express meaning. In this sense 1959 is often presented as the year of birth of *La Nouvelle Vague*. Three films presented in Cannes in 1959 were considered the starting points of the movement: *Orfeu Negro* by Marcel Camus, *les Quatre Cents Coups* by François Truffaut and *Hiroshima mon amour* by Alain Resnais.

As it was considered the showcase of world cinema, the Cannes Film Festival was avidly scrutinized by film critics. In this light the articles by François Truffaut (1932–1984), who wrote for many different journals and newspapers, are particularly interesting.[7] In 1954 Truffaut wrote the first of his articles (Truffaut 1954, 1955, 1956, 1957, 1958) on the Cannes Film Festival in the weekly *Arts*, entitled 'Where does French cinema stand? The Cannes Festival gives occasion for an assessment'. According to Truffaut (1954), of the about 100 films produced in France every year, 'only ten follow[ed] artistic intentions' and, in a sense, bore cultural value. He criticized the fact that these films were not short-listed in Cannes, adding: 'we would expect a cinema festival to be both a kind of economic barometer of the profession and, at the same time, a selection of the best films. Actually, this ideal has not been even remotely reached ...'

The following year, under the pseudonym of Robert Lachenay, Truffaut went further, stating that 'Festivals are film fairs and nothing else' and making fun of the prizes awarded: 'just as there is the Goncourt [France's best-known literature prize] psychology, there is the Oscar psychology, and also a festival psychology' (cited by Baecque and Toubiana 1996 and Cahoreau 1989). Although Truffaut thought better of Venice than Cannes, in 1955 he criticized the former, too, writing that 'the 10 or 12 excellent films [screened in Venice] were lost in the heap of about 30 others, which were pretty lousy'. According to Truffaut (1955), festivals oscillated between the necessity to screen only the best films, on the one hand, and, on the other, the need to discover foreign film-making in order to promote mutual understanding between nations. Given this, 'a festival will only make sense when the notion of selection has been reconsidered and ... official persons no longer have the power to throw films out of the competition'.

Truffaut was also of the opinion that all critics shared his negative views of the Cannes Film Festival, but did not dare to say so in order not to endanger their press accreditation. As if he wanted to prove that Truffaut was right, Favre Le Bret actually excluded him in 1958. Yet that was also the year when Truffaut managed to use the festival to his own advantage by succeeding in attracting funding for his first film. He persuaded his stepfather, Ignace Morgenstern, to buy the Soviet film *The Cranes are Flying* (Mikhail Kalatozov, 1957). When the film was awarded the Golden Palm it became a huge success and Morgenstern was able to fund young Truffaut's project, which became *The 400 Blows* and earned Truffaut the Best Director's Prize at the 1959 Cannes Film Festival (Baecque and Toubiana 1996: 197–201).

In cinema the 1960s were strongly determined by the opposition between the '*cinéma d'auteurs*' and commercial movie productions. Cannes was the place where a minority presented its movies, and yet they were still censored by the nation-states that selected the movies for competition in the first place. It was therefore difficult to access a diversified international film selection. Simultaneously, and despite the strong contradictions within it, the French cinema was undergoing important changes.

In 1968, and against the background of the growing social and cultural discontent among the French student population and working class, an attempt was made to oust Henri Langlois (1914–1977) from his post as artistic and technical director of the *Cinémathèque française*, which he had founded some thirty years earlier in 1936, and which nurtured a close relationship with the film directors of the *Nouvelle Vague*. This attempt was spearheaded by André Malraux, another great film aficionado and a major supporter of the French cinema, who was Minister of Cultural Affairs at the time. Malraux was himself an art critic and historian but did not entirely agree with Langlois' deference to the '*cinema d'auteurs*' and was keen to see a change in the directorship of the *Cinématheque* after thirty years.[8]

The film world was appalled by this coup. Under Truffaut's and Renoir's leadership the *Comité de Défense de la Cinémathèque* was brought to life, and demonstrations were organized as of 14 February, which were generally brutally repressed by the police. Following this pressure, Henri Langlois was finally reinstated on 22 April. The atmosphere of this fierce conflict would still be palpable when the socio-political crisis erupted in May 1968. Hence, the origins of the events that occurred in Cannes during the 21st Festival can be traced back to the broader context of a national crisis but also to an internal crisis in the French film world that had started earlier.

The politically and socially charged atmosphere soon reached the festival, which was scheduled to take place between 10 and 24 May. Opinions as to the identity of the Cannes Film Festival appeared to be as disoriented as those concerning the identity of French society as a whole. For this reason the festival became an arena of conflict. What did it mean? What did it stand for? How was it to be staged?

The student revolt reached the Cannes Film Festival on 13 May, three days after the opening. On 10 May the organizers managed to hold a calm and peaceful opening ceremony, without referring to the crisis already rocking French universities. But the absence of politicians during the opening gala was the first sign of trouble. 10 May is also famous as the 'night of the barricades' in Paris and notorious for the heavy-handed police treatment of demonstrators. And whilst the capital was the scene of these violent riots, Cannes peacefully welcomed celebrities from all over the world. What is more, the organizers deliberately tried to play down tensions by removing two films about the Vietnam War from the competition.

On 13 May the *Association Française pour la Critique du Cinéma* appealed for solidarity with the student movement and requested all festival participants to interrupt the festival that day and demonstrate in favour of the students and 'cultural liberty' (Thévenin 2008: 41). This was followed on 17 May by a call for a general strike by the students of the *Institut des Hautes Etudes Cinématographiques*, who then proceeded to occupy the premises of the CNC and demand an immediate end to the Cannes Film Festival. The movement was supported by the professionals of the movie world. On 18 May a small party of people supporting the students met Robert Favre le Bret in his office to inform him that the festival had been declared closed in Paris. As Robert Favre le Bret refused to declare an official end to the festival, this group of protesters occupied the festival palace and prevented further screenings.

The demonstrators challenged the institution of the Cannes Film Festival, but they also had to face disagreement from their own ranks and from the festivalgoers. The debate first concerned whether the festival had ended or not. Second, if the festival was over, the question remained as to whether movies should be shown or not. By the late afternoon of 18 May the board had decided to close the competition but to continue screenings when the filmmakers agreed to show their films (Thévenin 2008: 16). On 19 May a group led by Truffaut and Godard prevented further screenings from resuming. Eventually, at lunchtime, Robert Favre le Bret declared the official end of the 1968 Cannes Film Festival.

Towards a French stage for the cinemas of the world

At one level, the consequences of the 1968 crisis on the festival were less severe than feared; the dress codes remained, countries continued to select the movies and the events taking place in the palace and on the red carpet perpetuated the segregation between the glamorous elite and visitors longing to catch a glimpse of the stars. But, on taking a look at the films presented in 1969, especially the ones selected in the competition, it is remarkable to note that socio-political issues had finally and definitively entered the festival through the films it presented.

The year before, Jean-Luc Godard had complained about the dearth of films depicting the plight of workers and students, noting that '[t]here is not one film showing the problems of workers or students such as they are today, there is not a single one. Were it made by Forman, me, Polanski or François, there is none' (INA 1968). One year later, film directors with movies presenting contemporary issues were granted centre stage. *If* by Lindsay Anderson was awarded the *Grand prix international du festival*. This film tells the story of a rebellion in a British public school and reflects the ideas of counterculture and antiauthoritarian movements. Dennis Hopper was awarded the *Prix de la première oeuvre* for *Easy Rider*, a movie depicting the atmosphere of the late 1960s with sex, drugs and rock 'n' roll.

Many films with social and political dimensions shown in 1969 were not in the regular competition but in a new section called 'Directors' Fortnight' (*Quinzaine des Réalisateurs*). This section was completely organized by an association of French directors (mostly from the *Nouvelle Vague*) with the title '*Société des Réalisateurs de Films*'. Twenty-two nationalities were represented, exemplifying many different political issues: the Frenchman Louis Malle showed a kaleidoscope of stunning shots from Calcutta; Walter Lima presented a pessimistic science-fiction film about his country, *Brasil Ano 2000*, whereas *Barravento*, by his compatriot Glauber Rocha, was to be considered as the manifesto of Third World cinema; Evald Schorm, known as 'the conscience of the Czech New Wave', had trouble with the Czech police after showing his film *Five Girls Around the Neck*; Ed Emshwiller presented his first underground feature film with two dancers and other couples discussing their relationships and lives in a candid display of self-revelation. From its very first year on, the 'Quinzaine' was a success in democratizing the festival and opening it up to a wider range of directors.

In other words, 1968 had three major impacts. First, it allowed the world of the cinema to be defined as a sphere where socio-political and cultural issues could be staged. Second, it legitimized the international character of the Cannes Film Festival as an arena for New Waves from all over the world; a home was now guaranteed for new generations of filmmakers. Finally, what had already begun in the late 1950s was confirmed at the end of the 1960s: the move from diplomatic and governmental issues towards a greater focus on the cinema world itself, its heterogeneity in styles and origins. Indeed, the shift from 'inter-nationalism' to multiculturalism started to occur after 1968 and led progressively to the suppression of national censorships of the film selections. Cannes was no more the stage of the world of cinemas, but welcomed the cinemas of world.

The 'Directors' Fortnight' was, of course, the most important consequence of the 1968 revolution for the Cannes Festival, but as early as 1962 another section had been created to free the festival from political pressure, namely the 'Critics' Week', designed to showcase first and second feature films. From the outset it was organized by the Association of French Film Critics, independently of the official festival, although it was clear that it should take place in Cannes at the same time. The programme of the first event was clearly more exempt from political and diplomatic pressure than the official festival: of the ten films selected, *Strangers in the City* (Rick Carrier) depicted the life of a

Puerto Rican family in a Manhattan slum and *Adieu Philipinne* (Jacques Rozier) dealt with a young man's departure to Algeria. Even if the word Algeria was not mentioned, everyone could see the film as a manifesto against the French Army in this 'war without a name'. In 1968 the programme of 'Critics' Week' offered no fewer than seven of the twelve films selected on different aspects of revolution.

In conjunction with the general socio-political and cultural developments, the arrival of Gilles Jacob at the head of the festival in the mid 1950s heralded a new era. This had in great part to do with the fact that Gilles Jacob was a cinema aficionado, unlike both Maurice Bessy and Robert Favre Le Bret before him. His attention was therefore focused on promoting film as an art form, besides maintaining the glamour associated with the festival and playing the diplomatic game. The latter was still important, but not as paramount as it had been during the first years.[9]

Jacob initiated a new official section of the festival entitled 'A Certain Look' (*Un certain regard*) for promoting films that were less commercial but more artistic or innovative. Films selected for the '*Regard*' could use this in their advertising material and posters – just as those of the official selection could use '*en compétition*'. Thus, as of the late 1960s there were three equally prestigious programme components: the official selection, the '*Un certain regard*' and the Director's Week. This latter section gained much prominence thanks to its director, Pierre-Henri Deleau, who ran it from its beginning in 1969 until 1998. This rise in prominence partly explains the launch of '*Regard*' by Gilles Jacob.

Another component of the festival that gained prominence with time was the 'out of competition' screenings of, mainly, new Hollywood releases that did not qualify for the official selection but that nevertheless sought to use Cannes as a platform for gaining publicity. Last but not least, Jacob introduced the 'Golden Camera' award (*Camera d'Or*), which was awarded to the best first film by a director in any section of the festival.[10]

Recently the festival has launched a new section in order to highlight its role in the development of film as an art form and, more precisely, to promote the emergence of new talents. Headed by Georges Goldenstern, *Cinéfondation* consists of three main parts. The first part, introduced in 1998, is linked to the screening of short films during the festival as part of the official selection. The '*Résidence*', created two years later, assists six film directors from around the world to live and work in Paris for almost five months, all in a common flat, so that they can write the script of their first or second films and interact with one another. Since 2004 there has also been the '*Atelier*' (the studio): 15 projects are selected, each with the script and also at least 20 per cent of the budget already completed. The film directors in charge of the selected projects meet professionals in Cannes during the festival and '*Cinéfondation*' helps them to complete their budgets.

Commitment to cinema and critical reflection related to film and society have a long tradition in Cannes, even if other festivals such as that of Berlin are better known in this respect. This is, among other things, also evidenced by conferences organized occasionally within the framework of the festival. In 1977, when Roberto Rossellini accepted chairmanship of the jury, it was only on condition that he could hold a workshop on the 'social and economic commitment of cinema'.[11] In 1989 debates on democracy took centre stage. A symposium entitled 'Cinema and Liberty' was held to commemorate the 200th anniversary of the French Revolution, attracting over a hundred directors from all over the world.

The French Minister of Culture, Jack Lang, often employed the festival as a vehicle for announcing key elements of his policies, so it gradually grew to assume a European dimension. In his press conference in Cannes on the relations between Europe and cinema on 17 May 1985, Lang declared:

> In my view, these are the goals to be achieved and the conditions to be fulfilled to safeguard the future of European cinema. It cannot happen without a national endeavour on the part of every country, without forgetting egotism, without the participation of the creative themselves, who can do a lot to enhance public awareness, by the political representatives of the cultural and economic issues at stake. They also have to take responsibility for this future, making their experiences, their aspirations, joint issues; is not the 38th Cannes Festival, a crossroads and meeting point, the ideal place for these exchanges and the pursuit of this common idea?[12]

In the year 2000 the establishment of a 20-million-Franc funding programme was announced to promote Franco-German co-productions. On this occasion, Prime Minister Lionel Jospin commented that the future of French cinema was increasingly that of European cinema.[13]

Conclusion

> Cannes is everything that defines cinema: glamour and strictness, stupidity and gravity, sexual and cerebral, excessive and sophisticated, art and business, the ridiculous and the sublime. A strongly discriminatory elitism and at the same time the ability to change, to embrace the new trends in cinema. Competitive and very open.
>
> (Todd McCarthy, film director and critic,
> on the website of the City of Cannes)

Unlike the Berlin Film Festival, which is an open space attended by all strata of the population, Cannes stands for something that is comparable with an international conference of experts and government officials. Cannes is a closed circle, which only highly select people have the right to join, at least for the official selection. Cannes is ruled by strict dress codes and etiquette, and Cannes' paramount task is to assess films.

Recognized by all major stakeholders as the premier international film festival in the world, Cannes's influence on the world of film is a major one, and for this reason some people might now be on the lookout for 'Cannes-proof' films. But what are the specific characteristics of a 'Cannes-proof' film? Does it rely on its unpredictability and taking up diverse topics in a profoundly creative and innovative way? Or does the audience expect a certain film format, which is then produced as a result? Does Cannes then contribute to a certain fossilization of the art of the cinema, not only in form, but also in content? Does it present a 'discriminatory elitism', not only in the way the festival is organized, but also by excluding films that are not in keeping with the identity of the festival?

When the value of films came to the forefront of criticism, mainly started by the *Nouvelle Vague*, it became necessary to introduce a sense of modernity, whilst preserving a certain tradition. This implied a paradox in the raison d'être of the festival. This balance between tradition and innovation/modernity could be achieved thanks to the highlights described previously. May 1968 especially helped to reform the structures of the festival. From then on, the official selection could represent the festival tradition of prestige and the parallel sections (the '*Quinzaine*' and 'Critics' Week' even more so) stood for openness and the promotion of new generations. The next major step in this direction was taken in 1972, when the selection of films was handed over from national selection committees to a group of experts and specialists directly linked to Cannes. This move enhanced the legitimacy of the festival, as it now became a stage for films selected by cinema experts/lovers/critics for their inherent artistic and cultural value and removed from the bias of national concerns. This change in the selection mode also made the festival more political, since it could now be used more freely to express criticism.

Apart from the coexistence of the official and parallel sections, another warranty of the balance between tradition and modernity is the presence of highly committed film experts in the management of the festival. The current president of the festival, Gilles Jacob, is a person able to challenge cinema and the festival and always on the watch for new forms of cinema art. The same is true of Thierry Frémaux, the festival's general delegate. The organizers feel a real commitment to cinema. Yet critics like Antoine de Baecque still express the fear that Cannes encourages a format that some directors or producers try to copy in order to win a prize. The festival has constantly to be on the brink to avoid losing its ability for self-reflection and innovation.

For the 2009 event the Cannes Film Festival endeavoured to shape its image as much as possible by adapting to digital technologies and by giving broader accessibility to the films presented; a 3D animated film was shown at the opening ceremony and the first five minutes of a few selected films were available online. At the same time, traditions and rituals can be seen as responses to specific needs. After all, the glamorous dimension of the festival also contributes to another major aspect of cinema: it is not only about reflecting socio-political and contemporary issues. It is also about magic, dreams and escaping from reality for a little while, using aesthetics and emotion as means of affective communication in the cultural public sphere.

Finally, Cannes has a threefold reputation to uphold. First, with support from the national level it is a channel for promoting democratic values and a worldwide stage for dialogue and cultural exchange, and this is an important element for France's cultural diplomacy. Second, in order to remain in the leading position, it has to seek and find new directors and new film genres and be open to new technologies, thus acquiring the right to judge and give an impression of new trends in cinema. Third, it has to foster its established image and celebrate its achievements, making it into an arena where previous young generations can continue to grow and return again in the course of time to present their subsequent oeuvre.

Ultimately, even if the Cannes Film Festival manages to unite an important diversity of aspects and even if it derives its energy from a history shaped by major challenges, it is one of many events, larger and smaller festivals, that all contribute to pluralism and diversity in the world of cinema. Cannes has certainly left its mark on the map of film festivals all over the world, not least as an example to follow or one to question. This makes it into a fixed point in the cultural public sphere, a guarantee for the constant progression of the art of cinema.

Notes

1 Erlanger was of the opinion that a new festival was necessary not only because the *Mostra* had come under Mussolini's influence but also because Salzburg was gradually being brought under Nazi control.
2 The agreement was so called in honour of the persons who led the negotiations: Leon Blum and Jean Monnet on the French side, and James F. Byrnes on the American side.
3 All the translations from the French are the authors'. This quotation is taken from the Archive of the Cannes Festival, stored at the Cinémathèque in Paris (*Bibliothèque du film*), here FIFA14B4 (FIFAxxByy refers to documents from file XX, box YY in the archives of the Administration of the *Festival international du film*).
4 *Le Fascinateur*, the first cinema journal, established in 1903, and other reviews were the first arenas in which film criticism emerged and evolved. These reviews targeted professionals in the film industry and were intended to contribute to its prosperity.
5 FIFA93B13 pp. 6 and 7.
6 This is a reference to the Young Turk Revolution that restored the constitution in Turkey in 1908. The initiators of that revolution defined themselves as progressive and modernist.
7 The Truffaut archives are also located at the *Bibliothèque du film*.
8 It should be added that Langlois' contract was due to come to an end that year.
9 The very arduous negotiations with the Soviets held by Jacob in Moscow in February 1977 illustrate this important aspect of his work (Jacob 2009).
10 This programme was in part conceptualized to counteract the 'Critics' Week', which had selected the best second film by a director since 1962.

11 Jacob devoted a whole chapter of his autobiography to this workshop and insinuated that Rossellini's death a few months later might have been precipitated by his huge involvement in this venture (Jacob 2009: Ch. 24). A film has been made on the workshop, *Le colloque de Cannes*, by Jacques Grandclaude (1977).
12 Archives nationales, Fonds CNS, 20050582, article 197.
13 Report to the French National Assembly. Roland Blum, *Rapport d'information* n° 3197, recorded at the Record Office of the National Assembly, 26 June 2001, on the strengths and weaknesses of French cinema on the international market, 60 and 62.

References

Baecque, A. de and Toubiana, S. (1996) *François Truffaut*. Paris: Gallimard.

Bessy, M. (1946). Le festival de la liberté. *Le Film Français* hors-série, 1.

Blumenkranz-Onimus, N. (1971) Montjoie! ou l'héroïque croisade pour une nouvelle culture. In Brion-Guerry, L. (ed.) *L'Année 1913 – Les formes esthétiques de l'œuvre d'art à la veille de la première guerre mondiale*, 1105–1116. Paris: Klincksieck.

Cahoreau G. (1989) *François Truffaut: 1932–1984*. Paris: Julliard.

Deforseau, N. (2007) *Les Cahiers du Cinéma, une histoire étonnante d'une revue singulière*. Bruxelles: Presses de l'Université libre de Bruxelles.

Dubosclard, A. (2004) Le cinéma, passeur culturel, agent d'influence de la diplomatie française aux États-Unis dans l'entre-deux-guerres. *1895*, 42, 57–75.

Erlanger, P. (1974) *La France sans étoile – souvenirs de l'avant-guerre et du temps de l'occupation*. Paris: Plon.

Frodon, J.-M. (1995) *L'Age moderne du cinéma français*. Paris: Flammarion.

Gauthier, C. (2004) Le cinéma des nations: invention des écoles nationales et patriotisme cinématographique (années 1910 – années 1930). *Revue d'Histoire Moderne et Contemporaine* 51(4): 58–77.

Gimello-Mesplomb, F. (2006) The economy of 1950s popular French cinema. *Studies in French Cinema Journal* 6(2): 141–150.

Hess, J. (1974) La politique des auteurs, Truffaut's Manifesto (2). *Jumpcut, a review of contemporary media* 2: 20–22.

INA (1968) Newsreel from the French Audiovisual National Institute (INA) (http://www.ina.fr) May, archives used in Cinéma cinémas – 04/06/1989 – 10min25s, here at 3'20.

Jacob, G. (2009) *La Vie Passera Comme un Rêve*. Paris: Robert Laffont.

Le Forestier, L. (2004) L'accueil en France des films américains de réalisateurs français à l'époque des accords Blum-Byrnes. *Revue d'Histoire Moderne et Contemporaine*, 51(4): 78–97.

McGuigan. J., (2005) The Cultural Public Sphere. *European Journal of Cultural Studies* 8(4): 427–443.

Milliet-Mondon, C. (1986) *Cannes, 1835–1914. Villégiature, urbanisation, architecture*. Nice: Serre.

Monsigny, J. and Meeks, E. (2007) *Le Roman du Festival de Cannes*. Paris: Editions du Rocher.

Thévenin, O. (2008) *La SRF et la Quinzaine des Réalisateurs: 1968–2008: une construction d'identités collectives*. Paris: Aux Lieux d'être.

Truffaut, F. (1954) Où en est le cinéma français – Bilan et perspectives à l'occasion du Festival de Cannes. *Arts*, 17 March.

Truffaut, F. (1955) La Biennale de Venise – Excellente première semaine. *Arts*, 7 September.

Truffaut, F. (1956) Un palmarès ridicule. *Arts*, 16 May.

Truffaut, F. (1957) Cannes: un échec dominé par les compromis, les combines et les faux-pas. *Arts*, 22 May.

Truffaut, F. (1958) Si des modifications radicales n'interviennent pas, le prochain Festival de Cannes est condamné. *Arts*, 21 May.

11 'Space is the Place'

The global localities of the Sónar and WOMAD music festivals

Jasper Chalcraft and Paolo Magaudda[1]

> The music is different here, the vibrations are different here, not like Planet Earth.
>
> (Sun Ra, 1972 *Space is the Place*. Film directed by John Coney)

Introduction

This chapter discusses the relationships of two festivals with the localities where they are organized and take place. Festivals represent specific moments during which new interactions, relationships, cultures and practices are established. This means that the material and local dimensions where the festival is held are transformed, even if only temporarily, by festivals. The ways festivals articulate their relationships with the local and actual places where they are performed influence the forms through which they can define themselves as public places, both from an aesthetic and a cultural perspective. Therefore, the present chapter aims at tracing the different ways in which these two festivals perform and project local and global dimensions, and, moreover, how these relationships are of relevance for the ways in which festivals relate to a cultural public sphere.

The first case, the Sónar festival in Barcelona (Spain), is a music festival held in the same place over the last two decades and attended mostly by foreigners; the second case, WOMAD, consists of a travelling festival which is organized in different places around the world. Thus, the chapter presents the relationships and engagements these two festivals have with the local dimensions where they take place and with which their audience, organizers, workers and artists engage.

'Festivalscapes' and the cultural public sphere in music festivals

Music festivals are characterized by being places that enable 'intense' and concentrated interaction for people coming from different places and often involved in specific subcultures, cultural consumption patterns, and other kinds of mainly identity-based groups. Festivals have become occasions during which people spatially dispersed in a cultural global world are able to meet and to establish relations on the basis of the common sharing of aesthetics, cultural objects and practices. By pointing out this key dimension in music festivals, we want to outline and discuss the ways in which a music festival is based on the expression of distinctive relationships between the local and the global dimensions.

Here the relationships between festival, globality and locality will be discussed, and we point out that music festivals with strong international characteristics represent a very good case for discussing the relationship between cultural and aesthetic flows as the embodied dimension of actual publics and festivalgoers. Therefore, music festivals are here considered as examples of the 'concentred interaction' typical of late modernity, in which global cultural flows coexist with local cultures and habits and where their two dimensions are even more constantly intertwined with one another (Appadurai 1996).

Indeed, in some ways festivals can be seen as the terrain on which, following Appadurai's work, a variety of '-scapes' (ethnoscapes, mediascapes, technoscapes, financescapes and ideoscapes) are constantly at play. In this sense, the two international music festivals considered here are used to introduce a further description of the forms of interconnection between culture, people and space that we call 'festivalscapes'. Festivalscapes are a set of cultural, material and social flows, at both local and global levels, both concrete and imagined, both deliberate and unintended, which emerge and are established during a specific festival. In this sense, festivals can be seen and analysed as terrains where different cultural, aesthetic and political patterns and values temporarily converge and clash, constantly creating, stabilizing and redefining the setting of festival interaction, and in so doing stressing the problems raised by the multiple articulation of global cultural flows, local life and spatiality.

The cultural and spatial complexity of music festivals leads us to consider the ways in which these festivals represent the material symbolic crossings of different and divergent issues, strengths and experiences, which are understood as complex forms of 'Festivalscapes'. We also draw on Appadurai's idea that it is imagination that constitutes the ideological battleground of modernity; the deterritorialized hybridities of migrants and a global media represent new possibilities against the globalization pessimists and their fears of cultural homogenization. The definition of 'festivalscape' has been deliberately vague because we also imply that festivals have now become such a significant part of modernity's cultural production that they need to be considered as a further component of the global cultural economy, analogous to the other '-scapes' that Appadurai (1990) set out in his landmark essay 'Disjuncture and difference in the global cultural economy'.

The festivalscape also needs to be considered alongside the processes of 'festivalizing' – which other chapters in this volume explore (See Chapter 8 by Roche in particular). This is another ambiguous concept. On the one hand, it is the strategy of urban 'branding' pursued by city authorities as part of creating distinct city identities, often through festivals and mega-events whose cultural offerings are transnational (Roche, Chapter 8, this volume). Yet we suggest that 'festivalizing' also represents a shift away from the elite/popular culture axis towards an idealized, but nonetheless not entirely imaginary, new democratic space where the performance of culture requires the interaction of artists, audience and locality. Operatively, this partly depends on a specific form of authenticity generated within the festival.

Authenticity constitutes a crucial part of the audience experiences of the Sónar and WOMAD festivals, in terms of the aesthetic content itself (the music and dance), but also, and perhaps most importantly, in how the festival itself is experienced. Understanding this authenticity involves understanding what music festivals mean to their audiences, even across different genres and in very different localities. Authenticity is thus a corollary of 'festivalizing' culture; culture performed in this way, displayed, experienced and interacted with through the festival format, gains authenticity as a cultural product as much as it helps constitute the festival experience itself.

The considerations of the issues, problems and opportunities that emerge in reflecting the local–global relationships of music festivals are clearly of great relevance in analyzing the forms through which festivals in general and music festivals in particular can articulate themselves as 'cultural public spheres' (McGuigan 2005: 435). Indeed, starting from development of the Habermasian conception of the public sphere, McGuigan traces an evolved concept of the public sphere with a dominant emphasis on the affective, aesthetic and emotional dimensions of public life and people's participation (see Chapter 5 in this volume). Thus, the ways in which localities and globalities are actually addressed by music festivals are not a secondary element when the forms and degrees to which these festivals actually perform their openness, democracy, equality and so on are considered, by presenting cultural, aesthetic and musical products and commodities in specific local contexts.

The case-studies are presented as made up of 'global localities', a term that requires a minimum of justification. Localities represent a distinct scale, which, in this instance, enables comparison of a festival located in one of Europe's iconic cities (Barcelona) with the varied locations of WOMAD, ranging from a rural country estate in the UK to the constructed capitalist utopian urbanity of Abu Dhabi. Aware of the term's contentious history for geographers (e.g. Cook 1989; Jonas 1988; Massey 1993; May 1996; Urry 1987), here we nevertheless take 'locality' to encompass a local sphere of interaction that may or may not stretch beyond a city or site, and to be a term that recognizes the agency of various actors and institutions without making an a priori theoretical assumption about which factors were most instrumental in shaping it. Therefore, 'global localities' are those places whose identification, content or even just coincidental creation, is explicitly internationalist and overtly non-parochial.

The ways in which the two music festivals relate with their actual localities, as well as the form through which they talk to and for other places and spaces, constitute a doubly relevant issue. On the one hand, the declination of this relation is an element reflecting the ways these globally projected festivals 'speak about' and construct public, political and symbolical identity in the actual spaces where they are performed. On the other, the ways in which they are 'globally local' are crucial elements in constructing a cultural geography that helps develop artistic and cultural production and consumption. In the following sections the relevance of these issues will be explored by entering into the details of the actual ways these two festivals articulate their specific global localities.

The Sónar Festival and its global and international dimensions

The Sónar Festival represents a relevant case for reflecting on the relationship between music festivals, the aesthetic public sphere, and those questions raised by the complex and ambiguous relationship between the local and the global in contemporary society. Indeed, the Sónar Festival is probably the best-known electronic music festival in the world, and every year brings together about 80,000 young people for three days of concerts, exhibitions and dance events in the Mediterranean city of Barcelona. A vast majority of the more than 100 artists invited, half of the numerous audience, and more than half of the total of 800 journalists come to Barcelona from foreign countries just to attend the festival. Sónar's development over the 17 editions of the festival has proceeded together with the affirmation of electronic dance music genres in the markets, tastes and practices of new youth generations around the world. Therefore, its history is characterized by a strong evolution over the years, both in terms of dimensions and of legitimacy.

During its history the festival has acquired a pre-eminent role in the world of electronic music, and it has definitively contributed to legitimizing dance music in the realm of art and culture. The festival's musical events tend to favour electronic music in the broadest sense of the term, thus including techno, house, hip-hop and other, different, electronic musical genres more connected with a highbrow attitude, such as experimental and avant-garde music. It also proposes multimedia art events that involve the massive use of video and sound, in this way also opening the festival perspective to international contemporary visual and performing arts.

Launched in 1994 as a small festival with about 5,000 visitors, the Sónar Festival was at its outset already characterized by a clear international projection, defining itself as an 'International Festival of Advanced Music'. Its international and global dimensions can be articulated around four different elements: creative networks, audience, international representation of the festival and presence in foreign countries. All these elements contribute in different ways to constructing a specific international dimension to the festival, as will be seen more specifically in the following section.

The first element through which the Sónar Festival articulates its relationships with an international and global dimension consists of its embeddedness in different international and global creative networks. In pre-eminent position are those electronic music creative networks with respect to which the festival constitutes a crucial reference in terms of market and cultural legitimacy. All of the most important music artists and labels have played at Sónar at least once since its beginning in 1994, and presence at Sónar still represents a source of legitimacy for new acts and artists.

Moreover, other kinds of creative networks are relevant in the connections the festival establishes with the foreign context, such as those involved in the creation of art exhibitions hosted within the festival, a section that is called 'Sónarmatica'. Every year the work of the exhibition 'Sónarmatica' involves different topics and artists in some way connected to sound and the sonic dimension, and, in so doing, it involves the connection with networks characterized more explicitly in the direction of the 'art world' rather than electronic music. Specifically, every year this session activates networks of mainly young art curators from different places – especially from European countries – for the creation of the exhibitions presented at the festival.

The second element that helps one to understand the complex relation of the festival to a global dimension is represented by the composition of the audience: about 80,000 mostly young people, aged between 15 and 30 and from many different countries. Indeed, according to the official data released by the festival management, more than half of the public arrives in Barcelona from abroad expressly to attend the festival and associated events. What is of interest is not only the fact that the audience comes from outside Spain, but also that it is spread extensively across countries and continents, especially western and developed ones, such as the United States, Australia and Japan.

The geographical heterogeneity of the audience helps to introduce a third element in the analysis, consisting of the international strategies of representation and advertising set up by the festival. The centrality of the Sónar Festival in global electronic music production and dissemination is solidly connected with a network of actors, institutions and especially the press and media from all those countries where electronic music is affirmed and developed. In this respect, it is useful to consider that not only does the festival run a specific international media and press office, but more specifically that – according to management data – more than two-thirds of the 450 accredited journalists come from outside Spain and represent as many as 47 different countries from all over the world.

The international projection of the representation and advertising strategies of the festival is also carried out by organizing small musical events in different countries during the year. This work of displacement of the festival in different countries constitutes a fourth autonomous dimension of the articulation of an international dimension of the festival. These events that run parallel to the festival are defined as 'A taste of Sónar' and have regularly characterized the festival activity over the last eight years. In 2009 they were staged in New York and Washington (USA) and in London (UK). This 'physical' displacement of the festival to other places can be considered a fourth relevant dimension in the relation of the festival with the global scene. It is since 2002 that Sónar has organized itinerant musical events in different countries, among which a specific part has been played by those countries where electronic music has already gained a prominent position in the cultural production industry (i.e. the United States, the United Kingdom and Germany). Other international events are located in places where electronic music is not as attractive to young audiences as it is in the United Kingdom, but where it can be further developed as a musical genre together with the brand of the festival, such as in the cases of Argentina, Brazil, France, Italy and South Korea. Thus, for the festival, international events represent an occasion both for entering local markets and creative networks and for improving a global and cosmopolitan image and representing the festival in these different localities.

All the elements just considered clearly delineate a festival that is not only clearly oriented towards a global setting, even if it is western and economically and culturally developed. It also seems to lead to considering the Sónar Festival as a basically global festival, with loose connections not only to the physicality of the venues, but, more generally, also to their national and regional politics, cultures and peoples. In the following section some aspects of the festival will be considered that offer a different view of the relation of the Sónar Festival to its original locality, in order to understand how locality and globality constitute the two necessary sides of the same coin.

Sónar and its 'local globality'

It is interesting to note the ways in which an international and, to some extent, global festival such as Sónar is embedded in local material, cultural and political contexts, and how this local embeddedness has a role in constructing a specific global projection of this musical event. Considering the ways in which a markedly international and, to some extent, global festival is intertwined with its local roots, places and environment is not easy if we want not only to address the most obvious and superficial forms of relationships but also to endeavour to understand the deeper and more consistent elements of interaction between locality and festival.

The first and more evident dimension consists in the relation of the Sónar festival to the physical place where it is situated. In general, the material and spatial location of a festival is not an insignificant element, and Sónar confirms this aspect. Indeed, the festival presents two main venues; during the day it is hosted in the adjoining spaces of the Centre of Contemporary Culture of Barcelona (Cccb) and the Museum of Contemporary Art (Macba), which are located within the old and popular district of Raval, on the right of the well known and touristic street La Rambla. These locations are a constitutive element of the political culture of the festival. This becomes apparent when one considers that, since its beginnings, one of the main and more evident innovative dimensions of Sónar has been the mixing and conflating of, on the one hand, highbrow, experimental and 'serious' electronic music and, on the other, lowbrow, dance-based and entertaining musical genres. This attitude toward the combination of musical genres has been possible thanks to the possibility of mixing these different forms of music in the same legitimate 'frame' formed by the two art exhibition centres. In other words, the physical places hosting the Sónar Festival have been one of the required 'cultural tools' involved in the process of the cultural translation of electronic music that has been one of the characteristic elements of the same festival in the world.

The physical relation to the institutions and the district clearly does not represent the only element. Another one concerns the role of the broader cultural and social environment of the city, which is, in itself, a mixture of locality and globality, consisting of the distinct cultural identity of the city of Barcelona and the region of Catalonia and the creative, young and heterogeneous flows of people that have been attracted by this area since the rebirth of the city after the 1992 Olympic Games. The development of the Sónar Festival and its strong international projection cannot be fully addressed without considering, on the one hand, the historical openness of the city of Barcelona towards modernity and innovation. This is not a recent phenomenon, but can be traced back, for example, to the role of the city in the modernist artistic and architectural movement. In recent years this historical attitude has allowed the city to implement strategies appealing to a variety of external audiences and consisting of urban requalification and transformation and the development of ambitious cultural policies. These are only two minor aspects of the strong relationships between the innovativeness of the Sónar Festival and the qualities of innovation and modernity characterizing the city of Barcelona as a whole (Balibrea 2001; Smith 2005).

To understand the international development of the Sónar Festival requires not only a consideration of the general historical and socio-cultural attitude of the city of Barcelona towards modernity and innovation, but also, more specifically, a look at the ways in which an explicit cultural policy has played a role in the development and success of the festival. Indeed, the cultural policy of the region has developed a specific strategy around festivals and especially music festivals. This specific political strategy has consisted, for example, of recognizing a few music festivals – including Sónar – as strategic in order to develop the representation of the region outside the country, giving the city the opportunity to develop and invest within a mid-range temporal frame. Moreover, it is worth noticing that in 2009 the organization of Sónar was awarded the 'City of Barcelona Prize' in the category of 'International projection' of the city towards the foreign. Specific reference was made to the events organized in other countries and it was stressed that 'Sónar is a world reference for electronic music' and that it 'favoured the presence of audience, professionals and mass media from all over the world in the city of Barcelona over seventeen years' (Ajuntament de Barcelona 2009). The connections between Sónar's success and local cultural policies show that an international and global projection can be developed, especially when the original locality evolves an attitude toward the capitalization of music festivals as a tool to 'sell' the locality abroad.

The festival itself also causes a material and economic impact on the city where it is located. Concerning Sónar's economic influence on the city of Barcelona, it is relevant to note that an economic study sponsored by the festival management in 2004 estimated that the festival generated revenues of 47 million Euros, clearly showing its relevance for Barcelona's economy and tourism (Oliveras 2008; Van der Borg and Russo 2008). The economic and material impact of the Sónar Festival on the locality of the district and the city is only one example of a more general impact that also concerns music-related shops and professional activities, nightclubs and other associated activities. All these elements show some aspects of the complex relationships between the festival, which is clearly oriented towards an international and global dimension, and the material and economic consequences it may have on the locality where it has been designed and takes place.

Moreover, taken together, the aspects of internationalization and globality of the festival make it possible to develop some thoughts on the interwoven relationship between globality and locality. In this respect, the global projection of the festival and its local embeddedness compose two constitutive elements of the same process of shaping the festival. The first of these elements consists of the fact that the Sónar Festival started and developed as being strictly integrated into international, and, to some degree, global flows of aesthetic and cultural production, as in the cases of electronic music and digital culture. These cultural genres and styles have developed globally, though they have brought with them their own geographies, which consist of more relevant places (the UK, the USA and Japan), other more peripheral localities (Western Europe and other developed countries) and other sites that remain outside the flows of cultural production.

On the other hand, we have seen that the development of the Sónar Festival has been closely connected to the material, the cultural and the political aspects of its locality, which has affected not only the cultural and artistic landscape within which the project of the festival has been able to find its way, but also the political and managerial tools involved in the work of the global projection of the music festival. Thus, considering simultaneously the local and global dimensions of the Sónar festival, we can catch a glimpse of the complex relationship between local embeddedness and global cultural flows and, moreover, observe how the local and global are elements that constantly co-shape one another as they create the conditions where the festival is organized and actually experienced by artists and audience.

Is the Music Different Here? Introducing WOMAD

WOMAD is a successful global festival brand, and, whilst it is clearly born from the crucible of British festival culture (with its countercultural roots), it is impossible to understand it through its UK manifestations alone. Consequently, we can see this itinerant festival as a kind of meta-event. Thus, despite a clear attachment to certain places, WOMAD exists beyond place. After a brief history of the festival, WOMAD's role will be considered within world music; then attention will be given to WOMAD as a festivalscape and, finally, to the politics that inform the festival.

The World of Music, Arts & Dance (WOMAD) makes a claim to being the first and largest festival dedicated to those musical cultures of the world now subsumed under the genre of 'world music'. At the time of the first WOMAD in 1982, this still nascent genre was known variously as 'world beat', 'ethnic music', 'roots music' and even 'third-world music' (Frith 2000: 305–6), and it is worth noting a symbiosis between the festival and the genre that it now presents to audiences around the world. WOMAD itself notes the contrast between the difficult early years and the period following the invention of the term 'world music' in 1987, when festival organizers and sponsors became more interested in such events (Brooman 2007). Rather, as with Sónar, motivations for starting the festival were aesthetic rather than economic. In Peter Gabriel's own words, 'Pure enthusiasm for music from around the world led us to the idea of WOMAD [...] Cynical business-minded people said we'd never survive and a couple of times they were nearly right. But we're still here' (Gabriel 2008).

The first festival took place at the Royal Bath and West Showground in the UK in 1982. Covering everything from exhibitions and cinema to performances and workshops, the first WOMAD began with more than 7,000 schoolchildren participating in the Children's Day and establishing what has become one of WOMAD's staple features both in the UK and abroad: the children's parade. However, it proved a financial disaster, with losses running to a six-figure sum. Consequently, the organization was restructured, and the educational aspects of the festival were separated from the rest. Established in 1983, the WOMAD Foundation's charitable objectives were 'to promote, maintain, improve, and advance education and research in world cultures and multi-cultural education' (WOMAD Foundation 1983), objectives it has continued to pursue abroad as well as in the UK. Until 1990 WOMAD was itinerant within the UK, being staged in various places as the organizers experimented with locations, different kinds of partnerships and fluctuating budgets, until they gained the support of Reading Borough Council from 1990 onwards.

The growth of the new musical genre saw WOMAD consolidate into something recognizable as a global brand of sorts, undoubtedly because of its multiple international sites, a trend that started back in 1988 with events initially also staged in Denmark and Canada. Since their very first UK festival in 1982, the organizers have held more than 160 festival events (around six a year, and sometimes as many as ten) in 27 different countries. The range of countries is heavily weighted towards the affluent world, but still represents remarkable global coverage for a festival tied to a musical genre whose largest following lay for the most part – as it still does – in Europe.

One of the reasons for this success can be placed in the context of the establishment of 'world music' as a genre. It clearly also has something to do with the cultural (and probably financial) capital and contacts of pop musician Peter Gabriel, who by 1986 had become a member of the 'rock aristocracy', winning his first Grammy for his album *So*. This era is something Steven Feld (2000) has characterized as the 'popstar curation' of world music, picking up where the Beatles and Ravi Shankar left off. So when WOMAD took its genre of music to the world, it was to publics with ears that had been opened by rock and pop musicians. The greatest period of WOMAD's exploratory international activity seems to have been in the mid 1990s, by which time the symbolic significance of 'world music' events as a soundtrack to loudly pronounced multiculturalist ideals had become a strategically useful tool for western city councils, institutions and funding bodies, even whilst national governments often contradicted these ideals in practice. WOMAD's 'different' music had thus become a part of the mainstream of cultural programming – albeit a small part – though what this institutional acceptance has meant for the festival itself remains to be considered in the next section.

WOMAD's 'global localities'

WOMAD offers an insight into a festival culture that maintains a cohesive identity even though it has various local identities in its varied locales and varied publics. This is possible, not because WOMAD is a 'brand' or franchise, but by the way it operates, and the continuing relevance, and resonance, of its founding ethos. In the metaphor of one of the WOMAD Foundation's directors, putting on WOMAD events is like a play – like theatre. Consequently, staging a WOMAD event requires the flexibility to perform the same script whilst adapting to varied local contexts of production. Given the nature of the musical troupe that 'world music' artists represent, such practicalities are also global: visas, international flights and so on. Fortress Europe, and particularly the non-Schengen UK, have become genuinely problematic spaces to tour for 'world' artists, with visa issues impacting heavily on cultural programming. This is so much the case that, between acts, compères at the UK's WOMAD Charlton Park 2009 made impassioned pleas against those states whose immigration policies were unable to recognize that deliberately obstructive visa services contradicted their stated multicultural ideals. The campaigning organization Freemuse (www.freemuse.org) put the case in its universal context in a statement on its website announcing a white paper that it drafted and presented to the European Commission in 2009:

> If the European countries are serious about honouring their ratification of the UNESCO Convention on Cultural Diversity they need to make visa and work permit procedures and the general access to the European market for artists more flexible, transparent and homogenous.

Increased cultural capital and international following has not eased the global movement of world musicians. These political realities thus remain an integral part of the festival, something shared by organizers, audience and artists alike.

WOMAD operates pragmatically in slightly different ways around the world. In the UK, the festival is organized by WOMAD Ltd. (the festival company), whilst educational activities remain the domain of the WOMAD Foundation, a registered charity. For its two ongoing Spanish festivals (in Las Palmas and Cáceres), WOMAD Spain is run by an independent production company and has its own director, though educational activities are still centrally organized by the Foundation. Unlike the WOMAD at Charlton Park in the UK, the Spanish WOMADs enjoy substantial financial support from their host city councils, as well as local media and other sponsorship. Like that in Spain, the WOMADs in Australia and New Zealand are so well established that they, too, have their own directors, their own sponsorship and institutional support, and very much their own identity. In fact, WOMADelaide is the largest WOMAD worldwide, attracting attendances of 75,000 against Charlton Park's 30,000 in the UK. These are, of course, licensing issues, but they also directly reflect institutional subsidy and regional political and media profiles. WOMADelaide – rather like WOMAD Taranaki in New Zealand – has enjoyed political support from the highest level, as well as direct funding from the national arts body. In contrast, the UK's Arts Council only directly funds some of the educational activities of the WOMAD Foundation, and when WOMAD in the UK left its old site at Rivermeade in Reading it lost the financial support that the city council had offered it since 1990, something it has not yet managed to replace in rural Wiltshire. WOMADelaide is also established enough that it now runs its own educational programme, successfully including a number of Aboriginal groups. Even in Abu Dhabi, WOMAD's newest locality, the UK-based Foundation operates an extensive educational programme, as it did in WOMADs that no longer run, such as those of Singapore and South Korea. Artistic content, too, has a local flavour, with the directors of both WOMAD Spain and WOMAD Abu Dhabi detailing in interviews the considerable control they have over it. For Spain, in particular, this means that a quota of local acts have to be included, and anecdotal evidence has it that the situation is similar for Australasian WOMADs.

These elements – music and dance performance combined with workshops and educational and outreach activities – mean that, despite pragmatically adapting to its individual localities, to local funding opportunities, institutional collaborations and partnerships, and varying criteria for cultural programming, something identifiable as 'WOMAD' does seem to exist, its multiple manifestations notwithstanding. Importantly, WOMAD is recognizable not only to its audiences, organizers, sponsors and partners, who realize its symbolic value and valency, but also to the artists without whom the festival would not exist. For artists, WOMAD seems to be more than just one gig amongst a string of European or Antipodean touring dates; rather, it confers status within the industry, as well as representing a particular kind of performance space.

Like Sónar, WOMAD offers a source of legitimacy to artists within its genre. Most of the major names in world music have played at the festival, and it still represents the premier public showcase for the genre. As such, WOMAD is a truly international stage, with which artists, producers and promoters actively seek involvement. Whilst the locally and loyally experienced festival elements of WOMAD are clearly part of why this remains a vibrant event, its cultural caché, built up by actively shaping the world music genre, its numerous international events, its affiliated label Realworld, and the links to Peter Gabriel, mean that it maintains a distinctly global profile. In interviews, artists from the UK, Cameroon, China and Mali have all described how WOMAD launched their careers onto a global stage, whilst British and French producers have related that their artists see WOMAD audiences as particularly discerning: as connoisseurs. The fact that world music is now a staple feature of numerous other music festivals – and indeed other cultural events, as well as the soundtracks of Hollywood movies – testifies to WOMAD's crucial role in demonstrating that there is a broad audience for world music and imbuing the genre with a symbolic valency that far outstrips the actual size of its audience.

We need to ask whether world music festivals present anything particular and unique to the festivalscape. Is this a genre whose cultural content transcends more boundaries, transforms more localities into a kind of cultural meta-space? Firstly, we need to remember that world music began as a marketing category, though this rather prosaic beginning does not detract from the actual heterogeneity of the genre: multiple musical traditions and varied music scenes stretching from the 'traditional' and 'classical' to the most innovative, politicized and groundbreaking. The genre itself has permeable boundaries, and a review of WOMAD programming over nearly 30 years supports this; the festival has maintained a consistently heterogeneous and eclectic cultural programme, something exemplified by the collaboration during its first edition in 1983 between the Drummers of Burundi and the UK's Echo and the Bunnymen. In the accounts of festival organizers, producers and artists involved in WOMAD, such collaborative efforts are less about 'hybridity' or 'fusion' (terms that most of those involved seem to dislike intensely) but more about a natural organic desire to share one's art, though Taylor (2007: 126–9) has characterized 'collaboration' as a defining trope of the musical interactions of western and other musicians, one that masks inequalities and occasional exploitation. Even though there are now recognizable 'canonical' WOMAD artists, by bringing heterogeneous forms of music together in one festival event WOMAD disembeds its audiences, both from their national contexts and from the particular music scenes that they may be part of. The experiential side of the event thus hinges on a mixture of novelty and a sense of community, the first of which will now be considered in a little more detail.

In terms of aesthetic content, many of those interviewed as part of the empirical research underlying this chapter described the unique feature of WOMAD as its novelty, of wandering through the festival space and suddenly encountering as yet unheard sounds. With the relative dearth of recorded world music in the 1980s this was largely true. However, novelty is harder to find these days, a factor that may – according to the curator of World and Traditional Music at the British Library Sound Archive (interview 2009) – be driving the expansion of festivals abroad, especially new non-WOMAD festivals in the global south such as Mali's Festival in the Desert, the Festival on the Niger and Malawi's Lake of Stars. If the authenticity of a genuinely new musical encounter has become harder to create, then novelty and surprise can be produced through new venues and new spaces, whose location in 'source' countries relocates and repatriates music. What such festivalizing means in these 'new' contexts is still unclear. Where large local audiences make up the majority, this repatriation may redress the imbalance in favour of the source community's meanings and understandings of the music, rather than the partial connoisseurship of west-erners, for whom the lyrics, and sometimes the performance aesthetics, remain mysterious territories. The desire for novelty also drove WOMAD's expansion in the first place, something that can be seen in the incredible number of inter-national events that WOMAD put on during the 1990s. However, making WOMAD global was not about diversifying the festival company's financial portfolio, or about establishing it as a brand. Instead, organizers seem driven by the same love of novelty, of fresh cultural encounters, of new spaces, as their audiences. Alongside a genuine love for the music are motivations that distin-guish many world music professionals from people working in other music genres: those of politics.

WOMAD is a festival with intention. One of the WOMAD Foundation's directors claimed that the festival's programme choices are never deliberately political. This may be true, and it may well help the festival to operate in con-texts as diverse as the UK and Abu Dhabi. However, a certain ideological bent has been present from the festival's beginnings. Peter Gabriel's words express this credo and the festival's founding ethos clearly: 'Music is a universal lan-guage, it draws people together and proves, as well as anything, the stupidity of racism' (Gabriel 2008). In the context of the UK, the festival was born amidst the groundswell of the Rock Against Racism campaign, which saw crowds of 100,000 rally to its anti-Fascist event in London in 1978. Early on, WOMAD attracted involvement from NGOs like Amnesty International and Survival International; this was bolstered when the festival ran at Rivermeade, where the city council helped sponsor the One World Platform, a stage that pro-grammed debates on political and development issues. Importantly, and echo-ing the differences in organization and funding mentioned above, these NGO partnerships vary from country to country. Whilst Amnesty International, for example, remains a key presence at WOMAD in the UK, Las Palmas and Cáceres have created a strong link with Spain's national development organiza-tion Casa Africa, which deals firsthand with the boatloads of African immi-grants arriving in the Canary Islands, an uprooting known as *travesía*, but does so predominantly through culture rather than foreign policy.

These varied partnerships actually reflect a stronger underlying shared ethos, an engagement with issues that affect transnational communities. This is easy to

186 J. Chalcraft and P. Magaudda

find in the explicit politics of Gabriel's 1980 anti-apartheid song 'Biko', which brought South Africa's apartheid-era horrors into popular music. Significantly, he performed this song at the end of his set at the 2009 WOMAD Charlton Park festival in memory of the recently murdered Chechen journalist Natalya Esterimova, who was also a member of Gabriel's own NGO, Witness. WOMAD's founding goals of using music, art and dance for political ends – proving the stupidity of racism – have clearly endured.

Conclusion

Sónar and WOMAD are clearly distinct, yet both manifest the idea explored earlier that global localities have become an integral part of contemporary cultural production. In different ways, both festivals can be said to be cultural brokers. Sónar has acted as an intermediary between the subcultural dance scenes, from which contemporary electronic music arose, and the artworld, whilst WOMAD has quite explicitly brought together different cultures and actively promoted their collaboration. Was the emergence of 'electronic' or 'world' music inevitable? We offer no easy answers, but suggest that these festivals played key roles in brokering their success, whilst their own success is not entirely genre-symbiotic; modernity's creeping culturalism combined with the institutionalization of artworlds has created the conditions through which culture has become a discursive terrain, a space for debating politics, but also a locus of imaginaries. The festivals discussed are indeed bound up in their host localities, but they also transcend them through global networks and global imaginaries. As such, and like Sun Ra's film, which has the inspiration for the title of this chapter, they are essentially Garveyite, seeking new futures in an idealized elsewhere; if, two decades ago, Appadurai was right that imaginations were reconfigured by modernity, then these festivals bear witness to this reconfiguring.

Global imaginaries interact with locality through the experiential nature of these events, and this helps create and sustain spaces where publics actively reconstruct meaning around these forms of music. Aesthetically, both Sónar and WOMAD break down the elite/popular axis by programming material that ranges from serious experimental electronica and the ethnomusicologically authentic, to more danceable, even mainstream offerings. This diversity of content, along with workshops and children's activities, creates 'a sense of place' that is harder to define and is, to some degree, close to the 'no sense of place' that Joshua Meyrowitz (1985) has described as one of the main logics of the media revolution in post-Second World War western society. Our audience surveys point to a fiercely loyal following for the festivals, but one that is not territorial per se. WOMAD audiences in each host locality, for example, view the festival as their own, seemingly oblivious to the other WOMAD events around the world. Yet, for its UK followers, who have effectively pursued it around the country over the years, the actual physical location is seen as merely an enhancement of the festival, rather than as an essential part. The dynamics behind Sónar's international activities are more explicitly oriented towards promoting the festival, but Barcelona itself is only part of the picture. In this sense, the festivals help transform their localities into global spaces, and part of the 'global' nature of these festivals then lies in the simple fact that both are itinerant: for Sónar it is advertising; for WOMAD it is an integral part of what the festival itself does.

These two festivals offer us different global dispositions. With its aesthetic content predominantly from the global south, WOMAD's 'globality' is heavily influenced by other traditions and hybridities, though this is tempered by the pragmatic needs of music-making in the west (recording, touring, making money); for Sónar, the festival most instrumental in legitimizing electronic music as an artform, its compass points are clearly more western. Taken together, these very different parts of the same music industry demonstrate the legitimizing role of the festivalscape in establishing genres and shaping the careers of artists, promoters and directors, as well as the tastes of audiences. Within the culture industries, and within music in particular, festivals are crucial players in taking music scenes beyond their local embeddedness to global audiences, something echoed in the ways in which they are organized and managed, as much as in the cultural content itself. Moreover, within the culture industry, festivals are probably the cultural devices that most contribute to the reconfiguration of values of authenticity at a global scale and to the establishment of a global socio-cultural frame for the circulation of music abroad.

The transient nature of the festival experience leaves us with the question of whether their socio-political engagements are meaningful beyond the festivals themselves: are these just performed engagements and discussions? Experiencing a world music festival like WOMAD, for example, generally demonstrates a cosmopolitan disposition with implicit empathy for environmental and social issues, but does this really go any further? And what issues does a Sónar disposition imply? Or, indeed, taken at its global level, what issues does the 'festivalscape' imply? If 'festivalizing' is just a tool of those marketing the city, a branding strategy of established political and metropolitan elites, is there a counterproject within the festivals themselves? Peter Gabriel's performed public denunciation at the UK's 2009 WOMAD Charlton Park of the state-sponsored murder of a Chechen journalist, the WOMAD Foundation's ongoing global education work, the carbon-neutral status of WOMADelaide, and the Freemuse white paper on musicians and visas submitted to the European Commission (Reitov and Hjorth 2008) suggest that the festival and its networks are more than short-lived performances of ideals. Meanwhile, Sónar shows how popular musical subcultures have been able to transcend the elite/popular value boundary and to sediment a regional/urban identity that is globally rooted. This links up with Appadurai's (1995: 204) own understanding of locality as a 'complex phenomenological quality constituted by a series of links between the sense of the social immediacy, the technology of interactivity, and the relativity of contexts'. As festivals, Sónar and WOMAD contextualize technologies whose enaction temporarily engages with their localities, giving shape to some of their connected meanings and potentialities. In the end, what is transformed in these festivalscapes may be less the localities themselves than the configuration of ideological and aesthetic linkages that increasingly mean something to organizers, artists and audiences: performed, but public, culture that exists beyond place.

Note

1 In compliance with Italian academic folkways, the authors acknowledge that Paolo Magaudda wrote the first half of the chapter, and Jasper Chalcraft wrote the second.

References

Ajuntament de Barcelona (2009) *Premis Ciutat de Barcelona 2009*. From http://www.bcn.cat/cultura/premisciutatbcn/2009/secun3.shtml

Appadurai, A. (1990) Disjuncture and difference in the global cultural economy. *Public Culture* 2(2): 1–23.

Appadurai, A. (1995) The production of locality. In Fardon, R. (ed.) *Counterworks: Managing the Diversity of Knowledge*. London: Routledge.

Appadurai, A. (1996) *Modernity at Large: Cultural Dimensions of Globalization*. Minneapolis: University of Minnesota Press.

Balibrea, M. P. (2001) Urbanism, culture and the post-industrial city: challenging the 'Barcelona model'. *Journal of Spanish Cultural Studies* 2(2): 187–210.

Brooman, T. (2007) *Music & Rhythm: WOMAD 1982–2007* [3 CD set with booklet]. Box, Wiltshire: Real World Group.

Cooke, P. (ed.) (1989) *Localities: The Changing Face of Urban Britain*. London: Unwin Hyman.

Feld, S. (2000) A sweet lullaby for world music. *Public Culture* 12(1): 145–71.

Frith, S. (2000) The Discourse of World Music. In Born, G. and Hesmondhalgh, D. (eds.) *Western Music and its Others: Difference, Representation, and Appropriation in Music*. Berkeley: University of California Press.

Gabriel, P. (2008) Womad Festival in Gabriel's Words. *Sky News Online*. From, http://news.sky.com/skynews/Home/UK-News. Accessed September 2008.

Jonas, A. (1988) A new regional geography of localities. *Area* 20(2): 101–10.

Massey, D. (1993) Questions of locality. *Geography* 78: 142–9.

May, J. (1996) Globalization and the politics of place: place and identity in an inner London neighbourhood. *Transactions, Institute of British Geographers* NS 21: 194–215.

McGuigan, J. (2005) The Cultural Public Sphere. *European Journal of Cultural Studies* 8(4): 427–43.

Meyrowitz, J. (1985) *No Sense of Place: The Impact of Electronic Media on Social Behavior*. New York: Oxford University Press.

Oliveras, J. (2008) *Sónar – Festival Internacional de Música Avanzada y Arte Multimedia de Barcelona*. In Colombo, A. and Rosselló, D. (eds.) *Gestión Cultural: Estudios de Caso*. Barcelona: Ariel.

Reitov, O. and Hjorth, H. (2008) *Visas/the discordant note: a white paper on visa issues, Europe & artists mobility*. Public paper published by Freemuse, The European Live Music Forum and the European Council of Artists.

Smith A. (2005) Conceptualizing City Image Change: The 'Re-Imaging' of Barcelona. *Tourism Geographies* 7(4): 398–423.

Taylor, T. D. (2007) *Beyond Exoticism. Western Music and the World.* Durham: Duke University Press.

Urry, J. (1987) Society, space and locality. *Environment and Planning D: Society and Space* 5: 435–44.

Van der Borg, J. and Russo, P. (2008) *Regeneration and Tourism Development. Evidence from Three European Cities.* Working Papers Department of Economics, 21/2008.

WOMAD Foundation (1983) WOMAD Charitable Objectives. From, www.charity-commission.gov.uk. Accessed December 2008.

Conclusion

On the cultural significance of arts festivals

Gerard Delanty

The chapters collected in this volume illustrate the cultural significance of arts festivals.[1] The arts festival, including for visual arts the biennale, is an interesting example of the contemporary transformation of public culture and is of great interest to cultural sociology. The terms themselves, 'festival' and 'biennale', are interesting in that they have come to denote particular kinds of cultural experience and performance. Festivals, biennales and their derivatives[2] can be seen as the characteristically contemporary and, I argue, cosmopolitan form of public culture today. Indeed, it is possible to speak of a certain festivalization of culture more generally in that the festival genre, as found in a mixed arts festival, is having an impact on the more traditional kinds of social institutions, such as museums, political parties and universities.

Festivals and biennales have undergone not just a rapid period of expansion, but also a critical phase of differentiation from each other. There are now festivals and biennales that aim to showcase contemporary artistic practices and others which combine this function with a more critical focus on the process of innovation and intervention within global culture. It is this tension between the showcasing and the discursive model – the voice and the eye – that circulates within the genre of festivals and biennales and which is also expressive of the cosmopolitan form of public culture.

Festivals have always been sites of cultural reproduction and renewal, but generally they have been separate from the aesthetic world of production and consumption. The traditional carnivalesque festival and the world of high culture belonged to two different domains of culture. This distinction between popular and high culture has dissipated, if not disappeared, today with the vast proliferation of what has been referred to in the Introduction to this volume as post-traditional festivals, by which is intended arts festivals and biennales that are of relatively recent origin and have an international, as opposed to a local or national, identity or orientation in the world. However, this internationalism is increasingly being reworked as a cosmopolitan condition in which the national context is of diminished importance, and in place of being an organic experience the festival is rather a sphere in which a multiplicity of voices seek to be heard. I return to this later, but I would like to make the observation at the outset that the term 'public culture' captures in part this reworking of popular and high culture in a critical direction.

There has been an explosion of festivals throughout the world in the past decade or so. This is especially the case in Europe, the focus of several chapters in this volume, but is by no means confined to Europe, as is indicated by the chapters on festivals in Australia and Israel. It may be accounted in part as a consequence of migration, cultural globalization and the erosion of the distinction between high and low culture, changes in the nature of the public and the wider democratization and internationalization of culture. In this concluding reflection, I would like to comment on three considerations that emerge from the contributions to a cultural sociology of festivals presented in this volume: the underlying concept of public culture, the concept of the cultural public sphere, and cosmopolitanism. Connecting these three concepts is an emphasis on the public as mediator and interpreter. Signalled too in the notion of the public is a notion of critique, for all three concepts are forms of critical engagement.

As a self-constituting cultural phenomenon festivals are of particular interest to cultural researchers in social science. It is arguably the case, as Max Weber claimed, that social science is ultimately concerned with culturally constituted phenomena. Our concern with arts festivals highlights a number of aspects of culture more generally that are not easily accommodated by current theoretical approaches. The idea of public culture, for instance, which appears to be signalled by festivals and biennales, suggests a notion of culture that combines sociability, aesthetics and politics, and expresses the communicative notion of culture. There are now numerous ways in which culture can be theorized, and while many of these approaches share common views their presuppositions are often very different. Many theories of culture concern specific forms of life and are inadequate when it comes to expressions of culture that are less underpinned by a collective subject, as for example public culture. Placing the adjective 'public' before 'culture' qualifies the latter as a sphere of interpretation as opposed to a form of life.

This is not the place to review recent developments in cultural sociology and cultural theory more generally, but a few brief remarks can be made in order to point to future directions for cultural sociology. Theoretical approaches in recent sociological and cultural theory present a number of ways to conceive of culture that certainly go some way towards offering a theoretical framework for the analysis of culture that captures the logic of pluralization and festivalization that is at work in much of contemporary culture. Hermeneutical approaches suggest a notion of culture as a text that requires interpretation. This view of culture, which is also present in Foucauldian theory and more generally in discourse theory, stresses culture as a system of meaning that is always more than individual intentionality. Since the cultural turn in the social sciences, such views of culture have dominated cultural theory and offer an important corrective to traditional author-based conceptions of culture. The problem that such approaches present is the neglect of the social actor and of the possibility of meaningful action. Bourdieu's critical sociology stands for a different conception of culture from the textual model. Culture is instead theorized as a mode of capital that is accumulated and exchanged in a context underpinned by the habitus and by fields. In this analysis, culture is a resource in a field of power. Festivals and biennales are, after all, organizations that have to struggle for material resources and prestige. The forms of culture that they manifest are not pure texts but discourses that take place in the context of social struggles. Bourdieu's theory of cultural production, while an important corrective of postmodernist and hermeneutical conceptions of culture, offers only a very limited view of public culture as reflected in the global spread of biennales.

Against these alternatives, the notion of culture as performance has attracted considerable interest from those working in cultural analysis.[3] Performativity is of course already present in Bourdieu, who developed what had been a purely linguistic concept into a sociological one whereby individuals are endowed with symbolic authority to perform public acts, and which has been brilliantly applied by James English (2005) in his study on prizes as forms of economic and symbolic power (but see also his chapter in this volume). The concept has been invoked by Habermas in the universal pragmatics theory of language and famously by Judith Butler (1999) with her theory of gender as a repetition of acts. Dramaturgical accounts of social performance have become influential in sociology since Erving Goffman first introduced the concept of social drama, and this is also a feature of the recent cultural pragmatic sociology of Jeffrey Alexander, who stresses the objective domain of the cultural order of society on the one side and, on the other, individual actors who position themselves with respect to symbolic structures of meaning (Alexander *et al.* 2006). This is highly relevant to festivals, which clearly are examples of public performances and suggestive of a notion of public culture.

However, the problem with Alexander's approach is that it is places too much emphasis on what he calls cultural fusion between the diverse elements of a performance – authenticity, a script based on recognizable codes, capacity for collective identification, etc – which enable it to be successful. Public culture cannot in all its facets be understood in terms of performativity conceived of as cultural fusion. Indeed, much of it entails exchange and innovation, which is not always foreclosed as a performance. The dimension of public culture that escapes the aforementioned approaches is its critical function and its role in the shaping of new political subjectivities, an observation made by Papastergiadis and Martin in a chapter that could not be cast in the terms of a theory of cultural fusion (see their contribution in this volume). As a form of critique, public culture entails the raising of questions and the probing of new issues, and is often controversial about taste and boundaries. It is both discursive and showcasing, as mentioned earlier. As Liana Georgi argues in her chapter on literature festivals, much creative thinking today is about examining the limits of borders. The literature festival can be seen as the opening up of new spaces through conversation. The arts festival and the biennale are generally addressed to a critical public and, while retaining many of the conventions that might be associated with a public performance, have the additional function of experimentation, engaging in disputes over meaning and authority, and self-problematization.

Three theoretical approaches that highlight the critical dimension of culture can be mentioned. Habermasian approaches to culture stress its normative content and the resources it offers for criticism and self-problematization as well as consensus building. In repertoire theory, as advocated by Thevenot and Boltanski, culture is theorized in terms of evaluative criteria by which people justify their claims. They emphasize arguments and conflicts in which common norms are appealed to. Unlike Habermas's notion of justification, which appeals to the possibility for discursive consensus based on common presuppositions, Boltanski and Thevenot see a plurality of orders or repertoires of justification, each invoking different notions of it. For a theory of public culture as expressed in festivals and biennales where the emphasis is more on showcasing, this approach overestimates the role of argumentation and justification. Narrative approaches to culture stress the ways in which culture is constructed in sense-making activities such as biographies, memories and identities. Narratives are ways of experiencing and interpreting time, and situate the present in relation to the past and the future. Culture conceived of as a narrative is a medium of experience as well as including an interpretation of that experience. This is of relevance to public culture as a medium of critical reflection, since narratives entail the dialogic condition of communication. In addition to these conceptions of culture, it is pertinent to mention the notion of an imaginary signification, as highlighted by Castoriadis and Touraine's notion of a cultural model by which a society defines its self-identity on the level of a mode of self-interpretation that allows it to creatively renew itself. The imaginary component of culture and the idea of a socio-cognitive cultural model are relevant to the cultural logic of festivalization, which as indicated above is increasingly influencing the form for other cultural institutions.

Contemporary cultural theory clearly offers a rich if contested terrain of concepts and approaches that are variously relevant to the study of public culture. In this volume an explicit theory of culture was not applied, and all contributions draw from different approaches, including some of the aforementioned. To the extent to which a generalization can be made, and at the same time a possible course for further research outlined, there would appear to be agreement that the idea of culture points to the shaping of culture in discursive fields and offers a way to avoid essentialist notions of culture as the expression of an underlying subjectivity and simple views of a national culture. In that sense the notion of culture as public culture is presupposed. I would like to make a few general claims as to the nature of culture as illustrated by the example of festivals and biennales and the trend towards the festivalization of culture.

In the arts festival we find a post-representational notion of culture present. Culture is not something that exists prior to its representation, but is constituted in the act of presentation. The form that culture is increasingly taking in the arts, as in museums, biennales, exhibitions and festivals, is less the display or showcasing of already constituted objects than the exploration of contested meanings and identities. A second feature of public culture is that it entails its own interpretation. Interpretation is not entirely a separate activity or given over to a professional interpreter, but is integral not only to the mode of cultural representation but also to the aesthetic experience that the festival creates. A third characteristic of culture is that it is discursive in the sense of being a medium of communication. In this respect the role of the public is important in that, as the example of the arts festival illustrates, the public is integrated as an actor into the cultural form of the event (a development discussed in the chapter by Jean-Louis Fabiani). So the public is not a consumer as such but a participant in the event. As Papastergiadis and Martin also point out, the relationship between the artist and the public has changed from one in which the public is a witness to a spectacle to one in which the public is a participant and a constitutive partner that is active in the whole field of meaning. A fourth characteristic, which is especially pertinent to the arts festival, is sociability. As emphasized by Monica Sassatelli in her chapter, sociability is the key to the success of festivals. Festivals give expression to a significant sense of place and are usually place specific. It is possible that this explains the proliferation of festivals through the world in recent years. Festivals make possible the identification of individuals with a town or locality in ways that are inclusive as well as resonating with wider societal trends that give prominence to cultural regeneration, cultural consumption and increased mobility. Indeed, mobility is a presupposition of the post-traditional festival, which relies on travel and a greater emphasis on consumption. The fifth aspect of culture we can note is its transformative character: it does not merely transmit but transforms that which it communicates. It is this that gives to it its critical temperament. Finally, a sixth feature of culture is the increased importance of mediation between the world of artistic production and the social, political and economic context. Cultural managers – biennale and festival organizers, curators, etc – are more akin to mediators than to authoritative interpreters of culture, as Papastergiadis and Martin argue. This mediatory function is also linked to a reflective role that allows the festival to feed into other discourses outside the strictly artistic.

In an attempt to concretize further these characteristics of culture, the concepts of the cultural public sphere and aesthetic cosmopolitanism will be discussed. As indicated earlier and in the Introduction, the approach we have adopted in this volume is to explore the cultural significance of festivals. We situate the festival as a site of the public sphere, which is now one of the key concepts that emerged with the historical and cultural turn in social science since it was originally introduced by Habermas in the 1960s. Jim McGuigan's chapter provides an excellent elaboration of the more specific notion of the cultural public sphere and how festivals might be seen as an instance of it. This concept, as defined by McGuigan, refers to the articulation of politics as a contested domain through aesthetic modes of communication. It aims to capture the ways in which the world of art is not outside the public sphere, as in the original formulation by Habermas, who emphasized the role of the public sphere in generating political criticism that feeds into the organs of government. In view of the tie between art and politics – a tie that is underpinned by ethical issues – reduction of the public sphere to explicitly political communication and the interaction of civil society with the state is too limiting. The notion of the cultural public sphere makes some advance in opening the concept of the public sphere to a range of issues that include questions of cultural citizenship and democracy. The key to this is the dimension of cultural intervention, which McGuigan highlights, and which Jean-Louis Fabiani regards as linked to the critical role of the public in festivals.

Festivals are spaces and times of concentrated debate and 'collective effervescence', to use Durkheim's term. In recent times, these debates are increasingly politically charged ones relating to issues of representativity (gender, ethnicity, age-groups) and are thus relevant to what constitutes access to creativity and participation in not just the artistic community, but also the wider political community of which the cultural community is but a part. Democracy has now extended into the cultural domain, where, it has increasingly been recognized, is the arena in which much of the political is now articulated. The notion of the political that is at stake in this is more than one that can be formulated in terms of rights, but also includes questions of identity and participation. Citizenship, which is a component of democracy and relates to the dimension of participation in public life, cannot be conceived today outside the cultural sphere since much of what defines the citizen is cultural. This can be expressed in questions relating to place and belonging, communication, gender, age, identity and recognition, consumption, and living in a sustainable environment. Festivals explore the cultural politics that take place around these issues and in doing so give a particular salience to cultural citizenship and more generally to democracy.

As noted in most chapters in this volume the phenomenon of the festivals can be seen as an expression of cosmopolitanism and thus as a major site, not just of the cultural public sphere, but of the global cultural public sphere. It is possible to discern a general trend by which the biennale and festival have moved from a period of internationalization to one that can be termed cosmopolitan. As noted by Segal and Blumauer and also by Papastergiadis and Martin in their respective chapters, there is a clear pattern of internationalization of festivals since the 1950s whereby biennales increasingly entered the international arena. As Fabiani also notes in his chapter, festivals are a privileged space for developing critical interventions about global issues. But internationalization largely presupposes national cultures that compete on the international stage. It is possible to trace this back to the origins of the Venice Biennale in 1895. The trend towards internationalization is most vividly present in the case of the film festivals, such as Cannes, that are also funded by national governments and are major national icons. The Olympic Games is a clear example of the international festival that is of major importance for the nations competing in it and for the host city and country. In recent years it is possible to detect a shift from internationalism to cosmopolitanism in cultural developments as well as in politics and law. In this move the biennale or festival is no longer exclusively an arena for the international competition of nations, but a global site in which diverse cultural streams and influences are articulated. This development – which might be better characterized as one in which three narratives coexist in relations of tension rather than one replacing the other – is in part a consequence of a reaction to western dominance of global culture, but it is also a consequence of pluralization and changed relationships between the local and the global. The cosmopolitan turn takes place in the context of a double-edged movement in the direction of a global cultural arena – which we can term a global cultural public sphere – and a greater role for the local milieu to resituate itself.

The shift from internationalism to cosmopolitanism in the cultural logic of the festival is indicative of a wider cultural shift in the direction of the cosmopolitan. Cosmopolitanism is a term that is increasingly used to refer to internal pluralization and interaction of different cultures; it highlights moments of openness, exchange and dialogue. Cosmopolitanism is always about connecting global issues to particular contexts and as such it is different from globalization and internationalization; it refers to a particular kind of experience as well as the interpretation of such experiences. The field of cosmopolitanism covers specific forms of social, cultural and political experience as well as referring to particular forms of inquiry. Cosmopolitanism encourages the development of new ways of thinking that go beyond disciplinary boundaries and which challenge more broadly the very notion of borders. Cosmopolitanism has arisen as a response to the current predicament of political community and societal transformation. There has been a pronounced tendency in the cosmopolitan literature towards cultural topics and a general questioning of the association of cosmopolitanism with elites as well as a move away from purely normative analysis to a concern with empirical manifestations of what I have referred to as the cosmopolitan imagination (Delanty 2009). Included in this is the notion of aesthetic cosmopolitanism, to refer to the specific cultural context of public culture (Chaney 2002).

Cosmopolitanism as a concept was an important part of the 'cultural turn' in the human and social sciences. In place of an older cosmopolitan ideal of moral universalism and the desire to transcend the distinction between strangers and friends, the emphasis is now put on multiple forms of belonging and identity. But cosmopolitanism is a critical concept and highly pertinent to the forms of public culture that are associated with the biennale. For this reason I have used the term 'critical cosmopolitanism' in order to capture the transformational dimensions of global culture and cultural exchange. Cosmopolitanism thus conceived concerns self-transformation in light of the encounter with the other. As such it is more than the simple condition of internationalism or globality. A critical cosmopolitan approach with respect to cultural phenomenon concerns (1) the identification of openness to the world, (2) self-transformation in light of the encounter with the Other, (3) the exploration of otherness within the self, (4) critical responses to globality and (5) critical spaces between globality and locality. The significance of this for the analysis of post-national political community is that it provides a framework in which culture and identity can be examined in ways that do not reduce it to an underlying collective identity. From the perspective of critical cosmopolitanism the task is to assess processes of self-transformation in which new cultural models take shape and where spaces of discourse open up, leading to a socio-cognitive change. A critical cosmopolitan approach thus proceeds on the assumption that the cultural models of society contain learning potential in terms of moral and political normative criteria. It suggests a view of public culture as a sphere of cultural contestation and interpretation. Viewing it in these terms we can reconcile the contested conception of culture with a more general view that public culture can constitute itself as a site of conflicting interpretations of the world but in which there are possibilities for acts of signification and world disclosure. This essentially communicative concept of culture also opens up the cosmopolitan possibility for a reflexive relation between cultures. It is this that is enacted in the arts festival and biennale, which are places of exchange based on democratic values.

There is some evidence in the chapters collected in this volume for such an interpretation of contemporary arts festivals as the mediators of aesthetic cosmopolitanism. Maurice Roche argues that international mega-festivals can be interpreted as assisting in the integration of European societies and in promoting models of peaceful coexistence and co-presence. In a similar vein Segal and Blumauer cite the comment of the French Prime Minister, Lionel Jospin, in 2000 that the future of French cinema is increasingly European cinema. They note, too, the aspiration of Cannes to be a channel for promoting democratic values and a worldwide stage for dialogue and cultural exchange. In this context of a shift from a model of internationalism to one of cosmopolitanism, Papastergiadis and Martin discuss the idea of a global cultural public sphere wherein we can trace the signs of a new political imaginary that is not based on national models of identity. They make the important point that in a situation in which both the commercial and the political spheres have been aestheticized 'the formation of a "global cultural public sphere" takes on a greater urgency as both the destination of art and the focal point for shaping the politics of human life'. This is vividly illustrated by Chalcraft and Magaudda with respect to Sónar and especially the WOMAD festivals, which have a highly globalized sense of place. They demonstrate how global localities have become an integral part of contemporary cultural production.

The cosmopolitan model is also to be seen as a context in which the local and global interact, as opposed to the international model in which the national is promoted through international competition. The cosmopolitan can thus be found at either the local or the global level. Thus the space in which the critical inverventions of the festival takes place is often the exploration of the global within the specific context of the city. The chapters by Cummings, Woodward and Bennett and by Regev discuss examples of festivals that are situated in local contexts and often far from the sites of global metropolitan culture but can be considered nonetheless cosmopolitan. The position adopted in these chapters is that cosmopolitanism is primarily characterized by an attitude of openness to other cultures, and for Regev it takes the form of 'omnivorous cultural consumption'. While his analysis is confined largely to the national context, Cummings, Woodward and Bennett consider the festival experience as a means for generating green sensibilities and ethical consumption within youth culture. They argue that music festivals actively promote cosmopolitanism by advocating corporate and community responsibility. As such they are places of exchange and learning as much as they are carnivalesque.

Notes

1 I am grateful to Liana Giorgi, Monica Sassatelli and Nikos Papastergiadis for helpful comments on an earlier draft, and to all authors for their chapters, which have formed the basis of this contribution.
2 There are today triennials, quadriennials, etc. in the visual art world.
3 I draw here on Lloyd (2011).

References

Alexander, J. Giesen, B. and Mast, J. (eds.) (2006) *Social Performance: Symbolic Action, Cultural Pragmatics, and Ritual.* Cambridge: Cambridge University Press.
Butler, J. (1999) *Gender Trouble: Feminism and the Subversion of Identity.* London: Routledge.
Chaney, D. (2002) Cosmopolitan Art and Cultural Citizenship. *Theory, Culture, and Society* 19(1–2): 57–74.
Delanty, G. (2009) *The Cosmopolitan Imagination: The Renewal of Critical Social Theory.* Cambridge: Cambridge University Press.
English, J. (2005) *The Economy of Prestige: Prizes, Awards, and the Circulation of Cultural Capital.* Cambridge, MA: Harvard University Press.
Lloyd, M. (2011) From Linquistic Performativity to Social Performace: The Development of a Concept. In Delanty, G. and Turner, S. (eds) *International Handbook of Contemporary Social and Political Theory.* London: Routledge.

Index

*9 7 8 0 4 1 5 7 1 4 9 6 9 *

An environmentally friendly book printed and bound in England by www.printondemand-worldwide.com

PEFC Certified

This product is
from sustainably
managed forests
and controlled
sources

www.pefc.org

PEFC/16-33-415

This book is made of chain-of-custody materials; FSC materials for the cover and PEFC materials for the text pages.

#0261 - 261015 - C0 - 234/156/12 - PB - 9780415714969